Othello

SHAKESPEARE IN PERFORMANCE

Advisory Editors: **David Bevington, Barbara Gaines and Peter Holland**

D1494022

methuen | drama

To students, teachers, and lovers of Shakespeare

First UK edition published 2007

A & C Black Publishers Limited
38 Soho Square
London W1D 3HB
www.acblack.com

© 2005 Sourcebooks Inc.
First printed in the U.S. by Sourcebooks MediaFusion

ISBN 978-0-7136-8356-1

A CIP catalogue record for this book is available from the British Library.

This book is produced using paper that is made from wood grown in managed, sustainable forests. It is natural, renewable and recyclable. The logging and manufacturing processes conform to the environmental regulations of the country of origin.

Cover Design by Jocelyn Lucas

Cover Illustration © Ann Elson 2007

CD manufactured by Lemon Media

Printed and bound in Great Britain by The Bath Press, Bath

Contents

About Sourcebooks MediaFusion

Launched with the 1998 *New York Times* bestseller
We Interrupt This Broadcast and formally founded in 2000,
Sourcebooks MediaFusion is the nation's leading publisher
of mixed-media books. This revolutionary imprint is dedicated
to creating original content—be it audio, video, CD-ROM,
or Web—that is fully integrated with the books we create.
The result, we hope, is a new, richer, eye-opening,
thrilling experience with books for our readers.
Our experiential books have become both bestsellers
and classics in their subjects, including poetry (*Poetry Speaks*),
children's books (*Poetry Speaks to Children*),
history (*We Shall Overcome*), sports (*And The Crowd Goes Wild*),
the plays of William Shakespeare, and more.
See what's new from us at www.sourcebooks.com.

About the Text

Othello was not published in Shakespeare's lifetime. It first appeared in print in 1622, as a quarto (Q or Q1), printed by Nicholas Oakes for Thomas Walkley, and then appeared shortly afterwards among the tragedies in the First Folio (F) in 1623. Although they both print what is essentially the same play, there are a many differences (some of them quite small) between these two texts. Scholars have long debated the relationship of Q and F, and how both texts relate to what Shakespeare first wrote. The most detailed recent study of these questions is E. A. J. Honigmann's *The Texts of 'Othello' and Shakespearean Revision* (Routledge: London 1996), to which this edition is much indebted. Professor Honigmann thinks both Q and F were set from separate scribal copies of Shakespeare's original manuscript. There is some evidence that Q preserves a theatrical version of the play, cut in certain places for performance; it tends to have fuller stage directions than F. Q also includes a number of oaths and profanities, particularly in the speeches of Iago and Roderigo, which are not in F, and most scholars think that F has been expurgated (perhaps following the Act of Abuses in 1606 against profanity on the stage). A Second Quarto (Q2) was published in 1630 and seems to have drawn on both Q and F.

In preparing editions of the play, editors have usually drawn readings from both Q and F, as is the case with the present edition. For the most part, F has been the text followed here, unless there seems good reason to prefer a Q reading (or an emendation); Q's oaths and profanities have been accepted in place of the F alternatives, and Q's fuller stage directions amalgamated with F's. (Stage directions in square brackets are in neither Q nor F.) Punctuation and spelling have been modernized, on the whole from F, with the more usual form of rare or obsolete words given as in the *Oxford English Dictionary*. The result is a fairly conservative text, in keeping with the focus of the *Sourcebooks* series on performance, but listeners will note some differences between the text given here and some of the words used in the recordings.

There are a number of good scholarly editions of the play available: I have looked closely at the Oxford *Complete Works*, ed. Stanley Wells and Gary Taylor (Oxford 1986); the new Cambridge *Othello*, ed. Norman Sanders (Cambridge 1984, revised 2003); the Arden third series *Othello*, ed. E. A. J. Honigmann (1997); and the Oxford World's Classics *Othello*, ed. Michael Neill (Oxford 2006). I have used the Norton Facsimile of *The First Folio*, ed. Charlton Hinman (New York 1968) and the New Cambridge *First Quarto of Othello*, ed. Scott McMillan (Cambridge 2001). For performance history I am indebted to Lois Potter, *Shakespeare in Performance: Othello* (Manchester 2002) and Julie Hankey's *Othello* (Shakespeare in Production: Cambridge 1987, revised 2005).

Shakespeare was at the height of his powers when he wrote *Othello*, and it seems always to have been a popular play. Shakespeare based his play on an Italian short story by Giraldi Cinthio in his collection *Hecatommithi* (1565). Honigmann thinks the play might have been written as early as 1601 or 1602 [see his Arden third series edition (1997) p.1], though the first recorded performance was before the court on 1st November 1604; it was later one of twenty plays performed during the winter of 1612-13 at the wedding celebrations for Elizabeth, King James I's daughter, to Frederick, Elector Palatine. There is also a record of a performance in Oxford in 1610, when the boy playing Desdemona gave an especially moving performance [see Lois Potter, *Shakespeare in Performance: Othello* (Manchester University Press, Manchester 2002) p.5]. It remained popular until the theaters were closed in the mid 17th century and was revived when they opened again at the Restoration, and has remained popular ever since, attracting most leading actors of the day.

L. G. Black

On the CD

1. Introduction to the Sourcebooks Shakespeare *Othello*: Sir Derek Jacobi

ACT 1, SCENE 1, LINES 81-113
2. Narration: Sir Derek Jacobi
3. Peter Yapp as Brabantio, John McAndrew as Roderigo, and Anton Lesser as Iago
   Naxos • 2000

ACT 1, SCENE 3, LINES 77-95
4. Narration: Sir Derek Jacobi
5. Paul Robeson as Othello
   Columbia Masterworks • 1944
6. John Kani as Othello
   Johannesburg Market Theatre • 1987
7. Narration: Sir Derek Jacobi
8. F. Scott Fitzgerald as Othello, Lines 77-95 and 128-169
   F. Scott Fitzgerald Papers

ACT 1, SCENE 3, LINES 128-170
9. Narration: Sir Derek Jacobi
10. Hugh Quarshie as Othello
    Naxos • 2000
11. John Kani as Othello
    Johannesburg Market Theatre • 1987
12. Narration: Sir Derek Jacobi
13. Edwin Booth as Othello
    Private recording • 1890

ACT 1, SCENE 3, LINES 363-384
14. Narration: Sir Derek Jacobi
15. Anton Lesser as Iago
    Naxos • 2000

16. Jose Ferrer as Iago
    Columbia Masterworks • 1944

ACT 2, SCENE 1, LINES 173-203

17. Narration: Sir Derek Jacobi
18. Hugh Quarshie as Othello and Emma Fielding as Desdemona
    Naxos. • *2000*
19. Paul Robeson as Othello and Uta Hagen as Desdemona
    Columbia Masterworks • 1944

ACT 3, SCENE 3, LINES 157-193

20. Narration: Sir Derek Jacobi
21. Hugh Quarshie as Othello and Anton Lesser as Iago
    Naxos • *2000*
22. Paul Robeson as Othello and Jose Ferrer as Iago
    Columbia Masterworks • 1944

ACT 3, SCENE 3, LINES 292-330

23. Narration: Sir Derek Jacobi
24. Patience Tomlinson as Emilia and Anton Lesser as Iago
    Naxos • *2000*
25. Dorothy Gould as Emilia and Richard Haddon Haines as Iago
    Johannesburg Market Theatre • *1987*

ACT 4, SCENE 1, LINES 31-45

26. Narration: Sir Derek Jacobi
27. Hugh Quarshie as Othello and Anton Lesser as Iago
    Naxos • *2000*
28. Paul Robeson as Othello and Jose Ferrer as Iago
    Columbia Masterworks • 1944

ACT 4, SCENE 1, LINES 105-150

29. Narration: Sir Derek Jacobi
30. Anton Lesser as Iago, Roger May as Cassio,
    Hugh Quarshie as Othello, and Allison Pettit as Bianca
    Naxos • *2000*

Act 4, Scene 3, Lines 24-54
31. Narration: Sir Derek Jacobi
32. Emma Fielding as Desdemona and Patience Tomlinson as Emilia
Naxos • 2000

Act 4, Scene 3, Lines 57-101
33. Narration: Sir Derek Jacobi
34. Uta Hagen as Desdemona and Edith King as Emilia
Columbia Masterworks • 1944
35. Joanna Weinberg as Desdemona and Dorothy Gould as Emilia
Johannesburg Market Theatre • 1987

Act 5, Scene 2, Lines 1-22
36. Narration: Sir Derek Jacobi
37. Paul Scofield as Othello
BBC
38. Hugh Quarshie as Othello
Naxos • 2000

Act 5, Scene 2, Lines 134-165
39. Narration: Sir Derek Jacobi
40. Patience Tomlinson as Emilia and Hugh Quarshie as Othello
Naxos • 2000
41. Dorothy Gould as Emilia and John Kani as Othello
Johannesburg Market Theatre • 1987

Act 5, Scene 2, Lines 336-357
42. Narration: Sir Derek Jacobi
43. Paul Robeson as Othello
Columbia Masterworks • 1944
44. John Kani as Othello
Johannesburg Market Theatre • 1987

45. Introduction to Speaking Shakespeare: Sir Derek Jacobi
46. Speaking Shakespeare: Andrew Wade with Bill McCallum
47. Conclusion of the Sourcebooks Shakespeare *Othello*: Sir Derek Jacobi

Note from the Series Editors

For many of us, our first and only encounter with Shakespeare was in school. We may recall that experience as a struggle, working through dense texts, filled with unfamiliar words. However, those of us who were fortunate enough to have seen a play performed may have altogether different memories. It may be of an interesting scene or an unusual character, but it is most likely a speech. Often, just hearing part of one instantly transports us to that time and place. "Friends, Romans, countrymen, lend me your ears," "But, soft! What light through yonder window breaks?," "To sleep, perchance to dream," "Tomorrow, and tomorrow, and tomorrow."

The Sourcebooks Shakespeare series is our attempt to use the power of performance to help you experience the play. On these pages, you will see photographs from various productions, on film and on stage, historical and contemporary, known worldwide or in your community. You may even learn of some popular actors' surprising Shakespearean performances. You will see set drawings, costume designs, and scene edits, all reproduced from original notes. Finally, on the enclosed audio CD, you will hear scenes from the play as performed by some of the most accomplished Shakespeareans of our times. Often, we include multiple interpretations of the same scene, showing you the remarkable richness of the text. Hear the great Paul Robeson in a 1944 recording reciting Othello's speech to the Senate. Compare that to a private recording made by Edwin Booth in 1890. Listen to a modern version made in 2000. The performers are using the same words but creating different Othellos.

As you read the text of the play, you can consult explanatory notes for definitions of unfamiliar words and phrases or words whose meanings have changed. These notes appear on the left pages, next to the text of the play. The audio, photographs, and other production artifacts augment the notes, and they too are indexed to the appropriate lines. You can use the pictures to see how others have staged a particular scene and get ideas on costumes, scenery, and blocking. As for the audio, each track represents a particular interpretation of a scene. Sometimes, a passage that's difficult to comprehend opens up when you hear it out loud. Furthermore, when you hear more than one version, you gain a keener understanding of the characters and the larger themes. Was Emilia a victim of domestic violence? Was Mercutio in love with Romeo? Was Hamlet depressed or suicidal? The actors made their choices and so can you. You may even come up with your own interpretation.

The text of the play, the definitions, the production notes, the audio—all of these go together, and they are here for your enjoyment. The audio, being excerpts of performances, is meant to entertain. When you see a passage with an associated clip, you can read along as you hear the actors perform the scenes for you. Or, you can sit back, close your eyes, and listen, and then go back and reread the text with a new perspective. Finally, since the text is actually a script, you may find yourself reciting the lines out loud and doing your own performance!

You will undoubtedly notice that some of the audio does not exactly match the text. Also, there are photographs of and references to scenes that aren't in your edition. There are many reasons for this, but foremost among them is the fact that Shakespeare scholarship continues to move forward and the prescribed ways of dealing with and interpreting text are always changing. Thus a play that was edited and published in 1944 will be different from one published in 2005. It may also surprise you to know that there frequently isn't one definitive early edition of each play. *Othello*, for example, appeared in four editions before 1642. The First Quarto, published in 1622, was believed to have been a scribal transcript of his full, working draft of the play—his "foul papers." The First Folio, published in 1623, was thought to have been printed from a scribal transcript of his "fair copy" of the play. Finally, artists have their own interpretation of the play and they too cut and change lines and scenes according to their vision. Bianca's role was cut from the play in the eighteenth and nineteenth centuries, and the "willow scene," once thought of simply as an opportunity for a pathetic song from Desdemona, is now played to bring out the friendship between Desdemona and Emilia.

The ways in which *Othello* has been presented have varied considerably through the years. We've included essays in the book to give you glimpses into the range of the productions, showing you how other artists have approached the play and providing examples of just what changes were made and how. Janet Suzman's essay on her seminal production in 1987 in South Africa during apartheid is a compelling artistic and political statement. Lois Potter, in her essay, "In Production," steps back to provide an overview of how the play has been performed through the years, discussing its early history when mostly white actors played Othello to Paul Robeson's breakthrough portrayal to more recent productions: Raul Julia in 1979, Ben Kingsley in 1985, and Patrick Stewart in the so-called "photo-negative" version in 1997. Douglas Lanier's "It is the Green-eyed Monster" presents an intriguing look at how the play has been appropriated, twisted, and adopted by popular culture. He explores three key motifs in the play: Black self-representation, Black-White relations, and Relationships and Jealousy. Finally, for the actor in you (or for those of you who want to look behind the curtain), we have two essays that you may find intriguing. Andrew Wade, voice coach of the Royal Shakespeare Company for thirteen years, shares his point of view on how to understand the text and speak it; you will also hear him working with actors on the audio CD so that you too can learn the art of speaking Shakespeare. "The Cast Speaks" is actually from an interview we conducted: we talked to each member of a cast performing *Othello* (in this case, Actors From The London Stage) and asked about their characters and relationships. We found it fascinating to hear what they had to say on various topics: whether Emilia was abused, why Desdemona is not racist, Othello's willingness to be manipulated by Iago. The characters come to life in a way that's different from reading the book or watching a performance.

One last note: we are frequently asked why we didn't include the whole play, either in audio or video. While we enjoy the plays and are avid theatergoers, we are trying to do something more with the audio (and the production notes and essays) than just presenting them to you. In fact, our goal is to provide you tools that will enable you to explore the play on your own, from many different directions. Our hope is that the different pieces of audio, the voices of the actors, old production photos and notes, all these will engage you and illuminate the play in various ways so that you can construct your own understanding and create your own production, as it were.

Though the productions we have referenced and the audio clips we have included are but a miniscule sample of the play's history, we hope they encourage you to further delve into the works of Shakespeare. New editions of the play come out yearly, movie adaptations are regularly being produced, there are hundreds of theater groups in the U.S. alone, and performances could be going on right in your backyard. We echo the words of noted writer and poet Robert Graves, who said, "The remarkable thing about Shakespeare is that he is really very good—in spite of all the people who say he is very good."

We welcome you now to The Sourcebooks Shakespeare edition of *Othello*.

Dominique Raccah and Marie Macaisa
Series Editors

track 1

Introduction to the Sourcebooks Shakespeare *Othello*
Sir Derek Jacobi

In Production:

Lois Potter

The stage history of *Othello* is full of stories of audiences reacting in a way that we now associate only with the final moments of a football game: not only were they left in tears, they are said to have shouted warnings to the characters, or shot the hero, or attacked the villain. They saw the play in terms of hero, heroine, and villain, not of black man, white woman, and white villain. This is one respect in which it has changed in the last fifty years.

In the seventeenth and eighteenth centuries, great acting was about the expression of great emotions. Othello's role was dominated by love and jealousy (a complex emotion made up of fear and hatred), and thus allowed the actor to express more emotions than almost any other part in the theatrical repertoire. The play depended on Othello for its success, while Desdemona's role was never considered a major one. Iago seems not to have become a major character until the nineteenth century.

POETIC TO POIGNANT — OTHELLO IN THE 19TH CENTURY

The greatest Othello of the Romantic period, Edmund Kean (1787–1833), played both Othello and Iago but disliked playing the latter—apparently, because he did not want to be identified with a totally loathsome character. When Kean played his (heavily cut) Othello, the audience experienced the role as a series of infinitely melancholy events that he made them share with him. His greatest moment was the "now forever farewell" speech, in which his voice gave a sense of infinite loneliness. The focus was on the tragedy of this long-suffering man, who was to lose the source of all his happiness through the vilest treachery. Careful cutting of the text meant that the audience did not see him strike Desdemona or fall into a fit, nor did they hear any obscenities, either from him or from Iago. The play's effect was mainly poetic.

The greatest American nineteenth-century actor, Edwin Booth (1833–93), toured the country many times as both Othello and Iago, also playing both parts in England and on the European continent. Booth, who insisted in a letter that "my idea of Othello is not animal but poetic," was frequently contrasted with the Italian actor Salvini, who was applauded for throwing Iago to the floor and carrying a struggling Desdemona to her deathbed. Booth embraced Desdemona only "with delicacy" and promised the English actress Ellen Terry that he would always keep his robe in his hand when he touched her, so as to avoid marking her with his makeup. His Othello was light-skinned. Kean is supposed to have originated the "tawny" makeup, but the evidence is inconclusive; he may have adopted it because black makeup made his facial expression, an important part of his performance, hard to see in the large, candle-lit theaters. In Booth's case, given the racially charged situation in the United States, it was probably important to look like someone from the exotic East rather than from an American plantation. (Booth's brother, John Wilkes Booth, also an actor, is most famous as the assassin of Abraham Lincoln.)

However, a black American actor, of whom Booth probably never heard, had also played the part in the nineteenth century and toured perhaps even

Edmund Kean, Ira Aldridge, Tommaso Salvini

more widely. Ira Aldridge (1807–1867) seems never to have played Othello in the United States, although companies of black actors did exist in some of the northern states. Unable to achieve major roles at major theaters in England, he was much more successful on tour; he won honors and distinctions in Germany, eastern Europe, Scandinavia, and especially Russia, where liberal intellectuals, deeply involved in the contemporary debate over emancipating the serfs and aware of the abolition debate in the United States, found his performances profoundly moving. Aldridge played a still more heavily cut text than Kean's, since he gave most of his performances with a cast of local actors performing in their own language and relying on visual cues from him to tell them when to speak. It is evident that much of the enthusiasm that audiences felt for him came precisely from the fact that they heard what he said as the expression of his own feelings rather than Othello's. He is said to have thought of returning to the United States at the end of the Civil War, but died on tour in Poland before he could carry out his plan. His daughter, however, was to meet the next great black actor, Paul Robeson, when he was preparing to play Othello in 1930, and to help him with the work on his diction and blank verse rhythms that he felt was needed before he could confront an English audience.

CONFRONTING RACE

Robeson was already a famous singer, film actor, and musical comedy performer (in the English production of *Showboat*) when he first took on the role; he played it in England because it was still considered too risky for a black man to play it in the United States. The young Peggy Ashcroft, who was his Desdemona, received hate mail, something that had not happened to white actresses who played opposite Aldridge. The production was poor, as was the Iago, but Ashcroft went on to have a great career, while American directors almost immediately began trying to find a way to have Robeson play Othello in his own country.

It was only with the coming of World War II, the integration of the U. S. Army, and a more internationalist attitude, that it finally became possible to depict a black performer in a role where he would kiss and later kill a white woman. The two actors who played opposite Robeson, José Ferrer as Iago and Uta Hagen as Desdemona, went on themselves to be famous (although one effect of the production was the breakup of their marriage). The production started in two small theaters in university towns, but in the following year moved to Broadway and then to a national tour, refusing to play except to integrated audiences. Given that there was often a gasp when Robeson's Othello first kissed Uta Hagen's Desdemona, there was no way that Robeson could play the hero as anything other than a noble, gentle, and rather distant figure. But his personal charisma and beautiful voice, along with the same sense of identification with the role that had struck Aldridge's audiences, made the performance memorable.

Portrait of Paul Robeson as Othello, Carl Van Vechten Estate

To focus exclusively on race in a discussion of this play's history is, in many ways, unfair to the many fine white actors who have played Othello, not to mention the many fine Iagos. Some of these can be seen on video: Lawrence Olivier's powerful Othello (directed by John Dexter, adapted for video by Stuart Burge) plays opposite a deliberately pallid, scaled-down Iago from Frank Finlay; Anthony Hopkins, in the widely-distributed BBC Shakespeare series (directed by Jonathan Miller), is brought down by a small, giggling psychopath (Bob Hoskins). But there is no doubt that Robeson, like Aldridge before him, made Othello the center of the play, at a time when Iago was beginning to steal it from him. Audiences were finding Othello's emotionalism embarrassing. More encouragingly, perhaps, they were no longer prepared to believe that a man who murdered his wife on suspicion alone deserved to be seen as a tragic figure rather than a criminal. When a black actor played the part, it became easier to see him as a victim of prejudice (from Brabantio, Roderigo, and Iago) and cultural misunderstanding (from and towards Desdemona). The same effect could have been achieved, of course, by a white actor made up to look black, but this kind of impersonation, like the playing of Shylock by non-Jewish actors, began to seem insulting in the 1960s. First in the United States, then in the rest of the English-speaking world, it became more or less understood that no white actor should play Othello. The actor could be Puerto Rican, like Raul Julia (1940-1992), who first played it in Central Park in 1979, or could have an Indian father, like Ben Kingsley at Stratford, England, in 1985–1986, even if he did not look particularly different from the rest of the cast.

Janet Suzman's 1990 production in Johannesburg, South Africa, restored the shock effect to the play by emphasizing the background of apartheid and overtly expressed racism that was still part of people's lives. The Iago (Richard Haddon Haines) was modeled on a white supremacist leader and

Joanna Weinberg as Desdemona and John Kani as Othello in The Market Theater production, directed by Janet Suzman, 1987
Photo by Ruphin Coudyzer

his vicious performance, which involved threatening his wife with a knife, spitting, and mimicking Othello's supposedly monkey-like behavior, was intensified by the fact that he towered over the small, frail-looking African John Kani. There was really no hope for this hero from the beginning, in spite of the bravely honest Desdemona (Joanna Weinberg). His bewildered wretchedness at the end was almost unbearable, as was the recognition of Emilia (Dorothy Gould) that the tragedy was her fault. The racist background, in which Emilia shared, also made more poignant her choice to tell Othello the truth instead of protecting Iago.

In 1997, Patrick Stewart, a white actor whose success on television guaranteed him an audience for any theatrical role he chose, found a way to play Othello: directed by Jude Kelly, he starred in a "photo-negative" production where the rest of the cast was black (apart from the Cypriots, who were mainly mixed race or Hispanic). No lines were changed to accommodate this reversal, a fact that bothered some spectators but not others. The production emphasized the age difference between Othello and Desdemona (a charming,

Franchelle Stewart Dorn as Emilia, Ron Canada as Iago, Patrice Johnson as Desdemona, and Patrick Stewart as Othello in The Shakespeare Theatre's 1997-1998 production directed by Jude Kelly
Photo by Carol Rosegg

Othello on Stage: A Personal Note

Even though many Othellos have been famous before they ever played the part, and thus walked on stage to an audience that was already expecting something great, the play is so powerful that it can make an effect without such advantages. Some of the productions that have most moved me include an outdoor one in California, where the audience, mostly unfamiliar with the play, could hardly believe that anyone could be so evil as Iago; there were gasps and nervous laughs throughout, and absolute horror at the end. After a production by the students in the Professional Theatre Training Program at the University of Delaware, the colleagues and students I talked to wished they had not seen the tragedy at all, because it left them feeling so wretched, yet they agreed that it had been a beautiful experience. With the ethereal beauty of Desdemona's song lingering in my head, I remembered her words, as quoted by Othello in Act 1: the effect of his story, he says, was such that "She wished she had not heard it." At the same time, he goes on, she also said that "she wished/ That heaven had made her such a man."

and very young, Patrice Johnson) more than their racial difference. Stewart's mysterious, dreamy Othello, with a tragic past from which he hoped Desdemona would rescue him, was totally, even comically, besotted with her. Both female directors emphasized the brutality of Iago toward Emilia, which was so public as to make one wonder how the other characters could continue to tolerate and trust him. The answer, in each case, seemed to lie in the social setting. What apartheid was for Suzman, the military environment was for Kelly. Her Iago, Ron Canada, was a fat, lazy sergeant type, never happier than when writing things down in his notebook and barking out orders. The director's vision of the play contrasted the warmth of Cyprus (Venus' island) with the cold and rain of Venice, as well as emphasizing the oppression of the Cypriots by the militaristic Venetians. Iago was their representative, just as, in Suzman's production, he represented the full hideousness of apartheid.

FROM RACE TO SEX

A less heavily cut text made it possible to bring out a greater complexity in all the characters, not merely the hero. Desdemona, seen in the nineteenth century mainly as a timid and rather boring vision of sexless purity, benefited from a greater freedom to express her sexuality in the fact that she "did love the Moor to live with him". Restoring more of the text, so that the audience heard Iago's obscene language and saw the full extent of Othello's brutality toward her, also brought out, by contrast, her goodness and courage. For instance, Trevor Nunn's Royal Shakespeare Theatre Company production of 1989 depicted a vital, playful Desdemona (Imogen Stubbs) who could never have imagined herself dying at the hands of her husband (the opera singer Willard White). This production, like many other recent ones, also developed the relationship between Desdemona and Emilia (Zoe Wanamaker). The "willow scene," once thought of simply as an opportunity for a pathetic song from Desdemona, is now played to bring out the friendship between two women, originally separated by class, or difference in age, or by Emilia's feelings of guilt over an affair with Othello in her past, or by her revulsion at the mixed marriage or envy of its happiness. Almost too late, the two women finally achieve an understanding in their mutual unhappiness, an understanding that finally leads to Emilia's courageous and suicidal defiance of her husband. Even Bianca (whose role was cut from the play in the eighteenth and nineteenth centuries) has been reevaluated, seen not as a tart but a spirited woman who understands Cassio better than the great lady whom he idealizes. And of course the restoration of Bianca to the play affects the characterization of Cassio, no longer just an innocent victim of Iago but an ambitious young officer who has trouble fitting his sexual appetite into his career plans. Trevor Nunn's late nineteenth-century setting lent itself to a psychologically subtle reading of all the characters, particularly Ian McKellen's brilliant study of Iago's repressed sexuality.

FROM RACE TO RELIGION?

Othello was once a play about a passionate lover who is deceived into murdering the woman he loves. It is now a play about a black man who marries, and later murders, a white woman. The explosiveness of this subject matter is the result of history, which has intersected with the play to an alarming extent. Until recently, there was a tendency to assume that any production that made Othello a brown north African Moor instead of a black subequatorial African was being racist in ignoring the importance of the specific type of racial conflict that exists in North America. Given the extent of religious conflict in the twenty-first century and the increasing visibility of the Arab world, I should guess that in future productions the balance may tip in the other direction and religion may play as great a role in the tragedy as race.

As Performed

Janet Suzman

The year is 1987, the place Johannesburg. In only three years time Nelson Mandela will walk out of prison after twenty-seven years, but we weren't to know that at the time; to us it looked as if apartheid would continue to wreak its havoc until the crack of doom. The governing regime appeared unassailable, in spite of worldwide boycotts.

Us? We were the people who were involved in founding The Market Theatre in 1976—formerly a Victorian meat market and then transformed into a magical quasi-Globe in downtown Johannesburg, where apartheid was entirely banished and its absurdities and cruelties roundly mocked from the stage. When you live in a free country you take the theater for granted, but you can't imagine how exciting going to the theater can be in a police state—how exhilarating it is to mingle for a few talkative hours with like-minded people, to feel deliciously subversive watching plays that satirize the life outside—rule-bound and cruelly policed. Freedom of thought, richness of language, uncensored celebration of the human comedy—these become precious if you're not allowed them in the outside world. (That's not to say The Market didn't frequently have to answer to a Censorship Board when some individual complained that he was being corrupted and depraved.)

Memories are short and history moves on. I am so happy that apartheid is over, but perhaps a quick reminder to those who are too young to remember: the system of apartheid was based on separating the black and white races—and every shade in between—by law; laws made specifically by whites for the protection of the white minority. It was a system of discrimination based solely on a racist agenda. Acts of Parliament were passed to make bigotry legal. Can you imagine? It was against this context that we sought to mount a production of *Othello*.

PROTEST PLAY

In *Othello* the idea of "erring from nature" is raised several times whenever the marriage of Desdemona and Othello is mentioned. The doctrinaire Afrikaner Calvinist view was that Nature itself abhors miscegenation, and that since, in the natural world, like only propagates with like, the same natural embargo must prevail with human beings. In other words, they chose to see the human race as being made up of different species. This is the same viciously skewed argument that informed Nazi policies in the last World War—that certain peoples were "sub-human" and therefore had to be exterminated. The Afrikaner Nationalist view was that they must merely be separated at every level of social intercourse.

> *OTHELLO*
> And yet, how nature erring from itself,—
>
> *IAGO*
> Ay, there's the point. As, to be bold with you—
> Not to affect many proposèd matches
> Of her own clime, complexion, and degree,
> Whereto we see in all things nature tends—
> Foh! One may smell in such a will most rank,
> Foul disproportion, thoughts unnatural.

3.3.228–234

Othello, tussling with the alien notion that his beloved wife might be betraying him, fears that Desdemona's nature—loyal, honest, transparent—might have become its own opposite—disloyal, dishonest, opaque—i.e., erring from itself. Read again Iago's reply to this agonized lament, and you will read, in essence, a manifesto expressing the essential elements of Grand Apartheid. (Grand was applied to the overall concept of this vicious policy, Petty to the daily enforcement of its rules). Basically, Iago says this: "If you don't marry someone of your own kind—a rule which all of the natural world obeys—it is a willful, disgusting aberration that goes against the natural order."

Now perhaps you will begin to understand why I so much wanted to direct this great play in the South African context of the time. Shakespeare, entirely unaware of apartheid, has nevertheless imagined the sort of mindset that brought it into being. Someone once said that Shakespeare's plays, "like iron filings to a magnet, seem to attract whatever crisis is in the air." Again and again a play of his will hit a political/historical nail right on the head. To a South African eye, Iago seemed unmistakeably to represent the white enforcers intent on trashing the transgressing marriage of a black man and a white woman. Desdemona had not affected a match "of her own clime, complexion, and degree" and just deserts would surely follow, the subtext being that if they didn't he'd make them. The metaphor of the play, as we read it, was sound. (Although, strictly speaking, there is no subtext in Shakespeare: the clues to character and motivation being perfectly visible to the naked eye if you search thoroughly. The great scholar and teacher John Barton says that in Shakespeare, text *is* character.)

Because of the prevailing international cultural boycott, it was necessary to obtain permission from the Cultural Desk of the African National Congress in-exile to mount this play, which we did, on the grounds that we saw *Othello* as a protest play. Since Shakespeare has always been used subversively in societies where freedom of expression was restricted, we succeeded in getting the requisite nod to proceed.

CHARACTERS IN A RACIST SOCIETY
Armchair Liberal
Once you start to see this play through the prism of racist South Africa, it is astonishing how the characters emerge as a familiar cross-section of society. Brabantio is the all-too familiar armchair liberal, flaunting his openminded credentials by inviting the black general to dinner, but heaven forbid he should marry his daughter. His insulting language when he finds out that his child has gone betrays the prejudice sitting just beneath the skin:

> corrupted: 1.3.61
> for nature so preposterously to err: 1.3.63
> foul thief: 1.2.62
> Damned as thou art: 1.2.63
> sooty bosom: 1.2.70
> such a thing as thou, to fear not to delight: 1.2.71
> foul charms: 1.2.73
> an abuser of the world, a practiser of arts inhibited: 1.2.78–79

and then this outburst:

> … and she, in spite of nature,
> Of years, of country, credit, every thing,
> To fall in love with what she feared to look on!
> It is a judgment maimed and most imperfect
> That will confess perfection so could err
> Against all rules of nature and must be driven
> To find out practices of cunning hell…

1.3.97–103

So you see, Iago's "thoughts unnatural" have found a higher advocacy.

Bigots

Iago and Roderigo, from the start, are the out-and-out bigots. It is absolutely shocking to hear Roderigo call Othello "the thick lips" (1.1.65). Iago uses "gross" twice in describing Othello, and begins his nasty game of invoking animals to denigrate him:

> you'll have your daughter covered with a
> Barbary horse; you'll have your nephews neigh to you;

1.1.108–109

He calls Othello "an old black ram" and most famously conjures this image:

> …your daughter and the Moor are now
> making the beast with two backs

1.1.112–113

Donkeys, goats, and monkeys enter his malicious menagerie; he is foully insulting. South Africa once abounded with those openly racist types, their brutality protected by the prevailing laws sanctioning discrimination. They simply conduct themselves more covertly now, as they do in most countries where racist behavior is not legal. Leopards don't change their spots.

Perpetrator

If you search for the reason why Iago trashes the marriage, you will search in vain for an overridingly watertight one. He offers up several for your consideration: he's jealous of Cassio's advancement; he's suspicious that the Moor has had a fling with his wife Emilia; he despises Othello because he's black, or because he's credulous; he's disgusted with Desdemona for breaking the rules of white Venice. Put all these into the stewing-pot of Iago's character and they'll bubble away merrily, but do they measure up to the snarling rapaciousness of Iago's revenge? I think not.

There are two more revealing insights into his singular mind: of Cassio he says: "He hath a daily beauty in his life / Which makes me ugly." Think about what that tells us about Iago's character. And this is the final word from Iago in the play:

> Demand me nothing. What you know, you know.
> From this time forth, I never will speak word.

5.2.301–302

This is a flat refusal to explain or excuse himself. Now look at the beginning of the play and you might say that he places his being beyond rational explanation: "I am not what I am" (1.1.64). In the Bible, Jehova is described by the mighty enigma of "I am what I am"—what diametric opposite is Shakespeare suggesting here for his creation of Iago? The perpetrators of apartheid likewise never seemed bothered to excuse that abominable era in history. These resonant quotes should keep you discussing the mysteries of human behavior for hours. Othello calls Iago a demi-devil; is evil explicable, even to itself?

Richard Haddon Haines as Iago
Photo by Ruphin Coudyzer

CHARACTERS IN THE PLAY
Iago
The actor who played Iago was a friendly bear of a man with a huge talent, Richard Haddon Haines, and I can hardly bear to tell you that he died of a brain tumor barely two years after this production, having just played a fine King Lear for the Royal Shakespeare Company. A tragic waste. Richard knew well the threat of uniformed power in South Africa, and how its public face took pains to appear reliable. Othello sees Iago as a wholly trustworthy officer, he is described as "honest" about eighteen times in the play. His bedside manner, so to speak, is impeccable. (Shakespeare is fascinated, in all of his plays, with the idea of appearance and reality.) Only in his soliloquies, when he shares his wickedness with the audience, does gleeful malevolence seep through the armor of this sober ensign. Iago can be funny. Evil can be alluring, dangerous stuff.

Cassio
Cassio's sheer decency shows itself at every point; even more wonder that Othello's judgment goes so badly awry in condemning him solely on the evidence of Iago's plausible storytelling. (What an actor! No, what a dissembler—actors always try to be truthful; liars try to cover it up, and the trick is to sail as close to the truth as possible. Iago is a consummate con man.) Desdemona and Cassio are obviously out of the same social drawer, and feel easy with each other. Cassio is secretly and entirely honorably in love with Desdemona, rather like a schoolboy crush. Perceiving their fondness and friendliness, which plays right into his hands, Iago skews an innocent friendship into something it isn't. The slightest shift of viewpoint and comfortable familiarity becomes threatening intimacy. Jealousy, with its glaring green eyes, is spawned. It is significant that at the end, wise Lodovico acknowledges Cassio's qualities by appointing him ruler of Cyprus in Othello's place. (5.2.330)

Emilia
Emilia is often seen as the first feminist in literature. She seems to view her life with a certain clear-eyed reality, though she cannot do much about it. I always saw her as an abused wife; I can't imagine Iago not hurting her when he feels like it. Her speech to Desdemona in 4.3.80–99 bears that out. She is too obedient to be entirely sure of herself. She brings her husband the stolen handker-

chief as he has asked, but fear informs the giving. Her journey in the play hurtles towards a fatal self-awareness by the end. She dies telling the truth, she dies for telling the truth, and she knows what she is doing, which to me denotes a figure growing in tragic stature. Neither Desdemona nor Othello reach self-knowledge with the same fierce flame which, once lit, burns in her. I don't want to overly push the point, but South Africa had its full share of those brave enough to defy authority and be punished for fighting for a fairer world. In a great drama, the courage to stand up and shout out is given words.

Desdemona

Desdemona too has enormous courage. She defies her father, she presents a fine case to the Senate to accompany her husband to war-torn Cyprus, she outrides a storm at sea. We watch her bearing the ensuing humiliations as the drama unfolds with an unswerving steadiness of heart, as if waiting patiently

Dorothy Gould as Emilia and Joanna Weinberg as Desdemona
Photo by Ruphin Coudyzer

for yet another storm to pass. It hardly needs saying that she has not an ounce of her father's prejudice in her. "I saw Othello's visage in his mind" (1.3.249) has to be the ultimate reply to all those fools who cannot see beyond the color of a person's skin. Look, too, at the exquisite couplet that ends Act 4; only a supremely decent human being could find such generosity after being so hellishly used. Finally, with her dying breath she blames herself and excuses her husband. She finds, to my mind, an exquisite, almost oriental, fatalism. She holds herself ready to accept whatever comes her way and find good in it since it stems from the man she loves. But she can fight too, as she does for her life at the end—too late. It makes for good drama to wish so fervently that she'd fought before it was too late.

Othello

The sight of white actors blacking up is always faintly ludicrous to my eyes. Even the great Laurence Olivier I could not wholly believe in, though much seduced by his glamorous gleam and those unfurling pink palms. Olivier was a sophisticate, a worldly man, which Othello is not; by reputation a master on the battlefield, the strategies of the bedchamber quite defeat him. John Kani, on the other hand, was the real thing—a black African giving the impression of being at home in white society but most emphatically not of it. He speaks a magnificently vivid, colloquial English, but he dreams in Xhosa, his mother tongue. During those apartheid years, he surely despised the society that ruled his life, but he worked within its margins with authority and grace, biding his time. He kept his home life, his tribal affiliations—all those things nearest to his heart—entirely out of sight, yet, like the superb professional he is, worked hard on his public commitments.

I think John was the first black Othello who was a true exotic, the "wheeling stranger of here and everywhere," the man whose previous life is a mystery. More importantly, unlike previous great Othellos of American extraction, whose native tongue was English, John sounded foreign. In blank verse, the vowels need to be generous; they are like conduits that rush the feelings onwards eventually to pour into the open sea of meaning. The consonants are the sluice gates, controlling the flow, giving measure and smoothness to the speaking. The Xhosa accent in English tends to compress the diphthongs (beds for birds, eth for earth, stet for state, etc.) and in blank verse they need their full stretch. It took a huge effort to adjust his speaking

John Kani as Othello
Photo by Ruphin Coudyzer

habits and make the poetry live as vividly and movingly as John did. I salute him. I salute the whole cast in fact, because there were many youngsters who had never spoken blank verse before, not the least, luminous Desdemona and fiery Bianca, but after a few intense days of immersion in the structures that inform the speaking of it, they all came to inhabit the verse with great naturalness. No one need ever be in awe of Shakespeare—trust the verse and the sense will inevitably emerge. It's worth remembering that Shakespeare wrote for actors, not academics.

A FINAL WORD

I am sure that one of the legacies of this particular production of *Othello*, born in oppression, is that after John Kani it is no longer possible for a white actor to take the role without an uncomfortable feeling of usurpation. The same would go for Aaron in *Titus Andronicus*. Times have changed. I am not in the least an advocate of documentary casting—for instance, that only a Jewish actor should play Shylock and so on; however, for Othello, blackness starts with the right skin color. All other dramatic roles require a purely imaginative assumption. One other point—whereas a white actor would need to preserve a certain old-fashioned operatic distance between himself and the woman he suffers the pangs of hell for, a black actor need have no fear of leaving smudges on his Desdemona. Passion can have its moment in a play that pivots on physical enthrallment. If white people slammed out of the theater in disgust at the moments of tenderness between husband and wife, then that was more revealing of their closed minds than our unforced enactment of marital love. Likewise, if young black people from Soweto queued up in the hundreds to see this play, then that too revealed how much the tragic humiliation of a black man by a white thug spoke volumes to them in lives cursed by apartheid. Now that South Africa is bathed in the sunlight of democracy, it might be interesting to see how the shadows might fall if the situation was reversed—a white Othello holding office in a black state. Or would that be too contrived?

"It is the Green-eyed Monster":

Othello AND POP CULTURE

Douglas Lanier

Throughout much of the nineteenth and twentieth centuries *Othello* has been closely associated in the popular imagination with questions of racial identity, not with tragically misguided romantic passion. *Othello* has long been a vehicle in Anglo-American popular culture for addressing the vexed cultural status of black men in white society. Accordingly, the play has, on the one hand, perpetuated racist stereotypes and, on the other, garnered empathy for a noble black man brought low by prejudice and the demands of divided identity. Because Othello is Shakespeare's most prominent black character and yet has repeatedly been drafted into service for racist purposes, black actors and artists have often been interested in finding ways of reclaiming Othello as a figure for the dignity of black identity and culture.

BLACKFACE AND MINSTREL SHOWS

The 1840s were to see a complementary development in popular culture: the rise of the blackface minstrel Othello. Developing in the early 1800s and extending throughout the nineteenth century into the early twentieth, minstrel shows offered a mélange of musical numbers, comic banter, parodies of contemporary culture and farcical skits performed by white (and, in a few cases, black) musicians in burnt cork makeup and "plantation" dialect. Undeniably racist in their humor, such shows typically used stereotypical black characters to poke fun at social pretensions and mainstream "proper" culture, of which Shakespeare was a prime example. As the most famous blackface play in the classical theatrical repertory, Shakespeare's *Othello* was an irresistible target for minstrel lampoon. Minstrel performer T. D. Rice, the original "Jim Crow," produced a parody of *Othello* in 1844 (he billed it as a "burlesque opera" and modeled it after a British burlesque produced ten years earlier), the first of a long line of minstrel Othellos. In these parody versions of Shakespeare's play, with titles like "Desdemonum" and "Da's De Money," Othello's blackness is emphasized, imagined through the racist stereotypes of the minstrel show. In these plays Othello speaks with a thick plantation or West Indian accent, crudely pursues women or money (or both), lapses into jealousy with little motivation, and mangles the plot of Shakespeare's play by falling into slapstick brawls or minstrel songs. This version of Othello provided definitive evidence of his unrefined, uncivilizable nature, though, it should be added, these working-class burlesques often were ambivalent about being the value of conforming to standards of bourgeois "polite" behavior. From its American origins, minstrel Shakespeare was to become an international phenomenon in the nineteenth century whose popularity and effects would last well into the twentieth. Minstrelsy was thereby to become a powerful filter through which Shakespeare's Moor was perceived.

It is important to recognize that nearly all performances of the character of Othello up to the 1940s were in blackface, particularly in the United States. It was not until the 1940s, with Paul Robeson's Broadway performance, that the color barrier was definitively broken and the role was opened up to black actors.

BLACK SELF-REPRESENTATION AND RACIAL DIGNITY

Because it is the "classical" play most closely associated with the practice of blackface performance, *Othello* remains a lightning rod for issues of black self-representation on the stage and film. It is interesting, then, to note that in some popular works addressed to black audiences that the opportunity for a black man to play Othello carries symbolic resonance. In *Paradise in Harlem* (1939, Joseph Seiden), a so-called "race" film produced for predominantly African American audiences, the protagonist Lem's aspiration to play Othello is the centerpiece of his noble lifelong struggle against racism; tellingly, as the film opens he is stuck performing in a minstrel show. The film ends with a triumphal performance of the final scene of *Othello* with Lem as the Moor, the first film portrayal of Othello by a black actor. Interestingly Lem's performance of the murder of Desdemona slowly morphs into a musical number in which the black audience enthusiastically celebrates, and Othello's confession and suicide are silently excised. More recently, *True Identity* (1991, Charles Lane), written as a star vehicle for British comic Lenny

Henry, also features a struggling black actor, Miles Pope, who dreams of playing Othello. The twist is that when Miles becomes pursued by a hit man, he resorts to disguise as a white man—complete with whiteface makeup—to elude danger, in the process sending up white mannerisms and privilege, in effect reversing the racial polarity of minstrel show blackface. His performance of Othello at film's end becomes the means for him to expose the plot against him and thus to regain his true identity as a black man. In both films, these actors view Othello as a role through which they can assert racial dignity and cultural power.

BLACK-WHITE RELATIONS

Othello's close association with issues of racial identity and black-white relations also regularly surfaces in popular culture adaptations and references. This association can be played for comedy, as in "Lamont as Othello," an episode of the African American TV series *Sanford and Son* (broadcast September 14, 1973), in which irascible Fred Sanford (played by veteran black comic Redd Foxx) catches his son Lamont choking a white woman as they rehearse a scene from *Othello*. Fred's comic reaction—he thinks Lamont is really murdering her—uses *Othello* to lampoon the racist assumption that black young men are at bottom brutish, lusty louts, an assumption which Shakespeare's play has been used to exemplify. More often, however, popular adaptations of *Othello* make contemporary challenges of black identity the stuff of modern tragedy. Indeed, several recent adaptations of *Othello* have made subtle forms of racism in contemporary society their central concern. The American film *O* (2001, Tim Blake Nelson) recasts Othello as Odin, a black basketball star for a Southern prep school; the British TV film *Othello* (2002, Geoffrey Sax) depicts Othello as a black police captain who is elevated to his position as a way of quelling tensions during a racially-charged police scandal. Both films use *Othello* to demonstrate how, despite their outward success, these black professionals continue to find themselves plagued by inner doubt and subtle, rather than direct, forms of racism. This focus also found voice in journalism. Shakespeare's play was a ubiquitous touchstone in the media frenzy surrounding the 1995 trial of O. J. Simpson for the murders of Nicole Brown Simpson and Ronald Goldman, where a cross-racial marriage riven by jealousy and the precipitous fall of a black celebrity lionized by white society became the shaky foundation upon which all manner of comparisons between O. J. and Othello were erected. The comparison between the two even became the basis for the play *OJ / Othello* at the 1998 Edinburgh Fringe Festival. References to *Othello*, as well as several other Shakespeare plays, also made cameo appearances in Clarence Thomas's confirmation for the U.S. Supreme Court. It is striking that the critical issue that so exercised nineteenth-century critics, the enigma of Iago's motive for malignity, hardly registers in most pop culture, though Phil Willmott's play *Iago* (1992) and the heavy metal band Thorne's concept album *Iago* (1998) are interesting exceptions. Equally unexplored is Desdemona's plight: in most pop songs, she has become a mere type of the beautiful or long-suffering girlfriend, though a handful of writers have sought to reexamine her character from a feminist perspective, as in Paula Vogel's play *Desdemona: A Play About a Handkerchief* (in which Desdemona is gleefully, unapologetically promiscuous), Ann Marie MacDonald's play *Goodnight Desdemona (Goodmorning Juliet)*, and Louise Plummer's young adult novel *The Unlikely Romance of Kate Bjorkman*.

RELATIONSHIPS AND JEALOUSY

Certainly *Othello* has served as the touchstone for many popular tales of jealousy that do not directly engage the issue of race. Examples include the period melodrama *Les enfants du paradis* (1945, Marcel Carné), the western *Jubal* (1956, Delmer Daves), the horror film *The Flesh and Blood Show* (1974, Pete Walker), the police thriller *Internal Affairs* (1990, Michael Figgis), and the Mexican dance drama *Huapango* (2004, Ivan Lipkies). "Sergeant Iago," an episode of *Gomer Pyle*, broadcast on February 16, 1968, treats this theme less seriously, making Iago's generation of jealousy the stuff of sitcom romance rather than tragedy.

A fascinating theme closely linked with *Othello* addresses a different sort of vexed divided identity: that of the actor. *Othello* figures prominently in a series of stories on stage and screen that involve an actor playing the Moor who comes to murder or abuse women in his "real" life, compulsively prompted by the part he plays. Two of the earliest examples of this plotline can be found in Pordes-Milo's melodrama *Scirocco* and August Blom's silent short *Desdemona* (1911). In Blom's film, an actor who learns of his costar's affair with a gentleman takes his revenge upon her as he and she enact the final scene of *Othello*. (Remarkably, in Blom's film it is not the actor but the gentleman whom the audience blames.) Myriad variations were to follow, especially on film: *A Modern Othello* (1917), *Carnival* (1921, remade as a talkie in 1931), *Men are not Gods* (1937), and *Anna's Sin* (1955) all feature elements of this plotline. There are even comic versions. "Homicidal Ham," an episode of the TV series *Cheers* (broadcast October 27, 1983), turns on Diane Chambers' fears that her costar in an amateur production of *Othello*, a recently released criminal, is a homicidal maniac bent on murdering her in mid-performance. *A Double Life* (1947, George Cukor), an artful *film noir* for which Ronald Colman won an Oscar for best actor, offers an especially well-crafted variation on this theme. When he gets the part of Othello, Anthony John, a Broadway actor, finds that the Moor's suspicions and jealous rage invade his mind, fueling his anger against his ex-wife Brita, with whom he maintains a romantically ambiguous relationship, and against Pat Kroll, a seedy waitress at the Venice Café with whom he has begun an affair. When Kroll innocently tells him to "put out the light," John is compelled to murder her and later, convinced that Brita is attracted to Bill Friend, a reporter, John attempts to strangle him as well. The film is exceptionally skillful in portraying John's helpless descent into guilt, paranoia, and self-loathing, all of which converges on the film's climax, a performance of the final scene of *Othello* in which John nearly strangles Brita, confesses his guilt in character as Othello, and stabs himself in earnest onstage. In this version of *Othello*, the Moor comes to symbolize the "dark" unconscious of John's otherwise debonair demeanor, a "blackness" uncontrollably brought to the surface just by uttering Shakespeare's words.

This theme is by no means spent. Two recent films use *Othello* to explore the fluid line between acting and reality, but they develop the theme in novel ways. Roysten Abel's 2003 film *In Othello* (from his stage play) concerns an English-speaking troupe in New Delhi who, as they mount a cross-cultural production of *Othello*, find themselves riven by jealousy, professional rivalry, and ethnic tension, all of which bears striking resemblance to the details of Shakespeare's plays. Abel's film demonstrates the long cultural reach of *Othello*'s association with this metatheatrical theme. Richard Eyre's *Stage Beauty* (2004, from Jeffrey Hatcher's play) uses the final scene of *Othello* to consider the divided nature of the cross-dressed stage in the early Restoration. The film chronicles the downfall of Ned Kynaston, a man who specializes in women's parts, as he is challenged by his imitator, the actress Maria. Their rivalry turns on their competing depictions of Desdemona's death, both of which suffer from artificiality. At the film's climax, by pushing the final scene of *Othello* from a stylized spectacle to a seemingly real murder, Kynaston coaxes a realistic, Method-style performance from Maria and so resolves the problem of woman's divided identity on the stage. The film comedy *I Will Avenge You, Iago!*, currently in post-production, offers yet another contemporary variation on this perennial storyline. In all these works, race is hardly at issue; rather, all testify to the newly problematic nature of the theater in an age of cinema, even as they celebrate—albeit perversely—the overwhelming power of Shakespeare's language and characters, a power akin, they suggest, to the perverse power of Iago.

OTHELLO IN MUSIC—FROM OPERA TO HIP-HOP

Many have sought to popularize Shakespeare by transposing his work into musical forms. In this, *Othello* has been no exception, though the play has not been as popular a subject for music than some of Shakespeare's other works, perhaps because the sensitive racial issues in the play defy easy musical adaptation. Though Gioachino Rossini's operatic *Otello* (1816) was popular throughout the nineteenth century, it was eclipsed in popularity when Guiseppe Verdi's *Otello* premiered in 1887; both have become staples of the operatic repertoire. Verdi's version epitomizes a romantic conception of the play, emphasizing Othello's intense, finally tragic love for Desdemona rather than his racial victimization by Iago. Indeed, in his remarks on the opera librettist Arriga Boito speaks of Otello and Iago as deracialized personifications of elemental passion: "...Otello is Jealousy and Iago Envy." When jazz became a craze in mid-twentieth century America and Europe, it seemed to offer a new vehicle for adapting Shakespeare to popular musical form, one perhaps especially amenable to *Othello* because jazz was, at least initially, identified as "black" music. The film *Paradise in Harlem*, which melds the final scene of *Othello* with gospel and jazz music, illustrates the possibility of such a hybrid, as does Duke Ellington's *Such Sweet Thunder*, a 1957 jazz suite based on Shakespearean characters which gives Othello special prominence. Tellingly enough, both adaptations were produced by black artists. A fully-fledged jazzed-up *Othello* did finally appear in the form of the film *All Night Long* (1962, Basil Dearden). It tells the tale of ambitious drummer Johnny Cousin, who, on an effort to advance his career, poisons the marriage between black band leader Aurelius Rex (clearly modeled on Ellington) and his white wife Delia Lane, a singer. Especially deft is the Iago figure's use of an edited tape recording to incriminate Cass, the sax player with Rex's band who has been rehearsing privately with Delia. But for all the film's clever modernization and cameos by real jazz stars such as Charles Mingus, Johnny Dankworth, and Dave Brubeck, it arrived after jazz had moved from swing, a widely popular musical style, to bop and after, a coterie art. What is more, rather surprisingly *All Night Long* reveals little interest in the changing racial politics of the moment, in the jazz world or elsewhere. No one bats an eye at Rex and Delia's interracial marriage, and Cousin betrays Rex to advance his own flagging career, not because Rex is black.

By the mid-sixties, popular taste had moved in the direction of rock and roll (yet another "black" musical form), and the success of rock operas such as *Tommy* and *Jesus Christ Superstar* in the late sixties prompted the emergence of Shakespearean rock opera. *Othello* provided the basis for *Catch My Soul* (1969, lyrics and book by Jack Good, music by Ray Pohlman and Emil Dean Zoghby), a rock opera that reconceived Othello as the charismatic leader of a hippie religious commune undone by a demonic Iago. Patrick McGoohan's film version of *Catch My Soul* (1973) featured Richie Havens, the popular black folk singer, in the role of Othello, presenting him as a clearly Christ-like martyr dressed in a white robe who kills Desdemona and himself in a village church. Although the independent film is rather crudely made, its engagement with contradictions and conflicts within sixties counterculture make it a fascinating historical document. A number of other attempts have been made to recraft *Othello* in musical terms, among them the Canadian country-and-western musical *Cruel Tears* (1975), a German adaptation *Othello: Die Rock-oper* (1994, Hans von Chelius and Stefan Maro) and Mirta de la Torre Mulhare's *O.T.* (2001). Though the Reduced Shakespeare Company's *The Complete Works of Wllm Shkspr (Abridged)* (1994) wickedly lampooned the prospect of adapting *Othello* to hip-hop, the currently popular "black" musical idiom, it has not prevented that possibility from being explored: the student ensemble HWS-Rembiko presented *The Tragedy of Othella, the Hip Hop Diva of Venice Beach* at the Edinburgh Fringe Festival in 2003.

A FINAL WORD

Despite gains in the status of peoples of color in the past half-century and the extraordinary prevalence of black music in popular culture, *Othello* continues to reside in the long shadow of Anglo-American society's jaundiced attitudes toward black men, a fact amply demonstrated by the speed and ease with which Othello became a popular paradigm for discussing O. J. Simpson at the height of that *cause celebre*. As is so often the case with popular cultural appropriations of Shakespeare, *Othello*'s afterlife has been profoundly ambivalent, at once a means for perpetuating outmoded stereotypes and yet a vehicle for progressive representations of black identity and culture. But the firm association of *Othello* with questions of race has also worked to mute the play's potential in popular culture for engaging other, equally important themes, most notably questions of religious difference and marital abuse.

Dramatis Personae

DUKE OF VENICE

BRABANTIO, a senator

Other Senators

GRATIANO, brother to Brabantio

LODOVICO, kinsman to Brabantio

OTHELLO, a noble Moor in the service of the Venetian state

CASSIO, his lieutenant

IAGO, his ancient

RODERIGO, a Venetian gentleman

MONTANO, Othello's predecessor in the government of Cyprus

Clown, servant to Othello

DESDEMONA, daughter to Brabantio and wife to Othello

EMILIA, wife to Iago

BIANCA, mistress to Cassio

Sailor, Messenger, Herald, Officers, Gentlemen, Musicians, and Attendants

[Othello

Act 1

0: Scene: *Othello* is notable for the number of scenes that take place at night and sometimes in semi-darkness. This is one such scene: it opens on a street scene in semi-darkness, with the conversation between Iago and Roderigo. When Brabantio is roused and comes to his window (line 81) he cannot recognize who is below and Roderigo has to identify himself to him (line 94). The darkness suits Iago, who disappears before Brabantio comes out to the street with servants and torches (stage direction, line 155).

1: **Tush:** interjection suggesting mild contempt or impatience

3: **as if the strings were thine:** as if the money were Iago's own

4: **'Sblood:** a contraction of "God's Blood" used as an impolite curse word

4-6: **'Sblood...Despise me:** At various points in the play, the lineation in the First Folio differs from that in the First Quarto. In these lines, the lineation in the First Folio is observed.

9: **off-capped:** took off his cap (i.e., bowed in deference)

10: **price:** personal worth; **place:** position, rank

12: **bombast circumstance:** stuffy, inflated discourse

13: **epithets :** expressions, phrases

15: **nonsuits:** rejects a suit; **certes:** certainly

18: **forsooth:** In truth (here used with a suggestion of contempt)

20: **A fellow...fair wife:** editors debate this line; Cassio is unmarried in the rest of the play

23: **theoric:** theory (instead of practice)

24: **toga'd:** wearing a toga or gown; Iago the soldier is being scornful of civilian authority. ("toged" in the First Quarto, "tongued" in the First Folio and Second Quarto); **consuls:** senator

Act 1, Scene 1]

Enter RODERIGO and IAGO

RODERIGO

    Tush! Never tell me, I take it much unkindly
    That thou, Iago, who hast had my purse
    As if the strings were thine, shouldst know of this.

IAGO

    'Sblood, but you'll not hear me. If ever I did dream
    Of such a matter, abhor me.

RODERIGO

                Thou told'st me   5
    Thou didst hold him in thy hate.

IAGO

                Despise me
    If I do not. Three great ones of the city,
    In personal suit to make me his lieutenant,
    Off-capped to him, and, by the faith of man,
    I know my price, I am worth no worse a place.   10
    But he, as loving his own pride and purposes,
    Evades them, with a bombast circumstance
    Horribly stuffed with epithets of war,
    And, in conclusion,
    Nonsuits my mediators. For "Certes," says he,   15
    "I have already chose my officer."
    And what was he?
    Forsooth, a great arithmetician,
    One Michael Cassio, a Florentine,
    A fellow almost damned in a fair wife,   20
    That never set a squadron in the field,
    Nor the division of a battle knows
    More than a spinster—unless the bookish theoric,
    Wherein the toga'd consuls can propose

Set rendering of "Brabantio's House" from the 1951 staging by Orson Welles at St.
James Theatre

Rare Book and Special Collections Library, University of Illinois at Urbana-Champaign

29: **beleed:** placed on the lee (i.e., in a position unfavorable to the wind)
30: **counter-caster:** arithmetician; Iago is implying that Cassio is a mere accountant.
32: **ancient:** ensign or standard-bearer
35–37: **Preferment...to the first:** Promotions are granted by favoritism and not by
seniority (the traditional way)
38: **affined:** bound to, required. The First Quarto has "assigned", also a possible
reading (perhaps a confusion of "f" and long "s" which were similarly written in
Shakespeare's day).
44: **knee-crooking:** courtseying
47: **provender:** dry animal feed
47: **cashiered:** sold off; dismissed
49: **trimmed...duty:** maintaining the outward appearance of being dutiful

As masterly as he. Mere prattle without practice   25
Is all his soldiership. But he, sir, had th' election,
And I, of whom his eyes had seen the proof
At Rhodes, at Cyprus, and on other grounds
Christian and heathen, must be beleed and calmed
By debitor and creditor. This counter-caster,   30
He, in good time, must his lieutenant be,
And I, God bless the mark, his Moorship's ancient.

RODERIGO
By heaven, I rather would have been his hangman.

IAGO
Why, there's no remedy. 'Tis the curse of service;
Preferment goes by letter and affection,   35
And not by old gradation, where each second
Stood heir to th' first. Now sir, be judge yourself,
Whether I in any just term am affined
To love the Moor.

RODERIGO
                        I would not follow him then.

IAGO
O sir, content you.   40
I follow him to serve my turn upon him.
We cannot all be masters, nor all masters
Cannot be truly followed. You shall mark
Many a duteous and knee-crooking knave,
That, doting on his own obsequious bondage,   45
Wears out his time, much like his master's ass,
For nought but provender, and, when he's old, cashiered.
Whip me such honest knaves. Others there are
Who, trimmed in forms and visages of duty,
Keep yet their hearts attending on themselves,   50
And, throwing but shows of service on their lords,
Do well thrive by them, and when they have lined their coats,
Do themselves homage. These fellows have some soul,

Costume rendering for Roderigo from the 1951 staging by Orson Welles at St. James Theatre

Rare Book and Special Collections Library, University of Illinois at Urbana-Champaign

57: **In following...myself:** Iago is following the Moor in self-interest

59: **peculiar:** private

60-62: **For when...extern:** For when my behavior actually reflects my inner feelings

62: **complement:** This is the reading in both the First Quarto and First Folio, though some editors amend it to "compliment". Both senses were spelled "complement" in Shakespeare's time. In its modern sense, "complement" means the outward behavior that complements or completes the inner feelings, and "compliment" an outward show of politeness. Here, both senses are possible: Iago means "when my outward behavior actually reflects my inner feelings".

64: **daws:** jackdaws; the First Quarto has "doves", a less likely but possible reading (based on a confusion with the similarly written "daws").

65: **thicklips:** a derogatory reference to Othello

68: **Proclaim:** denounce

74: **timorous accent:** fearful tone

And such a one do I profess myself. For, sir,
It is as sure as you are Roderigo,   55
Were I the Moor, I would not be Iago:
In following him, I follow but myself.
Heaven is my judge, not I, for love and duty,
But seeming so, for my peculiar end;
For when my outward action doth demonstrate   60
The native act and figure of my heart
In complement extern, 'tis not long after
But I will wear my heart upon my sleeve
For daws to peck at; I am not what I am.

RODERIGO
What a full fortune does the thick-lips owe   65
If he can carry't thus!

IAGO
                                    Call up her father,
Rouse him, make after him, poison his delight,
Proclaim him in the streets, incense her kinsmen,
And though he in a fertile climate dwell,
Plague him with flies: though that his joy be joy,   70
Yet throw such changes of vexation on't
As it may lose some color.

RODERIGO
Here is her father's house, I'll call aloud.

IAGO
Do, with like timorous accent and dire yell
As when, by night and negligence, the fire   75
Is spied in populous cities.

RODERIGO
What ho! Brabantio, Signior Brabantio, ho!

IAGO
Awake! What, ho, Brabantio! Thieves, thieves, thieves!
Look to your house, your daughter, and your bags!
Thieves, thieves!   80

80: Stage Direction: Brabantio usually appears at an upper window or the playhouse balcony.

81–113:
Peter Yapp as Brabantio, John McAndrew as Roderigo,
Anton Lesser as Iago

85: **'zounds:** an exclamation indicating surprise or heavy stress (abbrev. for "God's wounds")

87: **an old black ram:** i.e., Othello

88: **tupping :** fornicating with

88: **white ewe:** i.e., Desdemona

89: **snorting:** snoring

BRABANTIO [appears] above, at a window

BRABANTIO
What is the reason of this terrible summons?
What is the matter there?

RODERIGO
Signior, is all your family within?

IAGO
Are your doors locked?

BRABANTIO
                    Why, wherefore ask you this?

IAGO
'Zounds, sir, you're robbed, for shame, put on your gown!   85
Your heart is burst, you have lost half your soul,
Even now, now, very now, an old black ram
Is tupping your white ewe. Arise, arise,
Awake the snorting citizens with the bell,
Or else the devil will make a grandsire of you.   90
Arise, I say!

BRABANTIO
                    What, have you lost your wits?

RODERIGO
Most reverend signior, do you know my voice?

BRABANTIO
Not I; what are you?

RODERIGO
My name is Roderigo.

BRABANTIO
                    The worser welcome—
I have charged thee not to haunt about my doors;   95

81–113:
Peter Yapp as Brabantio, John McAndrew as Roderigo,
Anton Lesser as Iago

98: **distempering draughts:** alcohol

99: **bravery:** bravado

100: **Sir, sir, sir...needs be sure:** Roderigo attempts to interrupt Brabantio, unsuccessfully, probably talking over Brabantio's lines. Both lines are thus marked as equally shared with the previous.

104: **grange:** a solitary farm house

106: **if:** even if

109: **Barbary horse:** a horse from Northern Africa (i.e., Othello). The phrase suggests an Arab stallion.

110: **coursers:** race horses or warhorses

110: **jennets:** small Spanish horses

110: **germans:** kin, family

111: **profane:** disrespectful

113: **making the beast with two backs:** engaging in sexual intercourse

In honest plainness thou hast heard me say
My daughter is not for thee. And now in madness,
Being full of supper and distempering draughts,
Upon malicious bravery, dost thou come
To start my quiet.

RODERIGO

            Sir, sir, sir—

BRABANTIO

                    But thou must needs be sure   100
My spirit and my place have in their power
To make this bitter to thee.

RODERIGO

            Patience, good sir.

BRABANTIO

What tell'st thou me of robbing? This is Venice—
My house is not a grange.

RODERIGO

                Most grave Brabantio,
In simple and pure soul I come to you.   105

IAGO

'Zounds, sir, you are one of those that will not serve God if the
devil bid you. Because we come to do you service, and you think
we are ruffians, you'll have your daughter covered with a
Barbary horse, you'll have your nephews neigh to you, you'll
have coursers for cousins and jennets for germans.   110

BRABANTIO

What profane wretch art thou?

IAGO

I am one, sir, that comes to tell you your daughter and the Moor
are now making the beast with two backs.

114: Thou...You are a senator: Brabantio's "Thou" is the impolite form, Iago's "You" the polite form, perhaps used ironically. Actors often pause at one of the words before "senator", creating a sense that Iago is about to make a rude reply.

114: a senator: (often said contemptuously)

119: odd-even: between midnight and 1 a.m.

132: wheeling: wandering, not settled

136: tinder: a flammable substance used to start a fire

140: Stage Direction: *Exit*: Brabantio here leaves his window or balcony and goes inside the house, coming out at street level at line 155, (in his night gown, according to the First Quarto stage direction) with servants carrying torches.

BRABANTIO
    Thou art a villain.

IAGO
                    You are a senator.

BRABANTIO
    This thou shalt answer. I know thee, Roderigo.   115

RODERIGO
    Sir, I will answer any thing. But I beseech you,
    If't be your pleasure and most wise consent—
    As partly I find it is that your fair daughter
    At this odd-even and dull watch o' th' night,
    Transported with no worse nor better guard   120
    But with a knave of common hire, a gondolier,
    To the gross clasps of a lascivious Moor.
    If this be known to you and your allowance,
    We then have done you bold and saucy wrongs.
    But if you know not this, my manners tell me   125
    We have your wrong rebuke. Do not believe
    That from the sense of all civility,
    I thus would play and trifle with your reverence.
    Your daughter, if you have not given her leave,
    I say again, hath made a gross revolt,   130
    Tying her duty, beauty, wit and fortunes
    In an extravagant and wheeling stranger
    Of here and everywhere. Straight satisfy yourself.
    If she be in her chamber or your house,
    Let loose on me the justice of the state   135
    For thus deluding you.

BRABANTIO
                    Strike on the tinder, ho!
    Give me a taper; call up all my people.
    This accident is not unlike my dream,
    Belief of it oppresses me already.
    Light, I say, light!

                                                   Exit [above]

141: **meet:** appropriate

142-143: **produced...against:** revealed not to be supporting

144: **gall:** harass, irritate

144: **check:** rebuke

145: **cast:** dismiss

148: **fathom:** ability

154: **Sagittary:** the inn or lodging where Desdemona is staying with Othello, under the sign of Sagittarius the Archer, sometimes depicted as a Centaur, a half man, half horse). See line 1.3.116.

157: **despisèd time:** remaining years when Brabantio is socially condemned (because his daughter eloped)

IAGO

     Farewell, for I must leave you.   140
 It seems not meet, nor wholesome to my place,
 To be produced—as, if I stay, I shall—
 Against the Moor. For I do know the state,
 However this may gall him with some check,
 Cannot with safety cast him, for he's embarked 145
 With such loud reason to the Cyprus wars,
 Which even now stands in act, that for their souls,
 Another of his fathom they have none
 To lead their business. In which regard,
 Though I do hate him as I do hell pains,   150
 Yet, for necessity of present life,
 I must show out a flag and sign of love,
 Which is indeed but sign. That you shall surely find him,
 Lead to the Sagittary the raised search,
 And there will I be with him. So farewell.   155

                Exit
   Enter, [below,] BRABANTIO in his night gown
          with Servants and torches

BRABANTIO

 It is too true an evil. Gone she is,
 And what's to come of my despisèd time
 Is nought but bitterness. Now, Roderigo,
 Where didst thou see her?—O unhappy girl!—
 With the Moor, say'st thou?—Who would be a father?— 160
 How didst thou know 'twas she?—O she deceives me
 Past thought!—What said she to you?—Get more tapers;
 Raise all my kindred.—Are they married, think you?

RODERIGO

 Truly, I think they are.

BRABANTIO

 O heaven, how got she out? O treason of the blood! 165
 Fathers, from hence trust not your daughters' minds
 By what you see them act. Is there not charms
 By which the property of youth and maidhood
 May be abused? Have you not read, Roderigo,
 Of some such thing?

174: **discover:** find

177: **I may command at most:** My authority allows me to demand help in most (homes)

179: **deserve your pains:** i.e., repay or reward you for your troubles

RODERIGO

                Yes, sir, I have indeed.   170

BRABANTIO

Call up my brother. O, would you had had her!
Some one way, some another. Do you know
Where we may apprehend her and the Moor?

RODERIGO

I think I can discover him, if you please
To get good guard and go along with me.   175

BRABANTIO

Pray you, lead on. At every house I'll call—
I may command at most. Get weapons, ho!
And raise some special officers of night.
On, good Roderigo; I will deserve your pains.

                                                Exeunt

Set rendering of "A Street" from the 1951 staging by Orson Welles at
St. James Theatre

Rare Book and Special Collections Library, University of Illinois at Urbana-Champaign

0: Scene: This street scene is again in semi-darkness until the two groups who are
looking for Othello arrive with their torches (lines 28 and 54). At first Iago and Othello
do not clearly see who the first group is (lines 28-34). When the second party arrives,
there is almost a scuffle until Othello stops it (line 59).

4: **to do me service:** to be useful to myself

5: **yerked:** stabbed (with a knife)

6: **prated:** bragged

7: **scurvy:** contemptible

10: **forbear:** leave alone, spare

12: **magnifico:** honorific title (referring to Brabantio)

17: **give him cable:** i.e., give him leeway, room to maneuver

18: **signiory:** rulers or governing body

19: **out-tongue:** get the better of, through talking

21: **promulgate:** publish, make known; the First Quarto has "provulgate", a rare but
possible reading, with a similar meaning; **fetch:** derive, draw as a source

22: **royal siege:** i.e., great social height (Othello comes from a royal family)

23: **unbonneted:** humbly

Act 1, Scene 2]

Enter OTHELLO, IAGO, and Attendants with torches

IAGO

Though in the trade of war I have slain men,
Yet do I hold it very stuff o' th' conscience
To do no contrived murder. I lack iniquity
Sometime to do me service. Nine or ten times
I had thought t' have yerked him here under the ribs. 5

OTHELLO

'Tis better as it is.

IAGO

              Nay, but he prated,
And spoke such scurvy and provoking terms
Against your honor
That, with the little godliness I have,
I did full hard forbear him. But I pray you, sir, 10
Are you fast married? Be assured of this,
That the magnifico is much beloved,
And hath in his effect a voice potential
As double as the Duke's. He will divorce you,
Or put upon you what restraint or grievance 15
The law, with all his might to enforce it on,
Will give him cable.

OTHELLO

              Let him do his spite.
My services which I have done the Signiory
Shall out-tongue his complaints. 'Tis yet to know,
Which when I know that boasting is an honor, 20
I shall promulgate. I fetch my life and being
From men of royal siege, and my demerits
May speak unbonneted to as proud a fortune

26: **unhoused:** unsettled, homeless

27: **circumscription:** restraint; confinement

28: **yond:** (short for "yonder") over there

29: **raised:** awakened and gathered (as in a raised army)

32: **Shall manifest me rightly:** Shall show me to be truthful and in the right

33: **Janus:** the Roman god of all beginnings, used here as an exclamation
(such as "By God"). Significantly, Janus is usually represented as having two faces.

37: **haste-post-haste:** very great haste/hurry

40: **heat:** importance

40: **galleys:** a flat-designed boat powered by oars

41: **sequent :** sequential, in a row

As this that I have reached. For know, Iago,
But that I love the gentle Desdemona,   25
I would not my unhousèd free condition
Put into circumscription and confine
For the sea's worth. But look, what lights come yond?

Enter CASSIO with Officers and torches

IAGO

Those are the raisèd father and his friends,
You were best go in.

OTHELLO

                    Not I; I must be found.   30
My parts, my title and my perfect soul
Shall manifest me rightly. Is it they?

IAGO

By Janus, I think no.

OTHELLO

The servants of the Duke? And my lieutenant?
The goodness of the night upon you, friends.   35
What is the news?

CASSIO

                    The Duke does greet you, general,
And he requires your haste-post-haste appearance,
Even on the instant.

OTHELLO

                    What is the matter, think you?

CASSIO

Something from Cyprus, as I may divine;
It is a business of some heat. The galleys   40
Have sent a dozen sequent messengers
This very night at one another's heels,
And many of the consuls, raised and met,
Are at the Duke's already. You have been hotly called for,

46: **quests:** messengers

48: **spend a word:** say something briefly

48: Editors usually add stage directions for Othello to exit at line 48 and re-enter after line 52, but there are no stage directions in either the First Quarto or the First Folio and he may simply go to the back of the stage and return.

49: **ancient:** Cassio draws attention to Iago's lower rank, possibly angering Iago

50: **boarded a land carack:** (Iago is being vulgar) boarded = enter a boat (with sexual connotation); carack = vessel which carries cargo (he is calling Desdemona a "land carack")

56: **comes to:** comes with

When, being not at your lodging to be found,   45
The Senate hath sent about three several quests
To search you out.

OTHELLO
                'Tis well I am found by you:
I will but spend a word here in the house
And go with you.

                                        [Exit]

CASSIO
                Ancient, what makes he here?

IAGO
Faith, he tonight hath boarded a land carrack.   50
If it prove lawful prize, he's made for ever.

CASSIO
I do not understand.

IAGO
                He's married.

CASSIO
                        To who?

                                [Enter OTHELLO]

IAGO
Marry, to—Come, captain, will you go?

OTHELLO
                Have with you.

CASSIO
Here comes another troop to seek for you.
                        Enter BRABANTIO, RODERIGO, with
                        Officers, Torches and weapons

IAGO
It is Brabantio: general, be advised;   55
He comes to bad intent.

59: **Keep up your bright swords:** Keep your swords sheathed

64: **refer me to all things of sense:** I'll appeal to things that have sense (i.e., people)

68: **wealthy curlèd darlings:** i.e., the young, handsome suitors appropriate to her class

69: **a general mock:** social ridicule

70: **guardage:** guards

70: **sooty bosom:** sooty = dark, i.e., Othello

71: **to fear, not to delight:** i.e., Desdemona should fear Othello, not take pleasure in his company

75: **motion:** sense; reason

77: **attach:** seize; arrest

79: **arts inhibited...warrant:** i.e., magical arts (inhibited = prohibited; out of warrant = illegal)

OTHELLO
Holla! Stand there;

RODERIGO
Signior, it is the Moor.

BRABANTIO
Down with him, thief!

[They draw on both sides]

IAGO
You, Roderigo! Come, sir, I am for you.

OTHELLO
Keep up your bright swords, for the dew will rust them.
Good signior, you shall more command with years   60
Than with your weapons.

BRABANTIO
O, thou foul thief, where hast thou stowed my daughter?
Damned as thou art, thou hast enchanted her,
For I'll refer me to all things of sense,
If she in chains of magic were not bound.   65
Whether a maid so tender, fair and happy,
So opposite to marriage that she shunned
The wealthy curlèd darlings of our nation,
Would ever have, t' incur a general mock,
Run from her guardage to the sooty bosom   70
Of such a thing as thou: to fear, not to delight?
Judge me the world, if 'tis not gross in sense
That thou hast practiced on her with foul charms,
Abused her delicate youth with drugs or minerals
That weakens motion. I'll have't disputed on,   75
'Tis probable and palpable to thinking.
I therefore apprehend and do attach thee
For an abuser of the world, a practicer
Of arts inhibited and out of warrant.
Lay hold upon him. If he do resist,   80
Subdue him at his peril.

82: **my inclining:** those who support or favor me

86: **course of direct session:** a session in court

95: **idle:** trifling, insignificant

98: **have passage free:** be allowed

OTHELLO

                 Hold your hands,
Both you of my inclining, and the rest.
Were it my cue to fight, I should have known it
Without a prompter. Whither will you that I go
To answer this your charge?

BRABANTIO

                 To prison, till fit time   85
Of law, and course of direct session
Call thee to answer.

OTHELLO

                What if I do obey?
How may the Duke be therewith satisfied,
Whose messengers are here about my side,
Upon some present business of the state   90
To bring me to him?

Officer

              'Tis true, most worthy signior;
The Duke's in council and your noble self
I am sure is sent for.

BRABANTIO

             How? The Duke in council?
In this time of the night? Bring him away;
Mine's not an idle cause. The Duke himself,   95
Or any of my brothers of the state,
Cannot but feel this wrong as 'twere their own;
For if such actions may have passage free,
Bond-slaves and pagans shall our statesmen be.

                                      Exeunt

Set rendering of "Council Chamber" from the 1951 staging by Orson Welles
at St. James Theatre
Rare Book and Special Collections Library, University of Illinois at Urbana-Champaign

Orson Welles's sketch of "Senate" from the staging at St. James Theatre
Rare Book and Special Collections Library, University of Illinois at Urbana-Champaign

0: **Scene:** This is the first clearly lit scene, with the Venetian council in urgent session in the middle of the night.
1: **composition:** agreement
2: **gives them credit:** lends them credence
2: **disproportioned:** inconsistent
3: **galleys:** oar-powered boats
5: **just:** accurate
9: **possible enough to judgment:** i.e., close enough for us to decide what to do
10: **not so secure me in the error:** i.e., not sure of the specifics

Act 1, Scene 3]

Enter DUKE and SENATORS, set at a table,
with lights, officers, and Attendants

DUKE OF VENICE
There is no composition in these news
That gives them credit.

First Senator
                Indeed, they are disproportioned.
My letters say a hundred and seven galleys.

DUKE OF VENICE
And mine, a hundred forty.

Second Senator
               And mine two hundred.
But though they jump not on a just account—   5
As in these cases, where the aim reports,
'tis oft with difference—yet do they all confirm
A Turkish fleet, and bearing up to Cyprus.

DUKE OF VENICE
Nay, it is possible enough to judgment.
I do not so secure me in the error,   10
But the main article I do approve
In fearful sense.

Sailor
                           [Within]

What ho, What ho, What ho!

                   [Enter a Sailor]

First Officer
A messenger from the galleys.

18: **How say you:** What do you say

19: **assay:** attempt

20: **keep us in false gaze:** distract us

24: **with more facile question bear it:** more easily win it in battle

25-27: **For that it stands...dressed in:** i.e., Cyprus is not as prepared for war as Rhodes

36: **injointed:** united

DUKE OF VENICE
> Now? What's the business?

Sailor
> The Turkish preparation makes for Rhodes, 15
> So was I bid report here to the state
> By Signior Angelo.

DUKE OF VENICE
> How say you by this change?

First Senator
> This cannot be,
> By no assay of reason. 'Tis a pageant
> To keep us in false gaze. When we consider 20
> Th' importancy of Cyprus to the Turk
> And let ourselves again but understand
> That, as it more concerns the Turk than Rhodes,
> So may he with more facile question bear it,
> For that it stands not in such warlike brace, 25
> But altogether lacks th' abilities
> That Rhodes is dressed in. If we make thought of this,
> We must not think the Turk is so unskillful
> To leave that latest which concerns him first,
> Neglecting an attempt of ease and gain, 30
> To wake and wage a danger profitless.

DUKE OF VENICE
> Nay, in all confidence he's not for Rhodes.

Officer
> Here is more news.

> > > *Enter a Messenger*

Messenger
> The Ottomites, reverend and gracious,
> Steering with due course toward the isle of Rhodes, 35
> Have there injointed them with an after fleet.

38: **restem:** retrace

39: **backward course:** course they followed

39: **frank appearance:** clear, obvious intention

41: **servitor:** servant

42: **free:** willing; eager

43: **believe:** Some editors prefer the conjecture "relieve" as being more forceful but both the First Quarto and the First Folio have "believe" and the messenger may merely be using a formal phrase.

47: **post-post-haste:** great hurry

57: **flood-gate:** overwhelming (like a flood)

58: **engluts:** swallows, consumes

First Senator
Ay, so I thought; how many, as you guess?

Messenger
Of thirty sail; and now they do restem
Their backward course, bearing with frank appearance
Their purposes toward Cyprus. Signior Montano,   40
Your trusty and most valiant servitor,
With his free duty recommends you thus,
And prays you to believe him.

DUKE OF VENICE
'Tis certain then for Cyprus.
Marcus Luccicos, is not he in town?   45

First Senator
He's now in Florence.

DUKE OF VENICE
Write from us to him, post-post-haste, dispatch.

First Senator
Here comes Brabantio and the valiant Moor.
                    Enter BRABANTIO, OTHELLO, CASSIO, IAGO,
                          RODERIGO, and Officers

DUKE OF VENICE
Valiant Othello, we must straight employ you
Against the general enemy Ottoman.—   50
[To BRABANTIO] I did not see you. Welcome, gentle signior.
We lacked your counsel and your help tonight.

BRABANTIO
So did I yours. Good your grace, pardon me,
Neither my place nor aught I heard of business
Hath raised me from my bed, nor doth the general care   55
Take hold on me, for my particular grief
Is of so flood-gate and o'erbearing nature
That it engluts and swallows other sorrows
And it is still itself.

61: **abused:** deceived

62: **mountebanks:** traveling con artists

70: **proper:** own

71: **Stood in your action:** i.e., was the accused party

DUKE OF VENICE
     Why? What's the matter?

BRABANTIO
  My daughter, O my daughter!

DUKE OF VENICE, *SENATORS*
     Dead?

BRABANTIO
           Ay, to me: 60
  She is abused, stol'n from me, and corrupted
  By spells and medicines bought of mountebanks,
  For nature so preposterously to err,
  Being not deficient, blind, or lame of sense,
  Sans witchcraft could not.   65

DUKE OF VENICE
  Whoe'er he be that in this foul proceeding
  Hath thus beguiled your daughter of herself,
  And you of her, the bloody book of law
  You shall yourself read in the bitter letter
  After your own sense—yea, though our proper son   70
  Stood in your action.

BRABANTIO
     Humbly I thank your grace.
  Here is the man, this Moor, whom now, it seems
  Your special mandate for the state-affairs
  Hath hither brought.

All
     We are very sorry for't.

DUKE OF VENICE
  [To OTHELLO] What in your own part can you say to this?   75

BRABANTIO
  Nothing, but this is so.

tracks 4-8

77–95:
Paul Robeson as Othello
John Kani as Othello
F. Scott Fitzgerald as Othello

84: **pith:** strength, force
85: **nine moons:** nine months
86: **tented field:** battlefield
88: **broil:** combat

Lines 90-92: "Yet, by your gracious patience, / I will a round unvarnished tale deliver / Of my whole course of love": The ensemble of The Shakespeare Theatre's 1997–1998 production directed by Jude Kelly

Photo: Carol Rosegg

91: **round:** plain
96: **motion:** impulses
100: **a judgment maimed:** bad judgment
104: **vouch:** declare, vow
107: **To vouch this is no proof:** i.e., To say something is true doesn't prove it is true
108: **Without...test:** without more conclusive proof

OTHELLO

Most potent, grave, and reverend signiors,
My very noble and approved good masters:
That I have ta'en away this old man's daughter,
It is most true; true, I have married her.   80
The very head and front of my offending
Hath this extent, no more. Rude am I in my speech,
And little blessed with the soft phrase of peace:
For since these arms of mine had seven years' pith,
Till now some nine moons wasted, they have used   85
Their dearest action in the tented field,
And little of this great world can I speak,
More than pertains to feats of broil and battle,
And therefore little shall I grace my cause
In speaking for myself. Yet, by your gracious patience,   90
I will a round unvarnished tale deliver
Of my whole course of love: what drugs, what charms,
What conjuration and what mighty magic—
For such proceeding I am charged withal—
I won his daughter.

BRABANTIO

                                    A maiden never bold,   95
Of spirit so still and quiet that her motion
Blushed at herself; and she, in spite of nature,
Of years, of country, credit, every thing,
To fall in love with what she feared to look on!
It is a judgment maimed and most imperfect   100
That will confess perfection so could err
Against all rules of nature, and must be driven
To find out practices of cunning hell
Why this should be. I therefore vouch again
That with some mixtures powerful o'er the blood,   105
Or with some dram conjured to this effect,
He wrought upon her.

DUKE OF VENICE

                                To vouch this is no proof,
Without more wider and more overt test

109: **thin:** (metaphorically) easily seen through

109: **habits:** clothing, outward appearance

110: **modern seeming:** common, ordinary appearances

112: **forced courses:** i.e., by force

115: **affordeth:** results in, yields

125: **justly:** truthfully, accurately

128–170:
Hugh Quarshie as Othello
John Kani as Othello
Edwin Booth as Othello

tracks 9-13

Than these thin habits and poor likelihoods
Of modern seeming do prefer against him.   110

First Senator
   But, Othello, speak:
   Did you by indirect and forced courses
   Subdue and poison this young maid's affections?
   Or came it by request and such fair question
   As soul to soul affordeth?

OTHELLO
                    I do beseech you,   115
   Send for the lady to the Sagittary,
   And let her speak of me before her father.
   If you do find me foul in her report,
   The trust, the office I do hold of you,
   Not only take away, but let your sentence   120
   Even fall upon my life.

DUKE OF VENICE
                    Fetch Desdemona hither.

OTHELLO
   Ancient, conduct them; you best know the place.
                    Exeunt [IAGO and] two or three [Attendants]
   And, till she come, as truly as to heaven
   I do confess the vices of my blood,
   So justly to your grave ears I'll present   125
   How I did thrive in this fair lady's love,
   And she in mine.

DUKE OF VENICE
                    Say it, Othello.

OTHELLO
   Her father loved me, oft invited me,
   Still questioned me the story of my life,
   From year to year: the battles, sieges, fortunes   130
   That I have passed.

128–170:
Hugh Quarshie as Othello
John Kani as Othello
Edwin Booth as Othello

134: **chances:** events

136: **scapes:** escapes

136: **breach :** gap in fortifications (military term)

138: **redemption:** release

139: **portance:** conduct (possibly referring to both traveling and behavior)

139: **travailous:** ("travel's" in the First Quarto, "traveller's" in the First Folio); G. R. Proudfoot (Notes & Queries, April 1974, 130) suggested the rare word "travailous", which most recent editors have adopted, with its quibble on "travel" and "travail" (hard labor). The word would sound much like "traveller's" on the stage. Othello's exotic vocabulary seems to have created difficulties for scribes and compositors.

140: **antres:** caves

140: **idle:** useless, infertile

144: **Anthropophagi:** cannibals

151: **pliant hour:** convenient time

153: **dilate:** expand upon, relate

154: **parcels:** in small increments

155: **intentively:** intently, with strong focus

I ran it through, even from my boyish days,
To th' very moment that he bade me tell it.
Wherein I spake of most disastrous chances,
Of moving accidents by flood and field,   135
Of hair-breadth scapes i' th' imminent deadly breach,
Of being taken by the insolent foe
And sold to slavery; of my redemption thence,
And portance in my travailous history.
Wherein of antres vast and deserts idle,   140
Rough quarries, rocks and hills whose heads touch heaven
It was my hint to speak,—such was my process.
And of the Cannibals that each other eat,
The Anthropophagi, and men whose heads
Do grow beneath their shoulders. This to hear   145
Would Desdemona seriously incline,
But still the house-affairs would draw her thence
Which ever as she could with haste dispatch,
She'd come again, and with a greedy ear
Devour up my discourse. Which I observing,   150
Took once a pliant hour and found good means
To draw from her a prayer of earnest heart
That I would all my pilgrimage dilate,
Whereof by parcels she had something heard,
But not intentively. I did consent,   155
And often did beguile her of her tears,
When I did speak of some distressful stroke
That my youth suffered. My story being done,
She gave me for my pains a world of sighs.
She swore, in faith, 'twas strange, 'twas passing strange,   160
'Twas pitiful, 'twas wondrous pitiful;
She wished she had not heard it, yet she wished
That heaven had made her such a man. She thanked me
And bade me, if I had a friend that loved her,
I should but teach him how to tell my story,   165
And that would woo her. Upon this hint I spake.
She loved me for the dangers I had passed,
And I loved her that she did pity them.
This only is the witchcraft I have used.
Here comes the lady; let her witness it.   170

Enter DESDEMONA, IAGO, and Attendants

172: take up...at the best: i.e., make the best of this disastrous situation

177: Light: fall

182: learn: teach

190: get: beget

Line 191-193: "Come hither, Moor. / I here do give thee that with all my heart / Which, but thou hast already": Joanna Weinberg as Desdemona, John Kani as Othello, and Stuart Brown as Brabantio in The Market Theater's 1987 production directed by Janet Suzman

Photo: Ruphin Coudyzer

196: For thy escape...tyranny: i.e., your elopement would teach him to be much more strict

197: hang clogs: encumber (clogs = objects hung on animals to hinder motion or escape)

DUKE OF VENICE
> I think this tale would win my daughter too.
> Good Brabantio, take up this mangled matter at the best.
> Men do their broken weapons rather use
> Than their bare hands.

BRABANTIO
>   I pray you, hear her speak.
> If she confess that she was half the wooer,   175
> Destruction on my head, if my bad blame
> Light on the man. Come hither, gentle mistress:
> Do you perceive in all this noble company
> Where most you owe obedience?

DESDEMONA
>   My noble father,
> I do perceive here a divided duty.   180
> To you I am bound for life and education;
> My life and education both do learn me
> How to respect you. You are the lord of duty;
> I am hitherto your daughter. But here's my husband,
> And so much duty as my mother showed   185
> To you, preferring you before her father,
> So much I challenge that I may profess
> Due to the Moor, my lord.

BRABANTIO
>   God be with you! I have done.
> Please it your grace, on to the state affairs.
> I had rather to adopt a child than get it.   190
> Come hither, Moor:
> I here do give thee that with all my heart
> Which, but thou hast already, with all my heart
> I would keep from thee. For your sake, jewel,
> I am glad at soul I have no other child,   195
> For thy escape would teach me tyranny,
> To hang clogs on them. I have done, my lord.

199: **grise:** degree, step

208: **bootless:** futile, useless

216: **are equivocal:** apply equally

222: **substitute:** delegate

222: **allowed sufficiency:** sufficient capability

223-224: **throws...you:** suggests you would ensure its safety more capably

224: **slubber:** sully, make dirty

224: **gloss:** luster, sheen

225: **stubborn:** rough, harsh

227: **flinty and steel couch:** Othello is referring to sleeping on stony, hard ground (flinty = full of hard stones; couch = bed)

228: **thrice-driven:** i.e., extremely soft

228: **agnize:** recognize, acknowledge

DUKE OF VENICE
   Let me speak like yourself, and lay a sentence
   Which as a grise or step may help these lovers
   Into your favor.   200
   When remedies are past, the griefs are ended
   By seeing the worst, which late on hopes depended.
   To mourn a mischief that is past and gone
   Is the next way to draw new mischief on.
   What cannot be preserved when fortune takes,   205
   Patience her injury a mockery makes.
   The robbed that smiles steals something from the thief;
   He robs himself that spends a bootless grief.

BRABANTIO
   So let the Turk of Cyprus us beguile,
   We lose it not so long as we can smile.   210
   He bears the sentence well that nothing bears
   But the free comfort which from thence he hears.
   But he bears both the sentence and the sorrow
   That, to pay grief, must of poor patience borrow.
   These sentences, to sugar, or to gall,   215
   Being strong on both sides, are equivocal.
   But words are words; I never yet did hear
   That the bruised heart was piercèd through the ear.
   I humbly beseech you, proceed to th' affairs of state.

DUKE OF VENICE
   The Turk with a most mighty preparation makes for Cyprus.   220
   Othello, the fortitude of the place is best known to you, and
   though we have there a substitute of most allowed sufficiency, yet
   opinion, a sovereign mistress of effects, throws a more safer voice
   on you. You must therefore be content to slubber the gloss of your
   new fortunes with this more stubborn and boisterous expedition.   225

OTHELLO
   The tyrant custom, most grave senators,
   Hath made the flinty and steel couch of war
   My thrice-driven bed of down. I do agnize
   A natural and prompt alacrity

233: **disposition:** arrangement, settlement

234: **reference:** appointment, assignment

234: **exhibition:** allowance, pension

235: **besort:** attendance, suitable company

239: **impatient:** angry

241: **unfolding:** explanation

241: **prosperous :** favorable

242: **charter:** privilege

243: **simpleness:** innocence

246: **scorn:** (from the First Quarto, "storm" is the reading in the First Folio and the Second Quarto); both "scorn" and "storm" are proverbial in this context and could be confused in handwriting. Though both are readings possible, "scorn" fits Desdemona's position better at this point in the play.

251: **consecrate:** devote

I find in hardness, and do undertake   230
This present war against the Ottomites.
Most humbly therefore bending to your state,
I crave fit disposition for my wife,
Due reference of place and exhibition,
With such accommodation and besort   235
As levels with her breeding.

DUKE OF VENICE
Why, at her father's.

BRABANTIO
                    I'll not have it so.

OTHELLO
Nor I.

DESDEMONA
                    Nor would I there reside
To put my father in impatient thoughts
By being in his eye. Most gracious Duke,   240
To my unfolding lend your prosperous ear,
And let me find a charter in your voice
T'assist my simpleness.

DUKE OF VENICE
What would you, Desdemona?

DESDEMONA
That I did love the Moor to live with him,   245
My downright violence and scorn of fortunes
May trumpet to the world. My heart's subdued
Even to the very quality of my lord:
I saw Othello's visage in his mind,
And to his honors and his valiant parts   250
Did I my soul and fortunes consecrate,
So that, dear lords, if I be left behind,
A moth of peace, and he go to the war,
The rites for which I love him are bereft me,

255: **a heavy interim:** a sad interval

258: **vouch:** bear witness

260: **heat:** passion

260: **young affects:** desires of youth

261: **defunct:** is ended, carried out, performed

264: **scant:** limit, short-change

265–266: **when light-winged toys...wanton dullness:** i.e., if I am ever blinded or distracted by amorous play

266: **seel:** blind (a term from falconry, where a young hawk's eyes are temporarily stitched up to prepare it for wearing a hood: see also 3.3.211)

267: **My...instrument:** Othello means his eyes

268: **disports:** sports, games

269: **helm:** helmet

270: **indign:** unworthy

271: **Make head:** surpass

275: **Tonight, my lord?:** This is only in the First Quarto. Its omission from the First Folio may be merely a copying error, but some scholars see it as part of a general toning down of Desdemona's character in the First Folio. This First Quarto passage suggests her surprise at being denied her wedding night with Othello.

And I a heavy interim shall support   255
By his dear absence. Let me go with him.

OTHELLO
   Let her have your voice.
   Vouch with me, heaven, I therefore beg it not
   To please the palate of my appetite,
   Nor to comply with heat the young affects   260
   In my defunct and proper satisfaction,
   But to be free and bounteous to her mind.
   And heaven defend your good souls that you think
   I will your serious and great business scant
   For she is with me. No, when light-winged toys   265
   Of feathered Cupid seel with wanton dullness
   My speculative and officed instrument,
   That my disports corrupt and taint my business,
   Let housewives make a skillet of my helm,
   And all indign and base adversities   270
   Make head against my estimation.

DUKE OF VENICE
   Be it as you shall privately determine,
   Either for her stay or going. Th' affair cries haste,
   And speed must answer it.

First Senator
              You must away tonight.

DEDEMONA
   Tonight, my lord?

DUKE OF VENICE
          This night.

OTHELLO
             With all my heart.   275

DUKE OF VENICE
   At nine i' th' morning here we'll meet again.

280: **import:** concern

289: Scene: **Look to her...eyes to see:** In some productions, Desdemona makes an attempt at reconciliation with her father, perhaps kneeling to seek his blessing, but is ignored.

294: **in the best advantage:** in the most opportune way (advantage = opportunity)

Set rendering "Outside Council Chamber" from the 1951 staging by Orson Welles at St. James Theatre

Rare Book and Special Collections Library, University of Illinois at Urbana-Champaign

Othello, leave some officer behind
And he shall our commission bring to you
And such things else of quality and respect
As doth import you.

OTHELLO
                    So please your Grace, my ancient.   280
A man he is of honesty and trust.
To his conveyance I assign my wife,
With what else needful your good Grace shall think
To be sent after me.

DUKE OF VENICE
          Let it be so.
Good night to every one. *[To BRABANTIO]* And, noble signior,   285
If virtue no delighted beauty lack,
Your son-in-law is far more fair than black.

First Senator
Adieu, brave Moor, use Desdemona well.

BRABANTIO
Look to her, Moor, if thou hast eyes to see:
She has deceived her father, and may thee.   290
                    Exeunt [DUKE OF VENICE, BRABANTIO,
                         CASSIO, Senators, Officers, &c]

OTHELLO
My life upon her faith! Honest Iago,
My Desdemona must I leave to thee,
I prithee, let thy wife attend on her,
And bring them after in the best advantage.
Come, Desdemona, I have but an hour   295
Of love, of worldly matter and direction,
To spend with thee. We must obey the time.
                    Exeunt OTHELLO and DESDEMONA

RODERIGO
Iago.

302: **incontinently:** immediately

309-310: **guinea hen:** disparaging euphemism for a woman

313: **fig:** disparaging euphemism for the female sex and sex organ, with an accompanying vulgar gesture

315: **hyssop:** a bushy, evergreen herb

316: **gender:** variety

318: **corrigible:** corrective

320: **poise:** balance

IAGO
What say'st thou, noble heart?

RODERIGO
What will I do, think'st thou?   300

IAGO
Why, go to bed, and sleep.

RODERIGO
I will incontinently drown myself.

IAGO
If thou dost, I shall never love thee after. Why, thou silly gentleman?

RODERIGO
It is silliness to live when to live is torment; and then have we a
prescription to die, when death is our physician.   305

IAGO
O villainous! I have looked upon the world for four times seven
years, and since I could distinguish betwixt a benefit and an
injury, I never found man that knew how to love himself.
Ere I would say, I would drown myself for the love of a guinea
hen; I would change my humanity with a baboon.   310

RODERIGO
What should I do? I confess it is my shame to be so fond, but it is not in
my virtue to amend it.

IAGO
Virtue? A fig! 'Tis in ourselves that we are thus or thus. Our bodies
are our gardens, to the which our wills are gardeners. So that if
we will plant nettles, or sow lettuce; set hyssop and weed up   315
thyme; supply it with one gender of herbs, or distract it with
many; either to have it sterile with idleness, or manured with
industry; why, the power and corrigible authority of this lies in
our wills. If the balance of our lives had not one scale of reason to
poise another of sensuality, the blood and baseness of our natures   320
would conduct us to most preposterous conclusions. But we have

322: **motions:** impulses

322: **unbitted:** unbridled

323: **sect or scion:** cutting (of a plant)

327: **knit to thy deserving:** dedicated to your cause

328: **perdurable:** lasting

328-329: **stead thee:** be of use to

330: **defeat:** disfigure

330: **favor:** face, appearance

330: **usurped:** false

334: **sequestration:** rupture, divorce

336: **locusts:** sweet tasting dessert (e.g. locust fruit)

337: **coloquintida:** colocynth, a plant with a sharp tasting fruit used for medicinal purposes

337: **for youth:** because she is young

342: **erring :** wandering, homeless

342: **supersubtle:** crafty, cunning

344-345: **It is clean out of the way:** entirely wrong to do

345: **compassing:** achieving

347: **be fast:** be true to, devoted to

347: **depend on the issue:** pursue this course

349: **hearted:** deeply felt, from the heart

350: **conjunctive:** united

351: **cuckold:** make a cuckold of him (cuckold = a man whose wife has been unfaithful)

353: **Traverse:** "March" (a military expression)

reason to cool our raging motions, our carnal stings, our unbitted
lusts; whereof I take this that you call love to be a sect or scion.

RODERIGO

It cannot be.

IAGO

It is merely a lust of the blood and a permission of the will. Come,   325
be a man! Drown thyself? Drown cats and blind puppies. I have
professed me thy friend, and I confess me knit to thy deserving
with cables of perdurable toughness. I could never better stead
thee than now. Put money in thy purse; follow thou the wars;
defeat thy favor with an usurped beard. I say, put money in thy   330
purse. It cannot be that Desdemona should long continue her love
to the Moor—put money in thy purse—nor he his to her. It was a
violent commencement in her, and thou shalt see an answerable
sequestration—put but money in thy purse. These Moors are
changeable in their wills.—Fill thy purse with money. The food   335
that to him now is as luscious as locusts, shall be to him shortly as
bitter as coloquintida. She must change for youth. When she is
sated with his body, she will find the errors of her choice. She
must have change, she must. Therefore, put money in thy purse.
If thou wilt needs damn thyself, do it a more delicate way than   340
drowning. Make all the money thou canst. If sanctimony and a
frail vow betwixt an erring barbarian and a supersubtle Venetian
be not too hard for my wits and all the tribe of hell, thou shalt
enjoy her—therefore, make money. A pox of drowning thyself, it
is clean out of the way. Seek thou rather to be hanged in compass-   345
ing thy joy than to be drowned and go without her.

RODERIGO

Wilt thou be fast to my hopes, if I depend on the issue?

IAGO

Thou art sure of me. Go, make money. I have told thee often, and
I retell thee again and again, I hate the Moor. My cause is hearted;
thine hath no less reason. Let us be conjunctive in our revenge   350
against him. If thou canst cuckold him, thou dost thyself a pleasure, me a sport. There are many events in the womb of time which
will be delivered. Traverse, go, provide thy money. We will have
more of this tomorrow. Adieu.

357-361: I'll be with thee...all my land: There is some confusion in this passage between the First Quarto and the First Folio texts over Iago's many repetitions.

357: betimes: early in the morning

tracks 14-16

363–384:
Anton Lesser as Iago
Jose Ferrer as Iago

364: profane: desecrate, pollute

365: snipe: simpleton

368: done my office: fulfilled Iago's duty i.e., engaged in marital relations with Emilia

370: surety: certainty

370: He holds me well: he (Roderigo) thinks well of me

373: plume up my will: triumph

375: abuse: deceive

RODERIGO

Where shall we meet i' th' morning?   355

IAGO

At my lodging.

RODERIGO

I'll be with thee betimes.

IAGO

Go to, farewell.—Do you hear, Roderigo?

RODERIGO

What say you?

IAGO

No more of drowning, do you hear?   360

RODERIGO

I am changed. I'll sell all my land.

IAGO

Go to, farewell, put money enough in your purse.

Exit RODERIGO

IAGO

Thus do I ever make my fool my purse:
For I mine own gained knowledge should profane,
If I would time expend with such a snipe   365
But for my sport and profit. I hate the Moor,
And it is thought abroad that 'twixt my sheets
He's done my office. I know not if 't be true,
But I, for mere suspicion in that kind,
Will do as if for surety. He holds me well,   370
The better shall my purpose work on him.
Cassio's a proper man; let me see now.
To get his place and to plume up my will
In double knavery. How? How? Let's see.
After some time, to abuse Othello's ears   375

tracks 14-16

363–384:
Anton Lesser as Iago
Jose Ferrer as Iago

377: **dispose:** disposition, temper

378: **framed:** fashioned, formed

379: **free:** candid

379: **open:** undisguised, straightforward

380: **but:** only

381: **tenderly:** readily

383: **engendered:** begotten, conceived

That he is too familiar with his wife.
He hath a person and a smooth dispose
To be suspected, framed to make women false.
The Moor is of a free and open nature,
That thinks men honest that but seem to be so,   380
And will as tenderly be led by th' nose
As asses are.
I have 't. It is engendered. Hell and night
Must bring this monstrous birth to the world's light.

Exit

[Othello

Act 2

Set rendering of "Arrival at Cyprus" from the 1951 staging by Orson Welles

Rare Book and Special Collections Library, University of Illinois at Urbana-Champaign

0: Stage Direction: **MONTANO:** The First Quarto stage direction describes Montano as Governor of Cyprus.

2: **highwrought:** with high waves

3: **heaven:** sky. This is the First Folio reading; the First Quarto has "haven", meaning the harbor, also a possible reading; **main:** the open sea

4: **descry:** discover, espy

7: **ruffianed:** raged

9: **mortise:** a wood joint (a carpentry term)

12: **chidden:** scolded, rebuked; **billow:** waves

13: **The wind-shaked...monstrous mane:** i.e., the waves are like wild beasts with huge heads

14-15: **Seems to cast...pole:** i.e., the crashing waves seem to soak all of the heavens and the earth;

14: **burning bear:** the constellation Ursa Minor

15: **the guards of th' ever-fixèd pole:** The "pole" is the Pole Star, which does not move from its position at the astronomical north pole, and the "guards" are the two bright stars in the constellation Ursa Minor ("the burning bear"). All these stars were important in navigation.

15: **ever-fixèd pole:** North Pole

16: **molestation:** disturbance

17: **enchafed:** furious, angry

19: **embayed:** sheltered in a bay

Act 2, Scene 1]

MONTANO
What from the cape can you discern at sea?

First Gentleman
Nothing at all: it is a highwrought flood.
I cannot 'twixt the heaven and the main
Descry a sail.

MONTANO
Methinks the wind hath spoke aloud at land,   5
A fuller blast ne'er shook our battlements;
If it hath ruffianed so upon the sea,
What ribs of oak, when mountains melt on them,
Can hold the mortise? What shall we hear of this?

Second Gentleman
A segregation of the Turkish fleet—   10
For do but stand upon the foaming shore,
The chidden billow seems to pelt the clouds,
The wind-shaked surge, with high and monstrous mane,
Seems to cast water on th' burning bear,
And quench the guards of the ever-fixèd pole.   15
I never did like molestation view
On the enchafèd flood.

MONTANO
If that the Turkish fleet
Be not ensheltered and embayed, they are drowned.
It is impossible to bear it out.   20

Enter a third Gentleman

23: **designment:** plan

24: **wrack:** ruin, shipwreck

24: **sufferance:** damage

27: **Veronese:** Both the First Quarto and the First Folio read "Veronessa", meaning from Verona, and the punctuation links this to Cassio, even though we have previously been told that Cassio is a Florentine (line 1.1.19). Most editors follow Theobald in repunctuating, so that it is the ship that is Veronese. The word has four syllables when pronounced.

30: **full:** accomplished, perfect

39: **throw out our eyes:** peer out, search for

40: **main:** the main sail

40: **aerial blue:** the sky

41: **an indistinct regard:** blend together (in our sight)

43: **arrivance:** arrivals, people arriving

Third Gentleman
    News, lads! Our wars are done.
    The desperate tempest hath so banged the Turks
    That their designment halts. A noble ship of Venice
    Hath seen a grievous wrack and sufferance
    On most part of their fleet.

MONTANO
                         How? Is this true?   25

Third Gentleman
    The ship is here put in.
    A Veronese; Michael Cassio,
    Lieutenant to the warlike Moor Othello,
    Is come on shore, the Moor himself at sea,
    And is in full commission here for Cyprus.   30

MONTANO
    I am glad on't. 'Tis a worthy governor.

Third Gentleman
    But this same Cassio, though he speak of comfort
    Touching the Turkish loss, yet he looks sadly
    And prays the Moor be safe, for they were parted
    With foul and violent tempest.

MONTANO
                         Pray heavens he be,   35
    For I have served him, and the man commands
    Like a full soldier. Let's to the seaside, ho!
    As well to see the vessel that's come in
    As to throw out our eyes for brave Othello,
    Even till we make the main and th' aerial blue   40
    An indistinct regard.

Third Gentleman
                         Come, let's do so,
    For every minute is expectancy
    Of more arrivance.

44: **valiant:** i.e., valiant soldiers

50: **approved allowance:** proven and tested

51: **surfeited:** fed excessively

51-52: **Therefore...cure:** i.e., my hopes are not yet dead and may still be fulfilled

52: **Stand in bold cure:** Wait to be remedied

52: Stage Direction: *A cry...a sail!:* from the First Folio; the First Quarto has a Messenger enter saying "A sail, a sail, a sail!" and speaking lines 54-5, and the Second Gentleman speak lines 57-8 and 60

57: **shot of courtesy:** a cannon salute indicating friendship, not hostility, used by ships as they approached a foreign shore

[Enter CASSIO]

CASSIO
    Thanks you, the valiant of this warlike isle,
    That so approve the Moor. O, let the heavens   45
    Give him defense against the elements,
    For I have lost him on a dangerous sea.

MONTANO
    Is he well shipped?

CASSIO
    His bark is stoutly timbered, and his pilot
    Of very expert and approved allowance;   50
    Therefore my hopes, not surfeited to death,
    Stand in bold cure.
                    A cry within "A sail, a sail, a sail!"

CASSIO
    What noise?

Gentleman
    The town is empty; on the brow o' th' sea
    Stand ranks of people, and they cry, "A sail!"   55

CASSIO
    My hopes do shape him for the governor.

                        A shot

Gentleman
    They do discharge their shot of courtesy,
    Our friends at least.

CASSIO
             I pray you sir, go forth,
    And give us truth who 'tis that is arrived.

61: **wived:** married

64: **blazoning:** trumpeting, proclaiming

65: **vesture:** clothing (metaphorically, the human body as that in which the soul is dressed)

66: **tire:** 1) "wear out", and 2) "clothe" (short for "attire")

66: **ingener:** engineer, inventor. Either she is God's masterpiece, or she defeats the artist who tries to describe her. (When pronounced, the stress is on the first syllable.)

70: **guttered:** indented, grooved

70: **congregated sands:** wind-swept sand piles (e.g., dunes, sandbanks)

71: **ensteeped:** lying underwater

73: **mortal:** deadly

78: **se'nnight:** seven night = a week

78: **Jove:** from mythology, the supreme god, a.k.a. Jupiter, also in charge of the sky and weather

81: **quick pants:** quickening heartbeat

Second Gentleman
    I shall.   60

                                           Exit

MONTANO
    But, good lieutenant, is your general wived?

CASSIO
    Most fortunately; he hath achieved a maid
    That paragons description and wild fame:
    One that excels the quirks of blazoning pens,
    And in th' essential vesture of creation   65
    Does tire the ingener.

                                  Enter Gentleman

                How now! Who has put in?

Gentleman
    'Tis one Iago, ancient to the general.

CASSIO
    He's had most favorable and happy speed.
    Tempests themselves, high seas, and howling winds,
    The guttered rocks and congregated sands,   70
    Traitors ensteeped to clog the guiltless keel,
    As having sense of beauty, do omit
    Their mortal natures, letting go safely by
    The divine Desdemona.

MONTANO
               What is she?

CASSIO
    She that I spake of, our great captain's captain,   75
    Left in the conduct of the bold Iago,
    Whose footing here anticipates our thoughts
    A se'nnight's speed. Great Jove, Othello guard,
    And swell his sail with thine own powerful breath
    That he may bless this bay with his tall ship,   80
    Make love's quick pants in Desdemona's arms,

82: **extincted:** extinguished

85: **let her have your knees:** kneel to her

88: **enwheel:** surround

Lines 86-88: "Hail to thee, lady, and the grace of heaven, / Before, behind thee, and on every hand, / Enwheel thee round!": Patrice Johnson as Desdemona and Teagle F. Bougere as Cassio in The Shakespeare Theatre's 1997-1998 production directed by Jude Kelly

Photo: Carol Rosegg

Give renewed fire to our extincted spirits
And bring all Cyprus comfort!
                    Enter DESDEMONA, IAGO, RODERIGO, and EMILIA

                    O, behold,
The riches of the ship is come on shore!
You men of Cyprus, let her have your knees.   85
Hail to thee, lady, and the grace of heaven,
Before, behind thee, and on every hand,
Enwheel thee round!

DESDEMONA
                    I thank you, valiant Cassio.
What tidings can you tell me of my lord?

CASSIO
He is not yet arrived, nor know I aught   90
But that he's well and will be shortly here.

DESDEMONA
O, but I fear—how lost you company?

CASSIO
The great contention of the sea and skies
Parted our fellowship.
                                        Within "A sail, a sail!"

                    But, hark! A sail!
                                                A shot

Gentleman
They give their greeting to the citadel;   95
This likewise is a friend.

CASSIO
                    See for the news.
                                        [Exit Gentleman]
Good ancient, you are welcome. *[To EMILIA]* Welcome, mistress.
Let it not gall your patience, good Iago,
That I extend my manners. 'Tis my breeding
That gives me this bold show of courtesy.   100
[Kissing her]

Costume rendering of "Desdemona and Emilia on Arrival at Cyprus" from the 1951 staging by Orson Welles at St. James Theatre

Rare Book and Special Collections Library, University of Illinois at Urbana-Champaign

102: of her tongue she oft bestows: Iago teases that Desdemona often scolds him (i.e., "bestows her tongue") but he also insinuates a sexual meaning to the phrase

105: list: desire, inclination

108: chides: quarrels, scolds

108: with thinking: in her mind

109: pictures out of doors: picturesque, i.e., the picture of propriety in public

112-113: Players in...your beds: i.e., you play at managing the household but you take your duties in bed seriously

117: What wouldst...praise me?: This is the first time we see Desdemona among her fellow Italians, relatively at ease with Iago's social banter, though concerned for Othello's welfare (line 92) and perhaps partly distracted in manner (line 120).

IAGO
Sir, would she give you so much of her lips
As of her tongue she oft bestows on me,
You'd have enough.

DESDEMONA
Alas, she has no speech.

IAGO
In faith, too much.
I find it still, when I have list to sleep.   105
Marry, before your ladyship, I grant,
She puts her tongue a little in her heart
And chides with thinking.

EMILIA
You have little cause to say so.

IAGO
Come on, come on. You are pictures out of doors,
Bells in your parlors, wildcats in your kitchens,   110
Saints in your injuries, devils being offended,
Players in your housewifery, and housewives in
Your beds.

DESDEMONA
O, fie upon thee, slanderer!

IAGO
Nay, it is true, or else I am a Turk;
You rise to play, and go to bed to work.   115

EMILIA
You shall not write my praise.

IAGO
No, let me not.

DESDEMONA
What wouldst thou write of me, if thou shouldst praise me?

120: **assay:** try, attempt
120: **one:** i.e., a messenger
122: **beguile:** deceive pleasingly

Lines 122-123: "I am not merry, but I do beguile / The thing I am by seeming otherwise": Virginia S. Burke as Emilia and Bill McCallum as Iago in the Guthrie Theater's 2003 production directed by Joe Dowling

Photo: T. Charles Erickson

126: **pate:** head
126: **birdlime:** a sticky substance used to catch birds
126: **frieze:** a coarse woolen material
127: **Muse:** one of the nine Greek goddesses who served as inspiration for artists, writers and musicians
131: **black:** dark-haired
131: **witty:** clever
133: **white:** a pun on white, the opposite of black, and "wight," meaning a person, in this case, a man
133: **her blackness fit:** a pun meaning that she will find her opposite to complement her blackness (again with a sexual suggestion)
136: **folly:** desire, wantonness

IAGO
>O gentle lady, do not put me to 't,
>For I am nothing if not critical.

DESDEMONA
>Come on, assay.—There's one gone to the harbor?   120

IAGO
>Ay, madam.

DESDEMONA
>I am not merry, but I do beguile
>The thing I am by seeming otherwise.
>Come, how wouldst thou praise me?

IAGO
>I am about it, but indeed my invention   125
>Comes from my pate as birdlime does from frieze.
>It plucks out brains and all. But my Muse labors,
>And thus she is delivered:
>>*If she be fair and wise, fairness and wit,*
>>*The one's for use, the other useth it.*   130

DESDEMONA
>Well praised. How if she be black and witty?

IAGO
>>*If she be black, and thereto have a wit,*
>>*She'll find a white that shall her blackness fit.*

DESDEMONA
>Worse and worse.

EMILIA
>>How if fair and foolish?

IAGO
>>*She never yet was foolish that was fair;*   135
>>*For even her folly helped her to an heir.*

137: **fond:** foolish

140: **foul pranks:** sexual acts (bawdy description)

143: **vouch:** testimony

145: **tongue at will:** could control her tongue/speak eloquently

146: **gay:** ostentatiously

151: ***To change the cod's head for the salmon's tail:*** An obscure passage, Iago is adapting some proverbial material with sexual innuendo. The general meaning seems to be to make a foolish exchange by exchanging something of value for something worthless. See the discussion by Balz Engler (Shakespeare Quarterly 35, 1984, 202).

154: **wight:** person

156: **chronicle small beer:** record trivial matters

159: **profane:** irreverent

159: **liberal:** wanton, licentious

160: **home:** without reserve, to the point

DESDEMONA
These are old fond paradoxes to make fools laugh i' th' alehouse.
What miserable praise hast thou for her that's foul and foolish?

IAGO
There's none so foul and foolish thereunto,
But does foul pranks which fair and wise ones do.   140

DESDEMONA
O heavy ignorance, thou praisest the worst best. But what praise
couldst thou bestow on a deserving woman indeed? One that, in the
authority of her merit did justly put on the vouch of very malice itself?

IAGO
She that was ever fair and never proud,
Had tongue at will and yet was never loud,   145
Never lacked gold and yet went never gay,
Fled from her wish and yet said, "Now I may;"
She that being angered, her revenge being nigh,
Bade her wrong stay and her displeasure fly;
She that in wisdom never was so frail   150
To change the cod's head for the salmon's tail,
She that could think and ne'er disclose her mind,
See suitors following and not look behind:
She was a wight, if ever such wights were, –

DESDEMONA
To do what?   155

IAGO
To suckle fools and chronicle small beer.

DESDEMONA
O, most lame and impotent conclusion! Do not learn of him,
Emilia, though he be thy husband. How say you, Cassio; is he not
a most profane and liberal counsellor?

CASSIO
He speaks home, madam. You may relish him more in   160
the soldier than in the scholar.

164: **gyve:** bind, ensnare, shackle

166-7: **kissed your three fingers:** a gesture, perhaps extravagant, of courtesy

167: **play the sir:** appear to be a gentleman

169-170: **clyster-pipes:** medical tubes (e.g., for enemas)

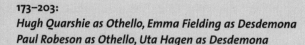

173–203:
Hugh Quarshie as Othello, Emma Fielding as Desdemona
Paul Robeson as Othello, Uta Hagen as Desdemona

Lines 174-175: "It gives me wonder great as my content / To see you here before me": John Kani as Othello and Joanna Weinberg as Desdemona in The Market Theater's 1987 production directed by Janet Suzman
Photo: Ruphin Coudyzer

178: **bark:** ship

178: **hills of seas:** tall waves

IAGO

[*Aside*] He takes her by the palm; ay, well said, whisper. With as
little a web as this will I ensnare as great a fly as Cassio. Ay, smile
upon her, do; I will gyve thee in thine own courtship. You say
true, 'tis so, indeed. If such tricks as these strip you out of your   165
lieutenantry, it had been better you had not kissed your three
fingers so oft, which now again you are most apt to play the sir
in. Very good, well kissed, and excellent courtesy: 'tis so, indeed.
Yet again your fingers to your lips? Would they were clyster-
pipes for your sake!   170

Trumpets within

The Moor! I know his trumpet.

CASSIO

'Tis truly so.

DESDEMONA

Let's meet him and receive him.

CASSIO

Lo, where he comes!

Enter OTHELLO and Attendants

OTHELLO

O my fair warrior!

DESDEMONA

My dear Othello!

OTHELLO

It gives me wonder great as my content
To see you here before me. O my soul's joy!   175
If after every tempest come such calms,
May the winds blow till they have wakened death,
And let the laboring bark climb hills of seas
Olympus-high and duck again as low
As hell's from heaven. If it were now to die,   180
'Twere now to be most happy, for I fear

173-203:
Hugh Quarshie as Othello, Emma Fielding as Desdemona
Paul Robeson as Othello, Uta Hagen as Desdemona

191: set down the pegs: loosen the strings

199: disembark my coffers: remove my trunks/luggage from the ship

200: master: ship's captain

202: challenge: demand, deserve

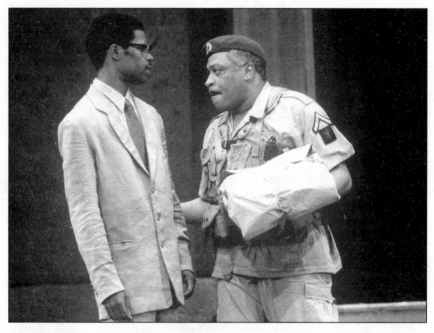

Jimmon Cole as Roderigo and Ron Canada as Iago in The Shakespeare Theatre's
1997-1998 production directed by Jude Kelly
Photo: Carol Rosegg

My soul hath her content so absolute
That not another comfort like to this
Succeeds in unknown fate.

DESDEMONA

The heavens forbid
But that our loves and comforts should increase,   185
Even as our days do grow.

OTHELLO

Amen to that, sweet powers!
I cannot speak enough of this content.
It stops me here; it is too much of joy:
And this, and this, the greatest discords be

They kiss

That e'er our hearts shall make.

IAGO

[*Aside*] O, you are well tuned now!   190
But I'll set down the pegs that make this music,
As honest as I am.

OTHELLO

Come, let us to the castle.
News, friends, our wars are done, the Turks are drowned.
How does my old acquaintance of this isle?
Honey, you shall be well desired in Cyprus,   195
I have found great love amongst them. O my sweet,
I prattle out of fashion, and I dote
In mine own comforts. I prithee, good Iago,
Go to the bay and disembark my coffers.
Bring thou the master to the citadel;   200
He is a good one, and his worthiness
Does challenge much respect. Come, Desdemona,
Once more, well met at Cyprus.

Exeunt OTHELLO, DESDEMONA,
[and all except Iago and Roderigo]

205-261: **Come hither...Farewell:** This is yet another scene between Iago and Roderigo where there are many small differences between the First Quarto and the First Folio texts (see 1.3.357).

205: **be'st:** are (archaic verb tense of "to be")

207: **list me:** listen to me

211: **lay thy finger thus:** i.e., alongside the nose or possibly over the mouth (both gestures imply keeping a secret)

212: **violence:** passion, strength

213: **prating:** bragging

216: **act of sport:** sexual intercourse

217: **saiety:** excessive gratification

220: **heave the gorge:** vomit

220: **disrelish:** loathe

223: **pregnant:** clear, natural

224: **very voluble:** of quick tongue, witty

225: **conscionable:** conscientious

226: **compass:** reach

226: **salt:** lechery

226-227: **hidden loose affection:** secret lasciviousness

227: **slipper:** slippery

228-229: **stamp and counterfeit advantages:** create or feign opportunity

231: **green:** young, immature

232: **pestilent:** disagreeable

234: **condition:** character, temper

IAGO

[*To attendant*] Do thou meet me presently at the harbour.
[*To Roderigo*] Come hither. If thou be'st valiant,—as, they say,   205
base men being in love have then a nobility in their natures more
than is native to them—list me. The lieutenant tonight watches
on the court of guard. First, I must tell thee this: Desdemona is
directly in love with him.

RODERIGO

With him? Why, 'tis not possible.   210

IAGO

Lay thy finger thus, and let thy soul be instructed. Mark me with
what violence she first loved the Moor, but for bragging and
telling her fantastical lies. To love him still for prating? Let not
thy discreet heart think it. Her eye must be fed, and what delight
shall she have to look on the devil? When the blood is made dull   215
with the act of sport, there should be a game to inflame it and give
satiety a fresh appetite—loveliness in favor, sympathy in years,
manners, and beauties, all which the Moor is defective in. Now,
for want of these required conveniences, her delicate tenderness
will find itself abused, begin to heave the gorge, disrelish and   220
abhor the Moor; very nature will instruct her in it and compel her
to some second choice. Now, sir, this granted,—as it is a most
pregnant and unforced position—who stands so eminent in the
degree of this fortune as Cassio does? A knave very voluble, no
further conscionable than in putting on the mere form of civil and   225
humane seeming for the better compass of his salt and most hidden loose affection. Why, none, why, none: a slipper and subtle
knave, a finder out of occasion that has an eye can stamp and
counterfeit advantages, though true advantage never present
itself. A devilish knave; besides, the knave is handsome, young,   230
and hath all those requisites in him that folly and green minds
look after. A pestilent complete knave, and the woman hath found
him already.

RODERIGO

I cannot believe that in her; she's full of most blest condition.

235: **fig's end:** an exclamation (with a bawdy undertone)

237: **paddle:** finger, toy with

240: **index:** preface

243: **mutualities:** intimacies

243: **marshal:** lead

244: **incorporate:** made one body

245: **Pish:** an interjection expressing contempt or disgust

249: **tainting:** discrediting

252: **choler:** anger (one of the four humors)

252: **haply:** perchance, by chance

255: **displanting:** removal from office

IAGO

Blest fig's end! The wine she drinks is made of grapes. If she had   235
been blest, she would never have loved the Moor. Blest pudding!
Didst thou not see her paddle with the palm of his hand? Didst
not mark that?

RODERIGO

Yes, that I did, but that was but courtesy.

IAGO

Lechery, by this hand: an index and obscure prologue to the   240
history of lust and foul thoughts. They met so near with their
lips that their breaths embraced together. Villanous thoughts,
Roderigo—when these mutualities so marshal the way, hard
at hand comes the master and main exercise, th' incorporate
conclusion. Pish! But, sir, be you ruled by me. I have brought you   245
from Venice. Watch you tonight. For the command I'll lay't upon
you. Cassio knows you not; I'll not be far from you. Do you find
some occasion to anger Cassio, either by speaking too loud, or
tainting his discipline, or from what other course you please which
the time shall more favorably minister.   250

RODERIGO

Well.

IAGO

Sir, he's rash and very sudden in choler and haply may strike at
you—provoke him that he may, for even out of that will I cause
these of Cyprus to mutiny, whose qualification shall come into no
true taste again but by the displanting of Cassio. So shall you have   255
a shorter journey to your desires by the means I shall then have to
prefer them, and the impediment most profitably removed, without the which there were no expectation of our prosperity.

RODERIGO

I will do this, if you can bring it to any opportunity.

260: **warrant:** assure

265: **howbeit:** although

269: **peradventure:** perhaps

273: **Hath leaped into my seat:** i.e., has had an affair with my wife

274: **inwards:** innards

280: **trash:** worthless object; **trace:** hold back, restrain (e.g. a hound with a collar)

281: **putting on:** provoking

282: **on the hip:** at a disadvantage

283: **rank garb:** lustful manner

284: **with my nightcap too:** in his bed (i.e., with Emilia)

IAGO

I warrant thee. Meet me by and by at the citadel. I must fetch his   260
necessaries ashore. Farewell.

RODERIGO

Adieu.

Exit

IAGO

That Cassio loves her, I do well believe 't;
That she loves him, 'tis apt and of great credit.
The Moor, howbeit that I endure him not,   265
Is of a constant, loving, noble nature,
And I dare think he'll prove to Desdemona
A most dear husband. Now I do love her too,
Not out of absolute lust—though peradventure
I stand accountant for as great a sin —   270
But partly led to diet my revenge,
For that I do suspect the lusty Moor
Hath leaped into my seat. The thought whereof
Doth, like a poisonous mineral, gnaw my inwards,
And nothing can or shall content my soul   275
Till I am evened with him, wife for wife.
Or failing so, yet that I put the Moor
At least into a jealousy so strong
That judgment cannot cure. Which thing to do,
If this poor trash of Venice, whom I trace   280
For his quick hunting, stand the putting on.
I'll have our Michael Cassio on the hip,
Abuse him to the Moor in the rank garb—
For I fear Cassio with my nightcap too—
Make the Moor thank me, love me, and reward me   285
For making him egregiously an ass
And practising upon his peace and quiet
Even to madness. 'Tis here, but yet confused;
Knavery's plain face is never seen till used.

Exit

2: **perdition:** destruction, ruin

1-6: **It is Othello's...nuptial:** It seems likely that these lines comprise the proclamation referenced in the stage direction. The rest of the speech is further comment added by the Herald.

5: **addiction:** inclination

Costume rendering of "Herald" from the 1951 staging by Orson Welles at St. James Theatre

Rare Book and Special Collections Library, University of Illinois at Urbana-Champaign

Act 2, Scene 2]

Enter Othello's Herald with a proclamation

Herald [reads]

It is Othello's pleasure, our noble and valiant general, that, upon
certain tidings now arrived importing the mere perdition of the
Turkish fleet, every man put himself into triumph: some to dance,
some to make bonfires, each man to what sport and revels his
addiction leads him. For besides these beneficial news, it is the   5
celebration of his nuptial. So much was his pleasure should be
proclaimed. All offices are open, and there is full liberty of feast-
ing from this present hour of five till the bell have told eleven.
Heaven bless the isle of Cyprus and our noble general Othello!

Exit

0: Scene: Both the First Quarto and the First Folio make this scene a continuation of the previous short scene. Doing so creates good opportunities for stage business, with singing and drunken revelry interrupted by sudden violence in the skirmish between Roderigo and Cassio and then the climactic entrance of Othello at line 139.

2: **honorable stop:** i.e., the socially responsible limits of drinking

3: **outsport:** celebrate excessively (in this case, more than discretion dictates)

7: **with your earliest:** i.e., at your earliest convenience

9: **purchase:** acquisition i.e., marriage

9: **fruits are to ensue:** i.e., the marriage has yet to be consummated

Lines 8-9: "Come, my dear love. / The purchase made, the fruits are to ensue": James Earl Jones as Othello and Julienne Marie as Desdemona in the Public Theater's 1964 production directed by Gladys Vaughan

Photo: George E. Joseph

14: **cast:** dismissed

16: **Jove:** from mythology, the supreme god, a.k.a. Jupiter, also known for sexual conquests

Act 2, Scene 3]

Enter OTHELLO, DESDEMONA, CASSIO, and Attendants

OTHELLO
Good Michael, look you to the guard tonight.
Let's teach ourselves that honorable stop
Not to outsport discretion.

CASSIO
Iago hath direction what to do,
But, notwithstanding, with my personal eye   5
Will I look to 't.

OTHELLO
                    Iago is most honest.
Michael, good night. Tomorrow with your earliest
Let me have speech with you. Come, my dear love,
The purchase made, the fruits are to ensue;
That profit's yet to come 'tween me and you.   10
Good night.
Exeunt OTHELLO, DESDEMONA, [and Attendants]
Enter IAGO

CASSIO
Welcome, Iago: we must to the watch.

IAGO
Not this hour, lieutenant; 'tis not yet ten o' th' clock. Our general
cast us thus early for the love of his Desdemona, who let us not
therefore blame; he hath not yet made wanton the night with her,   15
and she is sport for Jove.

CASSIO
She's a most exquisite lady.

Jordan Baker as Desdemona and Avery Brooks as Othello in The Shakespeare Theatre's 1990-1991 production directed by Harold Scott
Photo: Joan Marcus

18: **game:** i.e., sexual play

20: **sounds a parley:** calls for a conference (with an opponent)

22: **alarum:** call to arms (contrast to "love", i.e., the love-war metaphor also in line 20)

24: **stoup:** a drinking vessel

25: **without:** outside

25: **brace:** a couple

25: **gallants:** gentlemen

26: **fain:** gladly

31: **qualified:** mixed with water

IAGO

And, I'll warrant her, full of game.

CASSIO

Indeed she's a most fresh and delicate creature.

IAGO

What an eye she has! Methinks it sounds a parley to provocation.   20

CASSIO

An inviting eye, and yet methinks right modest.

IAGO

And when she speaks, is it not an alarum to love?

CASSIO

She is indeed perfection.

IAGO

Well, happiness to their sheets! Come, lieutenant, I have a stoup
of wine, and here without are a brace of Cyprus gallants that   25
would fain have a measure to the health of black Othello.

CASSIO

Not tonight, good Iago; I have very poor and unhappy brains for
drinking. I could well wish courtesy would invent some other
custom of entertainment.

IAGO

O, they are our friends! But one cup; I'll drink for you.   30

CASSIO

I have drunk but one cup tonight, and that was craftily qualified
too, and, behold, what innovation it makes here. I am unfortunate
in the infirmity and dare not task my weakness with any more.

IAGO

What, man? 'Tis a night of revels, the gallants desire it.

38: **fasten:** persuade

43: **caroused:** drunk hard

44: **potations:** liquor

44: **pottle:** two-quart tankard

45: **swelling:** proud, boastful

46: **hold...distance:** i.e., scrupulous about upholding their personal integrity

51: **offend the isle:** i.e., offend the people on the island

54: **rouse:** free and copious drinking

Line 56: "Some wine, ho!": Costume rendering for Wine Carrier from the 1951 staging by Orson Welles at St. James Theatre
Rare Book and Special Collections Library, University of Illinois at Urbana-Champaign

57: **cannikin:** little can

CASSIO
  Where are they?   35

IAGO
  Here at the door. I pray you call them in.

CASSIO
  I'll do't, but it dislikes me.

                                                                   Exit

IAGO
  If I can fasten but one cup upon him,
  With that which he hath drunk tonight already,
  He'll be as full of quarrel and offense   40
  As my young mistress' dog. Now my sick fool Roderigo,
  Whom love hath turned almost the wrong side out,
  To Desdemona hath tonight caroused
  Potations pottle-deep, and he's to watch.
  Three else of Cyprus, noble swelling spirits   45
  That hold their honors in a wary distance,
  The very elements of this warlike isle,
  Have I tonight flustered with flowing cups,
  And they watch too. Now 'mongst this flock of drunkards,
  Am I to put our Cassio in some action   50
  That may offend the isle.—But here they come.
               Enter CASSIO, MONTANO, and Gentlemen
  If consequence do but approve my dream,
  My boat sails freely, both with wind and stream.

CASSIO
  'Fore God, they have given me a rouse already.

MONTANO
  Good faith, a little one, not past a pint, as I am a soldier.   55

IAGO
  Some wine, ho!
                                                                [Sings]

        And let me the cannikin clink, clink;
        And let me the cannikin clink.

65: **potting:** drinking

65: **swag-bellied:** round, beer-bellied

68: **drinks you with facility:** outdrinks you with ease

68-69: **sweats not to overthrow:** effortlessly outdrinks

69: **Almain:** German

69-70: **gives...a vomit:** outdrinks (the Dutch) past the point of vomiting

74: **peer:** lord

75: **crown:** a coin (five shillings)

77: **lown:** loon (rogue or idler)

78: **wight:** man

81: **auld:** old

A soldier's a man,
O, man's life's but a span,   60
Why then let a soldier drink.
Some wine, boys!

CASSIO
'Fore God, an excellent song!

IAGO
I learned it in England, where indeed they are most potent in
potting. Your Dane, your German, and your swag-bellied Hollan-   65
der—Drink, ho!—are nothing to your English.

CASSIO
Is your Englishman so exquisite in his drinking?

IAGO
Why, he drinks you with facility your Dane dead drunk; he sweats
not to overthrow your Almain; he gives your Hollander a vomit
ere the next pottle can be filled.   70

CASSIO
To the health of our general!

MONTANO
I am for it, lieutenant, and I'll do you justice.

IAGO
O sweet England!
King Stephen was and a worthy peer,
His breeches cost him but a crown;   75
He held them sixpence all too dear,
With that he called the tailor lown.
He was a wight of high renown,
And thou art but of low degree.
'Tis pride that pulls the country down;   80
Then take thine auld cloak about thee.
Some wine, ho!

84: **hear 't:** a contraction for "hear it"

90: **quality:** rank

92–93: **lieutenant...ancient:** note that Cassio again makes reference to his superior rank over Iago

95-96: **my right hand:** Cassio begins by speaking of Iago ("his right hand man"), then in his drunkenness switches to a more literal meaning

CASSIO

'Fore God, this is a more exquisite song than the other!

IAGO

Will you hear 't again?

CASSIO

No, for I hold him to be unworthy of his place that does those   85
things. Well, God's above all, and there be souls must be saved,
and there be souls must not be saved.

IAGO

It's true, good lieutenant.

CASSIO

For mine own part, no offense to the general, nor any man of
quality, I hope to be saved.   90

IAGO

And so do I too, lieutenant.

CASSIO

Ay, but by your leave, not before me. The lieutenant is to be saved
before the ancient. Let's have no more of this. Let's to our affairs.
God forgive us our sins! Gentlemen, let's look to our business. Do
not think, gentlemen. I am drunk: this is my ancient; this is my   95
right hand, and this is my left. I am not drunk now: I can stand
well enough, and I speak well enough.

Gentlemen

Excellent well.

CASSIO

Why, very well then; you must not think then that I am drunk.

Exit

MONTANO

To th' platform, masters, come, let's set the watch.   100

104: **a just equinox:** of equal size, importance

107: **on:** at

107: **odd time of his infirmity:** when his defect overcomes him

110: **horologe:** clock

110: **a double set:** twice around (i.e., 24 hours)

112: **put in mind of it:** told about it

119: **second:** second in command

120: **ingraft infirmity:** deeply rooted character weakness

Set rendering for "The Brawl" from the 1951 staging by Orson Welles at St. James Theatre

Rare Book and Special Collections Library, University of Illinois at Urbana-Champaign

IAGO

You see this fellow that is gone before?
He is a soldier fit to stand by Caesar
And give direction; and do but see his vice,
'Tis to his virtue a just equinox,
The one as long as th' other. 'Tis pity of him—   105
I fear the trust Othello puts him in
On some odd time of his infirmity
Will shake this island.

MONTANO

But is he often thus?

IAGO

'Tis evermore the prologue to his sleep:
He'll watch the horologe a double set,   110
If drink rock not his cradle.

MONTANO

It were well
The general were put in mind of it.
Perhaps he sees it not, or his good nature
Prizes the virtue that appears in Cassio
And looks not on his evils. Is not this true?   115

[Enter RODERIGO]

IAGO

[Aside to him] How now, Roderigo?
I pray you, after the lieutenant, go.

[Exit RODERIGO]

MONTANO

And 'tis great pity that the noble Moor
Should hazard such a place as his own second
With one of an ingraft infirmity.   120
It were an honest action to say so
To the Moor.

126: **twiggen:** wicker work

128: **prate:** brag, speak idly

130: **mazard:** head, also drinking bowl

Lines 130: "Let me go, sir, / Or I'll knock you o'er the mazzard": Neil McCarthy as Cassio in The Market Theater's 1987 production directed by Janet Suzman
Photo: Ruphin Coudyzer

IAGO

                Not I, for this fair island.
I do love Cassio well and would do much
To cure him of this evil.

                        [Cry] within: "Help! Help!"
             But, hark! What noise?
               Enter CASSIO, pursuing RODERIGO

CASSIO

    Zounds, you rogue! You rascal!

MONTANO

                  What's the matter, lieutenant?   125

CASSIO

    A knave teach me my duty! I'll beat the knave into a twiggen bottle.

RODERIGO

    Beat me?

CASSIO

    Dost thou prate, rogue?

MONTANO

    Nay, good lieutenant! I pray you, sir, hold your hand.

CASSIO

    Let me go, sir, or I'll knock you o'er the mazard.   130

MONTANO

    Come, come, you're drunk.

CASSIO

    Drunk!

                             They fight

133: **cry a mutiny:** rouse the neighbors with yelling
135, 142: **Sir Montano:** The punctuation in both the First Quarto and the First Folio suggests that Iago is using "sir" respectfully in addressing Montano.
137: **Diablo:** the devil
139: Stage Direction: ***Enter OTHELLO:*** Othello usually appears half undressed, as if he has been disturbed from his bed.

Line 140-141: "'Zounds, I bleed still. I am hurt to th' death. He dies!": Sean Michael Dooley as Citizen of Cyprus, Shawn Hamilton as Montano, Lester Purry as Othello, Bill McCallum as Iago, and Robert O. Berdahl as Cassio in the Guthrie Theater's 2003 production directed by Joe Dowling
Photo: T. Charles Erickson

145: **whence:** what place
147: **Which...Ottomites:** It was thought at the time that the Koran forbade Muslims from fighting one another (see L. Danson in Journal for Early Modern Cultural Studies 2, 2002, 1-25).
149: **carve for:** indulge
150: **light:** unimportant, of little value
150: **upon his motion:** as soon as he moves
152: **propriety:** proper state

IAGO
[*Aside to RODERIGO*] Away, I say. Go out and cry a mutiny.

Exit RODERIGO

Nay, good lieutenant! God's will, gentlemen!
Help, ho! Lieutenant! Sir Montano! sir!   135
Help, masters!—Here's a goodly watch indeed!

A bell rings

Who's that which rings the bell? Diablo, ho!
The town will rise. God's will, lieutenant, hold!
You'll be ashamed forever.

Enter OTHELLO and Attendants

OTHELLO
What is the matter here?

MONTANO
                    'Zounds, I bleed still.   140
I am hurt to th' death. He dies!

OTHELLO
                    Hold, for your lives!

IAGO
Hold, ho! Lieutenant! Sir Montano! Gentlemen!
Have you forgot all sense of place and duty?
Hold! The general speaks to you—hold, for shame!

OTHELLO
Why, how now, ho! From whence ariseth this?   145
Are we turned Turks, and to ourselves do that
Which heaven hath forbid the Ottomites?
For Christian shame, put by this barbarous brawl.
He that stirs next to carve for his own rage
Holds his soul light; he dies upon his motion.   150
Silence that dreadful bell; it frights the isle
From her propriety. What is the matter, masters?
Honest Iago, that looks dead with grieving,
Speak, who began this? On thy love, I charge thee.

156: **like bride and groom:** i.e., like Othello and Desdemona

157: **Divesting:** disrobing, undressing

158: **unwitted:** deprived of understanding

161: **peevish odds:** silly conflict

164: **you are thus forgot:** i.e., you have forgotten your manners

166: **wont:** accustomed to

169: **censure:** judgment

171: **spend your rich opinion:** compromise your reputation

173: **hurt to danger:** dangerously hurt

176: **aught:** anything

178: **Unless self-charity...vice:** unless it is wrong to care for one's own well being

181: **blood:** anger

IAGO

I do not know. Friends all but now, even now,   155
In quarter, and in terms like bride and groom
Divesting them for bed. And then, but now,
As if some planet had unwitted men,
Swords out, and tilting one at other's breasts,
In opposition bloody. I cannot speak   160
Any beginning to this peevish odds,
And would, in action glorious, I had lost
Those legs that brought me to a part of it.

OTHELLO

How comes it, Michael, you are thus forgot?

CASSIO

I pray you pardon me, I cannot speak.   165

OTHELLO

Worthy Montano, you were wont to be civil;
The gravity and stillness of your youth
The world hath noted, and your name is great
In mouths of wisest censure. What's the matter,
That you unlace your reputation thus   170
And spend your rich opinion for the name
Of a night-brawler? Give me answer to it.

MONTANO

Worthy Othello, I am hurt to danger.
Your officer Iago can inform you,
While I spare speech, which something now offends me,   175
Of all that I do know; nor know I aught
By me that's said or done amiss this night
Unless self-charity be sometimes a vice,
And to defend ourselves it be a sin
When violence assails us.

OTHELLO

                    Now, by heaven,   180

182: **collied:** blackened

183: **assays:** tries

186: **rout:** brawl

188: **Though he had...at a birth:** even if he were my own twin

194: **affined:** bound by duty of friendship

194: **leagued in office:** bound in service

205: **entreats his pause:** begs him to hold/stop

209: **then rather:** more rapidly

Line 210: "For that I heard the clink and fall of swords": Sir Derek Jacobi as Cassio
and Ensemble in Stuart Burge's 1965 movie production
Courtesy: Douglas Lanier

212: **high in oath:** swearing loudly

My blood begins my safer guides to rule,
And passion, having my best judgment collied,
Assays to lead the way. Zounds, if I once stir
Or do but lift this arm, the best of you
Shall sink in my rebuke. Give me to know   185
How this foul rout began, who set it on,
And he that is approved in this offense,
Though he had twinned with me, both at a birth,
Shall lose me. What, in a town of war
Yet wild, the people's hearts brimful of fear,   190
To manage private and domestic quarrel?
In night and on the court and guard of safety?
'Tis monstrous! Iago, who began 't?

MONTANO

If partially affined or leagued in office,
Thou dost deliver more or less than truth,   195
Thou art no soldier.

IAGO

                      Touch me not so near.
I had rather have this tongue cut from my mouth
Than it should do offense to Michael Cassio.
Yet I persuade myself to speak the truth
Shall nothing wrong him. This it is general: 200
Montano and myself being in speech,
There comes a fellow crying out for help,
And Cassio following him with determined sword
To execute upon him. Sir, this gentleman
Steps in to Cassio and entreats his pause;   205
Myself the crying fellow did pursue,
Lest by his clamour, as it so fell out,
The town might fall in fright. He, swift of foot,
Outran my purpose. And I returned then rather
For that I heard the clink and fall of swords   210
And Cassio high in oath, which till tonight
I ne'er might say before. When I came back,
For this was brief, I found them close together
At blow and thrust, even as again they were

221: **indignity:** insult, contemptuous injury

222: **patience:** calmness, composure

222: **pass:** ignore

223: **mince:** soften, lessen

Lines 224-225: "Cassio, I love thee, / But nevermore be officer of mine": Cheyenne Casebier as Desdemona, Lester Purry as Othello, and Robert O. Berdahl as Cassio in the Guthrie Theater's 2003 production directed by Joe Dowling

Photo: T. Charles Erickson

When you yourself did part them.   215
More of this matter cannot I report,
But men are men; the best sometimes forget.
Though Cassio did some little wrong to him,
As men in rage strike those that wish them best,
Yet surely Cassio, I believe, received   220
From him that fled some strange indignity,
Which patience could not pass.

OTHELLO
                    I know, Iago,
Thy honesty and love doth mince this matter,
Making it light to Cassio. Cassio, I love thee,
But never more be officer of mine.   225
                              Enter DESDEMONA, attended

Look if my gentle love be not raised up!
I'll make thee an example.

DESDEMONA
What is the matter, dear?

OTHELLO
                    All's well now, sweeting;
Come away to bed. [To MONTANO] Sir, for your hurts
Myself will be your surgeon. Lead him off.   230
                              [MONTANO is led off]

Iago, look with care about the town
And silence those whom this vile brawl distracted.
Come, Desdemona, 'tis the soldiers' life
To have their balmy slumbers waked with strife.
                              Exeunt [all but IAGO and CASSIO]

IAGO
What, are you hurt, lieutenant?   235

CASSIO
Ay, past all surgery.

IAGO
Marry, God forbid!

239: **immortal:** i.e., in the sense that one's reputation lives on even after one dies, a common theme in Shakespeare's sonnets

246: **recover the general:** regain his favor

246: **cast in his mood:** dismissed because of his mood (i.e., his anger)

248: **Sue to him:** entreat him, beg your case to him

252: **parrot:** squawk like a parrot, babble

253: **fustian:** nonsense

260: **nothing wherefore:** no reasons why

262: **pleasance:** merriment

CASSIO

Reputation, reputation, reputation! O, I have lost my reputation!
I have lost the immortal part of myself and what remains is bes-   240
tial. My reputation, Iago, my reputation!

IAGO

As I am an honest man, I thought you had received some bodily
wound; there is more of sense in that than in reputation. Reputation is an idle and most false imposition, oft got without merit and
lost without deserving. You have lost no reputation at all, unless   245
you repute yourself such a loser. What, man, there are more ways
to recover the general again. You are but now cast in his mood, a
punishment more in policy than in malice, even so as one would
beat his offenseless dog to affright an imperious lion. Sue to him
again, and he's yours.

CASSIO   250

I will rather sue to be despised than to deceive so good a com-
mander with so slight, so drunken, and so indiscreet an officer.
Drunk? And speak parrot? And squabble? Swagger? Swear? And
discourse fustian with one's own shadow? O thou invisible spirit
of wine, if thou hast no name to be known by, let us call thee devil!

IAGO   255

What was he that you followed with your sword? What had he
done to you?

CASSIO

I know not.

IAGO

Is 't possible?

CASSIO

I remember a mass of things, but nothing distinctly; a quarrel, but   260
nothing wherefore. O God, that men should put an enemy in their
mouths to steal away their brains! That we should, with joy,
pleasance, revel and applause, transform ourselves into beasts!

267: **moraller:** moralizer

271: **Hydra:** a creature from Greek mythology said to look like a many-headed snake; each time a head was cut off, two would grow in its place

273: **inordinate:** immoderate

275: **creature:** anything created, including food and drink.

278: **approved:** experienced

282: **denotement:** making known

283: **importune:** eagerly solicit

286: **broken joint:** broken connection/friendship

287: **splinter:** bind back together, fix with a splint

287: **lay:** bet

IAGO

Why, but you are now well enough—how came you thus recovered?

CASSIO

It hath pleased the devil drunkenness to give place to the devil   265
wrath; one unperfectness shows me another to make me frankly
despise myself.

IAGO

Come, you are too severe a moraller. As the time, the place, and
the condition of this country stands, I could heartily wish this had
not befallen; but since it is as it is, mend it for your own good.

CASSIO   270

I will ask him for my place again, he shall tell me I am a drunk-
ard. Had I as many mouths as Hydra, such an answer would stop
them all. To be now a sensible man, by and by a fool, and
presently a beast! O strange! Every inordinate cup is unblessed
and the ingredient is a devil.

IAGO   275

Come, come, good wine is a good familiar creature if it be well
used; exclaim no more against it. And, good lieutenant, I think
you think I love you.

CASSIO

I have well approved it, sir. I drunk?

IAGO

You or any man living may be drunk at a time, man. I'll tell you   280
what you shall do. Our general's wife is now the general. I may
say so in this respect, for that he hath devoted and given up himself to the contemplation, mark, and denotement of her parts and
graces. Confess yourself freely to her; importune her help to put
you in your place again. She is of so free, so kind, so apt, so blessed   285
a disposition, she holds it a vice in her goodness not to do more
than she is requested. This broken joint between you and her husband entreat her to splinter, and, my fortunes against any lay
worth naming, this crack of your love shall grow stronger than it
was before.

291: **protest:** declare (affection)

292: **betimes:** early

294: **check:** stop, repress

299: **Probal to thinking:** probable, likely to be good

301: **inclining:** favorably disposed

302: **framed:** formed, fashioned

302: **fruitful:** bountiful, generous

303: **free elements:** basic elements of nature

304: **win:** persuade

306: **enfettered:** chained

307: **list:** desires

309: **function:** ability

CASSIO

You advise me well.   290

IAGO

I protest, in the sincerity of love and honest kindness.

CASSIO

I think it freely; and betimes in the morning I will beseech the
virtuous Desdemona to undertake for me. I am desperate of my
fortunes if they check me here.

IAGO   295

You are in the right. Good night, lieutenant, I must to the watch.

CASSIO

Good night, honest Iago.

                                                                Exit

IAGO

And what's he then that says I play the villain
When this advice is free I give and honest,
Probal to thinking, and indeed the course
To win the Moor again? For 'tis most easy   300
Th' inclining Desdemona to subdue
In any honest suit. She's framed as fruitful
As the free elements. And then for her
To win the Moor, were't to renounce his baptism,
All seals and symbols of redeemèd sin,   305
His soul is so enfettered to her love
That she may make, unmake, do what she list,
Even as her appetite shall play the god
With his weak function. How am I then a villain
To counsel Cassio to this parallel course,   310
Directly to his good? Divinity of hell!
When devils will the blackest sins put on,
They do suggest at first with heavenly shows
As I do now. For whiles this honest fool
Plies Desdemona to repair his fortune,   315

318: **repeals him:** tries to have Cassio restored to his position

321: **pitch:** black tar

Lines 321-23: "So will I turn her virtue into pitch, / And out of her own goodness make the net / That shall enmesh them all": Richard Haddon Haines as Iago in The Market Theater's 1987 production directed by Janet Suzman

Photo: Ruphin Coudyzer

326: **fills up the cry:** merely runs along with the others; **cry:** a pack of hounds

327: **cudgelled:** beaten

327: **issue:** final result

333: **dilatory:** full of delays

335: **hast cashiered Cassio:** have gotten Cassio dismissed from office

340: **billeted:** lodged

343: **move for:** plead for

346: **jump:** exactly

348: **Dull not device:** do not dampen his plot; **coldness:** want of zeal

And she for him pleads strongly to the Moor,
I'll pour this pestilence into his ear:
That she repeals him for her body's lust.
And by how much she strives to do him good,
She shall undo her credit with the Moor.   320
So will I turn her virtue into pitch,
And out of her own goodness make the net
That shall enmesh them all.

                                         [Enter RODERIGO]

How now, Roderigo!

RODERIGO   325
    I do follow here in the chase, not like a hound that hunts, but one
that fills up the cry. My money is almost spent; I have been
tonight exceedingly well cudgelled; and I think the issue will be,
I shall have so much experience for my pains; and so, with no
money at all, and a little more wit, return again to Venice.

IAGO
    How poor are they that have not patience!   330
What wound did ever heal but by degrees?
Thou know'st we work by wit and not by witchcraft,
And wit depends on dilatory time.
Does't not go well? Cassio hath beaten thee,
And thou by that small hurt hast cashiered Cassio.   335
Though other things grow fair against the sun,
Yet fruits that blossom first will first be ripe.
Content thyself awhile. By the mass, 'tis morning!
Pleasure and action make the hours seem short.
Retire thee, go where thou art billeted.   340
Away, I say! Thou shalt know more hereafter:
Nay, get thee gone.

                                         Exit RODERIGO

               Two things are to be done.
My wife must move for Cassio to her mistress;
I'll set her on.
Myself the while to draw the Moor apart,   345
And bring him jump when he may Cassio find
Soliciting his wife—ay, that's the way—
Dull not device by coldness and delay.

                                         Exit

[Othello

Act 3

0: Scene: Being a long play, *Othello* is almost always cut in performance; 3.1 and 3.2 are candidates for omission.

1: **masters:** the musicians

1: **content your pains:** i.e., pay for your services

3: **instruments:** musical instruments (also, pun on penis)

4: **i' th' nose:** nasally (also an allusion to syphilis, a venereal disease that also causes nasal deformity and was reputed to have first appeared in Naples)

8: **a tail:** a tale, story (also pun on penis)

Act 3, Scene 1]

Enter CASSIO with Musicians

CASSIO
  Masters, play here. I will content your pains.
  Something that's brief, and bid "Good morrow, general."

They play
Enter Clown

Clown
  Why masters, have your instruments been in Naples, that they
  speak i' th' nose thus?

First Musician
  How sir? How?   5

Clown
  Are these, I pray you, wind instruments?

First Musician
  Ay marry are they, sir.

Clown
  O, thereby hangs a tail.

First Musician
  Whereby hangs a tale, sir?

Clown
  Marry, sir, by many a wind instrument that I know. But, masters,   10
  here's money for you; and the general so likes your music that he
  desires you, for love's sake, to make no more noise with it.

First Musician
  Well, sir, we will not.

21: **quillets:** clever and tricky banter

23: **favor:** indulgence (of her time)

25: **In happy time:** i.e., just in time

Set rendering of "Street" from the 1951 staging by Orson Welles at
St. James Theatre

Rare Book and Special Collections Library, University of Illinois at Urbana-Champaign

26: **a-bed:** to bed

29: **suit:** petition

Clown

If you have any music that may not be heard, to 't again. But, as
they say, to hear music the general does not greatly care.   15

First Musician

We have none such, sir.

Clown

Then put up your pipes in your bag, for I'll away. Go, vanish into
air, away!

Exeunt Musicians

CASSIO

Dost thou hear, mine honest friend?

Clown

No, I hear not your honest friend; I hear you.   20

CASSIO

Prithee keep up thy quillets—there's a poor piece of gold for thee. If the
gentlewoman that attends the general's wife be stirring, tell her there's
one Cassio entreats her a little favor of speech. Wilt thou do this?

Clown

She is stirring, sir; if she will stir hither, I shall seem to notify unto her.

CASSIO

Do, good my friend.

Exit Clown
Enter IAGO

In happy time, Iago.   25

IAGO

You have not been a-bed, then?

CASSIO

Why, no; the day had broke before we parted.
I have made bold, Iago,
To send in your wife. My suit to her
Is that she will to virtuous Desdemona   30
Procure me some access.

32: **a mean:** a means, a way

42: **affinity:** relations; connections

42: **wholesome:** reasonable

43: **might not but refuse:** i.e., had no choice but to refuse

44: **suitor:** petitioner

44: **likings:** inclination

51: **speak your bosom:** i.e., say what is in your heart

IAGO
                    I'll send her to you presently,
And I'll devise a mean to draw the Moor
Out of the way, that your converse and business
May be more free.

CASSIO
  I humbly thank you for 't.

                                                    Exit [IAGO]
                    I never knew   35
A Florentine more kind and honest.

                                            Enter EMILIA

EMILIA
  Good morrow, good Lieutenant. I am sorry
  For your displeasure, but all will sure be well.
  The general and his wife are talking of it,
  And she speaks for you stoutly. The Moor replies   40
  That he you hurt is of great fame in Cyprus
  And great affinity, and that in wholesome wisdom,
  He might not but refuse you. But he protests he loves you
  And needs no other suitor but his likings
  To take the safest occasion by the front   45
  To bring you in again.

CASSIO
                    Yet I beseech you,
  If you think fit, or that it may be done,
  Give me advantage of some brief discourse
  With Desdemon alone.

EMILIA
                    Pray you come in,
  I will bestow you where you shall have time   50
  To speak your bosom freely.

CASSIO
  I am much bound to you.

                                                    Exeunt

1: **pilot:** (of the ship that took Othello to Cyprus)

2: **do my duties:** send my compliments, do homage

3: **works:** fortifications

Lines 3–4: "That done, I will be walking on the works. / Repair there to me": Patrick Stewart as Othello and Ron Canada as Iago in The Shakespeare Theatre's 1997–1998 production directed by Jude Kelly
Photo: Carol Rosegg

4: **repair:** come

Act 3, Scene 2]

OTHELLO
 These letters give, Iago, to the pilot,
 And by him do my duties to the Senate;
 That done, I will be walking on the works.
 Repair there to me.

IAGO
     Well, my good lord, I'll do't.

OTHELLO
 This fortification, gentlemen, shall we see't?   5

Gentleman
 We'll wait upon your lordship.

                 Exeunt

2: **all my abilities:** i.e., all I can

3: **warrant:** declare

Lines 7-9: "Bounteous madam, / Whatever shall become of Michael Cassio, / He's never any thing but your true servant": Sir Derek Jacobi as Cassio and Maggie Smith as Desdemona in Stuart Burge's 1965 movie production
Courtesy: Douglas Lanier

12: **in strangeness:** with reserve, in aloofness

15: **nice:** petty, trifling

15: **waterish:** insubstantial, thin

16: **breed...circumstances:** root by accident or due to chance

17: **supplied:** filled by another

Act 3, Scene 3]

Enter DESDEMONA, CASSIO, and EMILIA

DESDEMONA
Be thou assured, good Cassio, I will do
All my abilities in thy behalf.

EMILIA
Good madam, do. I warrant it grieves my husband
As if the cause were his.

DESDEMONA
O, that's an honest fellow. Do not doubt, Cassio,   5
But I will have my lord and you again
As friendly as you were.

CASSIO
             Bounteous madam,
Whatever shall become of Michael Cassio,
He's never any thing but your true servant.

DESDEMONA
I know't; I thank you. You do love my lord;   10
You have known him long, and be you well assured
He shall in strangeness stand no farther off
Than in a politic distance.

CASSIO
             Ay, but lady,
That policy may either last so long,
Or feed upon such nice and waterish diet,   15
Or breed itself so out of circumstances,
That I being absent and my place supplied,
My general will forget my love and service.

20: **give thee warrant of:** promise you

21: **perform it:** fulfill my obligation

22: **article:** detail

23: **watch him tame:** (from falconry) the practice of forcing a bird to stay awake in order to domesticate it

24: **board:** dining table

24: **shrift:** confessional

27: **thy solicitor:** petitioner, i.e., Desdemona

28: **give thy cause away:** i.e., give up

33: **purposes:** i.e., pleading his case

34: **your discretion:** as you see fit

DESDEMONA
    Do not doubt that: before Emilia here
    I give thee warrant of thy place. Assure thee,   20
    If I do vow a friendship I'll perform it
    To the last article. My lord shall never rest,
    I'll watch him tame and talk him out of patience;
    His bed shall seem a school, his board a shrift,
    I'll intermingle every thing he does   25
    With Cassio's suit. Therefore be merry, Cassio,
    For thy solicitor shall rather die
    Than give thy cause away.

EMILIA
    Madam, here comes my lord.

                        Enter OTHELLO and IAGO

CASSIO
    Madam, I'll take my leave.   30

DESDEMONA
    Why, stay, and hear me speak.

CASSIO
    Madam, not now; I am very ill at ease,
    Unfit for mine own purposes.

DESDEMONA
    Well, do your discretion.

                        Exit CASSIO

IAGO
    Ha! I like not that.

OTHELLO
               What dost thou say?   35

IAGO
    Nothing, my lord; or if—I know not what.

OTHELLO
    Was not that Cassio parted from my wife?

42: **suitor:** petitioner

47: **his present reconciliation take:** i.e., immediately restore Cassio to your (Othello's) favor

49: **That errs...cunning:** i.e., his fault was an accident, not deliberate

IAGO
　Cassio, my lord? No, sure, I cannot think it
　That he would steal away so guilty-like,
　Seeing your coming.

OTHELLO
　　　　　　　　I do believe 'twas he.　　　　　　　　40

DESDEMONA
　How now, my lord?
　I have been talking with a suitor here,
　A man that languishes in your displeasure.

OTHELLO
　Who is 't you mean?

DESDEMONA
　Why, your lieutenant, Cassio. Good my lord,　　　45
　If I have any grace or power to move you,
　His present reconciliation take;
　For if he be not one that truly loves you,
　That errs in ignorance and not in cunning,
　I have no judgment in an honest face.　　　　　50
　I prithee, call him back.

OTHELLO
　　　　　　　Went he hence now?

DESDEMONA
　Yes, faith, so humbled
　That he hath left part of his grief with me
　To suffer with him. Good love, call him back.

OTHELLO
　Not now, sweet Desdemon, some other time.　　　55

DESDEMONA
　But shall 't be shortly?

OTHELLO
　　　　　　The sooner, sweet, for you.

58: **dinner:** lunch, midday meal (supper = evening meal)

64: **trespass:** offense

67: **private check:** personal rebuke

70: **mamm'ring on:** hesitantly

72: **dispraisingly:** disparagingly

74: **bring him in:** i.e., back into Othello's favor

Franchelle Stewart Dorn as Emilia, Ron Canada as Iago, Patrice Johnson as
Desdemona, and Patrick Stewart as Othello in The Shakespeare Theatre's
1997–1998 production directed by Jude Kelly
Photo: Carol Rosegg

76: **boon:** granted favor, fulfilled wish

79: **sue to:** beg, entreat

79: **peculiar profit:** special benefit

DESDEMONA
  Shall 't be tonight at supper?

OTHELLO
                No, not tonight.

DESDEMONA
  Tomorrow dinner then?

OTHELLO
                I shall not dine at home:
  I meet the captains at the citadel.

DESDEMONA
  Why, then, tomorrow night, or Tuesday morn,   60
  On Tuesday noon or night, on Wednesday morn.
  I prithee, name the time, but let it not
  Exceed three days. In faith, he's penitent,
  And yet his trespass, in our common reason—
  Save that, they say, the wars must make examples   65
  Out of their best—is not almost a fault
  T' incur a private check. When shall he come?
  Tell me, Othello. I wonder in my soul
  What you would ask me that I should deny
  Or stand so mamm'ring on? What? Michael Cassio,   70
  That came a-wooing with you, and so many a time,
  When I have spoke of you dispraisingly,
  Hath ta'en your part, to have so much to do
  To bring him in? By'r lady, I could do much—

OTHELLO
  Prithee no more—let him come when he will;   75
  I will deny thee nothing.

DESDEMONA
                Why, this is not a boon:
  'Tis as I should entreat you wear your gloves,
  Or feed on nourishing dishes, or keep you warm,
  Or sue to you to do a peculiar profit
  To your own person. Nay, when I have a suit   80

81: **touch:** test by the touchstone, probe

82: **poise:** weight, importance

82: **weight:** consequence, importance

83: **fearful:** uncertain

88: **Be as...teach you:** do whatever you want

90: **wretch:** creature (used as a word of tenderness, perhaps mixed with pity)

Set rendering of "First Jealousy" from the 1951 staging by Orson Welles at St. James Theatre

Rare Book and Special Collections Library, University of Illinois at Urbana-Champaign

Wherein I mean to touch your love indeed,
It shall be full of poise and difficult weight,
And fearful to be granted.

OTHELLO

              I will deny thee nothing.
Whereon, I do beseech thee, grant me this,
To leave me but a little to myself.   85

DESDEMONA

Shall I deny you? No, farewell, my lord.

OTHELLO

Farewell, my Desdemona, I'll come to thee straight.

DESDEMONA

Emilia, come. Be as your fancies teach you.
Whate'er you be, I am obedient.

                      Exeunt DESDEMONA and EMILIA

OTHELLO

Excellent wretch! Perdition catch my soul   90
But I do love thee! And when I love thee not,
Chaos is come again.

IAGO

My noble lord—

OTHELLO

              What dost thou say, Iago?

IAGO

Did Michael Cassio, when you wooed my lady,
Know of your love?

OTHELLO

             He did, from first to last.   95
Why dost thou ask?

IAGO

But for a satisfaction of my thought,
No further harm.

98: **why:** of what consequence, what

102: **Discern'st thou...that:** i.e., Did you perceive something in that (discern'st = discern, perceive, aught = anything)

106: **for aught I know:** i.e., to my knowledge (Cassio is honest)

113: **of my counsel:** in Othello's confidence

OTHELLO

Why of thy thought, Iago?

IAGO

I did not think he had been acquainted with her.

OTHELLO

O yes, and went between us very oft.   100

IAGO

Indeed?

OTHELLO

Indeed? Ay, indeed. Discern'st thou aught in that?
Is he not honest?

IAGO

Honest, my lord?

OTHELLO

Honest? Ay, honest.   105

IAGO

My lord, for aught I know.

OTHELLO

What dost thou think?

IAGO

Think, my lord?

OTHELLO

Think, my lord? By heaven, thou echo'st me
As if there were some monster in thy thought
Too hideous to be shown. Thou dost mean something;   110
I heard thee say even now, thou lik'st not that,
When Cassio left my wife. What didst not like?
And when I told thee he was of my counsel
In my whole course of wooing, thou cried'st, "Indeed?"

115: **purse:** crease, press together

117: **conceit:** idea

120: **for:** because

122: **stops:** pauses, hesitations

124: **tricks of custom:** customary tricks

124: **just:** honest

125: **close:** hidden, secret

125: **dilations:** accusations

129: **Or those...seem none:** i.e., Men who are not honest should not appear to be honest

And didst contract and purse thy brow together, 115
As if thou then hadst shut up in thy brain
Some horrible conceit. If thou dost love me,
Show me thy thought.

IAGO

My lord, you know I love you.

OTHELLO
I think thou dost;
And for I know thou 'rt full of love and honesty 120
And weigh'st thy words before thou giv'st them breath,
Therefore these stops of thine fright me the more.
For such things in a false disloyal knave
Are tricks of custom, but in a man that's just,
They're close dilations, working from the heart, 125
That passion cannot rule.

IAGO

For Michael Cassio,
I dare be sworn, I think, that he is honest.

OTHELLO
I think so too.

IAGO

Men should be what they seem,
Or those that be not, would they might seem none.

OTHELLO
Certain, men should be what they seem. 130

IAGO
Why then I think Cassio's an honest man.

OTHELLO
Nay, yet there's more in this.
I prithee, speak to me as to thy thinkings,
As thou dost ruminate, and give thy worst of thoughts
The worst of words.

137: **all slaves are free to:** i.e., slaves can keep their thoughts private

139-140: **As where's...intrude not:** i.e., whose soul or mind hasn't occasionally entertained bad thoughts?

141: **uncleanly apprehensions:** filthy, impure thoughts

142: **leets:** manor court, courts which oversee a private jurisdiction

142: **law-days:** court days

144: **thy friend:** i.e., himself, Othello

145–146: **If thou...thoughts:** i.e., If you think he has been wronged and do not tell him

147: **vicious:** wrong

148: **plague:** torment

149: **to spy into:** seek out

149: **jealousy:** suspicion

150: **shapes:** creates, imagines

151: **conceits:** judges

153: **his:** i.e., Iago's

153: **scattering:** scattered, distracted

157-193:
Hugh Quarshie as Othello, Anton Lesser as Iago
Paul Robeson as Othello, Jose Ferrer as Iago

161: **filches:** steals, pilfers

IAGO

                    Good my lord pardon me;   135
Though I am bound to every act of duty,
I am not bound to that all slaves are free to—
Utter my thoughts? Why, say they are vile and false?
As where's that palace whereinto foul things
Sometimes intrude not? Who has that breast so pure,   140
But some uncleanly apprehensions
Keep leets and law-days and in sessions sit
With meditations lawful?

OTHELLO

Thou dost conspire against thy friend, Iago,
If thou but think'st him wronged and mak'st his ear   145
A stranger to thy thoughts.

IAGO

                    I do beseech you,
Though I perchance am vicious in my guess—
As, I confess, it is my nature's plague
To spy into abuses and oft my jealousy
Shapes faults that are not—that your wisdom yet,   150
From one that so imperfectly conceits,
Would take no notice, nor build yourself a trouble
Out of his scattering and unsure observance.
It were not for your quiet nor your good,
Nor for my manhood, honesty, and wisdom,   155
To let you know my thoughts.

OTHELLO

                  Zounds! What dost thou mean?

IAGO

Good name in man and woman, dear my lord,
Is the immediate jewel of their souls;
Who steals my purse steals trash; 'tis something, nothing;
'Twas mine, 'tis his, and has been slave to thousands.   160
But he that filches from me my good name
Robs me of that which not enriches him
And makes me poor indeed.

tracks 20-22

157-193:
Hugh Quarshie as Othello, Anton Lesser as Iago
Paul Robeson as Othello, Jose Ferrer as Iago

Line 166: "O, beware, my lord, of jealousy": Raul Julia as Othello and Christopher Walken as Iago in the Public Theater's 1991 production directed by Joe Dowling
Photo: George E. Joseph

168: **the meat it feeds on:** i.e., the jealous person
168–169: **that cuckold...wronger:** Iago suggests that the man who knows his wife has been unfaithful is much happier if he does not love her or her lover (unlike Othello, who loves Desdemona and Cassio)
173: **Poor...enough:** proverb
174: **fineless:** infinite
183: **exsufflicate and blown surmises:** i.e., overblown, inflated guesses or conjectures
184: **inference:** suggestion, allegation

OTHELLO
By heaven, I'll know thy thoughts.

IAGO
You cannot, if my heart were in your hand,
Nor shall not, whilst 'tis in my custody.   165

OTHELLO
Ha!

IAGO
O beware, my lord, of jealousy!
It is the green-eyed monster which doth mock
The meat it feeds on. That cuckold lives in bliss
Who, certain of his fate, loves not his wronger,
But O, what damnèd minutes tells he o'er   170
Who dotes, yet doubts, suspects, yet soundly loves!

OTHELLO
O, misery!

IAGO
Poor and content is rich and rich enough,
But riches fineless is as poor as winter
To him that ever fears he shall be poor.   175
Good God, the souls of all my tribe defend
From jealousy!

OTHELLO
Why, why is this?
Think'st thou I'd make a life of jealousy
To follow still the changes of the moon
With fresh suspicions? No, to be once in doubt   180
Is once to be resolved. Exchange me for a goat
When I shall turn the business of my soul
To such exsufflicate and blown surmises
Matching thy inference. 'Tis not to make me jealous
To say my wife is fair, feeds well, loves company,   185
Is free of speech, sings, plays, and dances well—
Where virtue is, these are more virtuous.

tracks 20-22

157-193:
Hugh Quarshie as Othello, Anton Lesser as Iago
Paul Robeson as Othello, Jose Ferrer as Iago

189: **revolt:** indiscretion

Lines 190–191: "For she had eyes and chose me. No, Iago, / I'll see before I doubt; when I doubt, prove": André Braugher as Iago and Avery Brooks as Othello in The Shakespeare Theatre's 1990–1991 production directed by Harold Scott
Photo: Joan Marcus

196: **franker:** more honest or open
199: **wear your eyes thus:** keep wary and alert (probably spoken with a specific gesture)
201: **self-bounty:** inherent kindness
202: **country disposition:** the character of our countrymen (i.e., the Venetians)
203: **pranks:** licentious tricks
204: **best conscience:** i.e., the best they can hope for (for their conscience)
208: **looks:** facial expressions, moods
210: **seeming:** facade, false front
211: **seel:** blind (see 1.3.266)
211: **close as oak:** i.e., entirely blind (possibly referring to the close grain of oak)

Nor from mine own weak merits will I draw
The smallest fear or doubt of her revolt,
For she had eyes and chose me. No, Iago,   190
I'll see before I doubt; when I doubt, prove;
And on the proof, there is no more but this:
Away at once with love or jealousy!

IAGO

I am glad of this, for now I shall have reason
To show the love and duty that I bear you   195
With franker spirit. Therefore, as I am bound,
Receive it from me. I speak not yet of proof.
Look to your wife' observe her well with Cassio;
Wear your eyes thus, not jealous nor secure;
I would not have your free and noble nature,   200
Out of self-bounty be abused—look to 't.
I know our country disposition well:
In Venice they do let God see the pranks
They dare not show their husbands. Their best conscience
Is not to leave 't undone but keep 't unknown.   205

OTHELLO

Dost thou say so?

IAGO

She did deceive her father, marrying you,
And when she seemed to shake and fear your looks,
She loved them most.

OTHELLO

                And so she did.

IAGO

                   Why, go to then.
She that, so young, could give out such a seeming   210
To seel her father's eyes up close as oak —
He thought 'twas witchcraft—but I am much to blame.
I humbly do beseech you of your pardon
For too much loving you.

218: **your love:** i.e., my love of you; **moved:** distressed

219–220: **strain my speech to grosser issues:** exaggerate the meaning or consequences of my words

223: **success:** outcome

Line 225: "My lord, I see you're moved": James Earl Jones as Othello and Mitchell Ryan as Iago in the Public Theater's 1964 production directed by Gladys Vaughan
Photo: George E. Joseph

230: **affect:** like, be pleased with

230: **proposèd matches:** suitors

231: **clime:** country, region

231: **degree:** social rank

OTHELLO

I am bound to thee forever.

IAGO

I see this hath a little dashed your spirits.   215

OTHELLO

Not a jot, not a jot.

IAGO

I' faith, I fear it has.
I hope you will consider what is spoke
Comes from your love. But I do see you're moved;
I am to pray you not to strain my speech
To grosser issues nor to larger reach   220
Than to suspicion.

OTHELLO

I will not.

IAGO

Should you do so, my lord,
My speech should fall into such vile success
As my thoughts aimed not at. Cassio's my worthy friend—
My lord, I see you're moved.

OTHELLO

No, not much moved.   225
I do not think but Desdemona's honest.

IAGO

Long live she so; And long live you to think so.

OTHELLO

And yet how nature erring from itself,—

IAGO

Ay, there's the point. As, to be bold with you,
Not to affect many proposèd matches   230
Of her own clime, complexion, and degree,
Whereto we see in all things nature tends—

233: **rank:** foul smelling, corrupted (with a pun referring to degree)
234: **Foul...unnatural:** disproportionate number of unnatural thoughts
235: **in position:** in making this assertion
237: **will:** desire (a pun meaning both her willfulness and sexual desire)
238: **her country forms:** look and appearance of her countrymen
244: **unfolds:** tells

Lines 243-244: "Why did I marry? This honest creature doubtless / Sees and knows more, much more, than he unfolds": Avery Brooks as Othello in The Shakespeare Theatre's 1990–1991 production directed by Harold Scott

Photo: Joan Marcus

246: **scan:** analyze
247: **have his place:** i.e., have his rank and position returned to him
251: **strain his entertainment:** press hard for his case
252: **importunity:** urgency
254: **too busy:** intrusive, meddlesome
256: **free:** (of suspicion)
257: **government:** self-control

Foh! One may smell in such a will most rank,
Foul disproportions, thoughts unnatural.
But pardon me, I do not in position   235
Distinctly speak of her, though I may fear
Her will, recoiling to her better judgment,
May fall to match you with her country forms;
And happily repent.

OTHELLO
                Farewell, farewell.
If more thou dost perceive, let me know more;   240
Set on thy wife to observe. Leave me, Iago.

IAGO
                                [Going]

My lord, I take my leave.

OTHELLO
Why did I marry? This honest creature doubtless
Sees and knows more, much more, than he unfolds.

IAGO
                          [Returning]
My lord, I would I might entreat your honor   245
To scan this thing no farther; leave it to time.
Although 'tis fit that Cassio have his place —
For sure he fills it up with great ability —
Yet, if you please to hold him off a while,
You shall by that perceive him and his means: 250
Note, if your lady strain his entertainment
With any strong or vehement importunity,
Much will be seen in that. In the meantime,
Let me be thought too busy in my fears—
As worthy cause I have to fear I am—   255
And hold her free, I do beseech your honor.

OTHELLO
Fear not my government.

260: **qualities:** character, aspects of human nature
261: **haggard:** 1) intractable, wild, 2) a wild untrained hawk
262: **jesses:** straps of leather and silk with which hawks were tied by the legs
263: **let her down the wind:** set her free, release her
264: **Haply:** perhaps
265: **soft parts of conversation:** gracious or pleasant sociability
266: **chamberers:** courtly gentlemen with drawing room graces and elegant turns of phrase

Lines 264–265: "Haply, for I am black / And have not the soft parts of conversation / That chamberers have": John Kani as Othello in The Market Theater's 1987 production directed by Janet Suzman

Photo: Ruphin Coudyzer

267: **vale:** valley
272: **vapour:** dank fumes
275: **prerogatived:** privileged
275: **base :** lowly ranked people
276: **destiny unshunnable:** i.e., inevitable
277: **forked plague:** i.e., horned cuckold (in popular iconography, a cuckold was depicted as having horns)
278: **quicken:** come to life

IAGO
  I once more take my leave.

  Exit

OTHELLO
  This fellow's of exceeding honesty
  And knows all qualities, with a learned spirit,   260
  Of human dealings. If I do prove her haggard,
  Though that her jesses were my dear heart-strings,
  I'd whistle her off and let her down the wind
  To prey at fortune. Haply, for I am black
  And have not those soft parts of conversation   265
  That chamberers have, or for I am declined
  Into the vale of years,—yet that's not much—
  She's gone. I am abused, and my relief
  Must be to loathe her. O, curse of marriage,
  That we can call these delicate creatures ours   270
  And not their appetites! I had rather be a toad
  And live upon the vapour of a dungeon
  Than keep a corner in the thing I love
  For others' uses. Yet, 'tis the plague of great ones;
  Prerogatived are they less than the base;   275
  'Tis destiny unshunnable, like death.
  Even then this forked plague is fated to us
  When we do quicken.

                    Enter DESDEMONA and EMILIA

  Look where she comes:
  If she be false, O then heaven mocks itself;   280
  I'll not believe 't.

DESDEMONA
                    How now, my dear Othello?
  Your dinner, and the generous islanders
  By you invited, do attend your presence.

OTHELLO
  I am to blame.

DESDEMONA
                    Why do you speak so faintly?
  Are you not well?   285

286: **upon my forehead here:** his temples (also suggesting the horns of a cuckold)

287: **with watching:** from lack of sleep

292–330:
Patience Tomlinson as Emilia, Anton Lesser as Iago
Dorothy Gould as Emilia, Richard Haddon Haines as Iago

289: **napkin:** handkerchief

289: Stage Direction: *He puts the handkerchief...it drops:* It is important that the audience can see the business with the handkerchief. On stage, Othello often knocks it from Desdemona's hand and so is partly to blame for the fact that she drops it. Neither notices that it has fallen.

294: **wayward:** contrary, capricious

296: **he:** i.e., Othello

296: **conjured:** solemnly entreated

297: **reserves:** keep (the handkerchief) close to her

298: **ta'en out:** copied

301: **I nothing:** possibly "I am nothing" or "I know nothing"

303: **chide:** scold

303: **a thing:** an object (in general) with a vulgar pun

304: **common:** a taunt, left dangling to suggesting Emilia is loose

OTHELLO
I have a pain upon my forehead, here.

DESDEMONA
'Faith, that's with watching; 'twill away again.
Let me but bind it hard, within this hour
It will be well.

OTHELLO
                    Your napkin is too little.
                        [He puts the handkerchief from him, and it drops]
Let it alone. Come, I'll go in with you.   290

DESDEMONA
I am very sorry that you are not well.
                    Exeunt OTHELLO and DESDEMONA

EMILIA
I am glad I have found this napkin.
This was her first remembrance from the Moor.
My wayward husband hath a hundred times
Wooed me to steal it, but she so loves the token,   295
For he conjured her she should ever keep it,
That she reserves it evermore about her
To kiss and talk to. I'll have the work ta'en out,
And give 't Iago. What he will do with it
Heaven knows, not I,   300
I nothing but to please his fantasy.
                                                    [Enter Iago]

IAGO
How now? What do you here alone?

EMILIA
Do not you chide; I have a thing for you.

IAGO
A thing for me? It is a common thing—

EMILIA
Ha!   305

292–330:
Patience Tomlinson as Emilia, Anton Lesser as Iago
Dorothy Gould as Emilia, Richard Haddon Haines as Iago

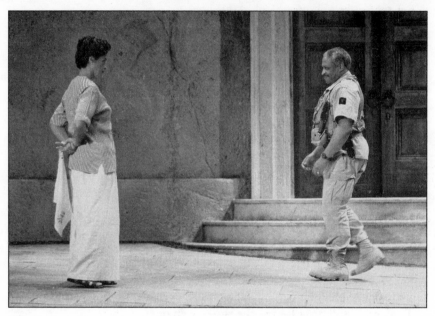

Line 307–308: "What will you give me now / For that same handkerchief?":
Franchelle Stewart Dorn as Emilia and Ron Canada as Iago in The Shakespeare
Theatre's 1997–1998 production directed by Jude Kelly
Photo: Carol Rosegg

313: **faith:** interjection "in faith"

315: **wench:** woman (not necessarily used in contempt)

318: **import:** importance

319: **run mad:** become mad

320: **lack it:** find it missing

IAGO
    To have a foolish wife.

EMILIA
    O, is that all? What will you give me now
    For that same handkerchief?

IAGO
                    What handkerchief?

EMILIA
    What handkerchief?
    Why, that the Moor first gave to Desdemona,   310
    That which so often you did bid me steal.

IAGO
    Hast stol'n it from her?

EMILIA
    No, faith, she let it drop by negligence,
    And, to th' advantage, I being here, took 't up—
    Look, here it is.

IAGO
                    A good wench, give it me.   315

EMILIA
    What will you do with 't, that you have been so earnest
    To have me filch it?

IAGO
                                        [Snatching it]
                    Why, what's that to you?

EMILIA
    If it be not for some purpose of import,
    Give 't me again. Poor lady, she'll run mad
    When she shall lack it.

tracks 23-25

292–330:
Patience Tomlinson as Emilia, Anton Lesser as Iago
Dorothy Gould as Emilia, Richard Haddon Haines as Iago

320: **Be not...on 't:** i.e., do not confess to knowing where it is

327: **conceits:** ideas

328–329: **Which....blood:** at first they do not seem distasteful (i.e., dangerous) but with a little persistence begin to work

331: **poppy:** the source for opium, which dulls the senses

331: **mandragora:** mandrake, a soporific

334: **owedst:** had

336: **Avaunt:** exclamation of contempt uttered to drive one away

336: **the rack:** a torture device on which victims hands and feet were attached and stretched in opposite directions

339: **sense:** understanding, knowledge

343: **wanting:** having need for (i.e., not knowing it was stolen)

IAGO

                Be not acknown on 't.   320

I have use for it. Go, leave me.

                               Exit EMILIA

I will in Cassio's lodging lose this napkin,

And let him find it. Trifles light as air

Are to the jealous confirmations strong

As proofs of holy writ. This may do something: 325

The Moor already changes with my poison.

Dangerous conceits are in their natures poisons,

Which at the first are scarce found to distaste,

But with a little act upon the blood

Burn like the mines of Sulphur.

                           Enter OTHELLO

                I did say so.   330

Look, where he comes. Not poppy, nor mandragora,

Nor all the drowsy syrups of the world

Shall ever medicine thee to that sweet sleep

Which thou owedst yesterday.

OTHELLO

                Ha, ha, false to me?

IAGO

Why, how now general? No more of that.   335

OTHELLO

Avaunt, be gone! Thou hast set me on the rack:

I swear 'tis better to be much abused

Than but to know 't a little.

IAGO

                How now, my lord?

OTHELLO

What sense had I in her stol'n hours of lust?

I saw 't not, thought it not, it harmed not me;   340

I slept the next night well, fed well, was free and merry,

I found not Cassio's kisses on her lips;

He that is robbed, not wanting what is stol'n,

Let him not know 't, and he's not robbed at all.

347: **Pioneers:** pioneers, i.e., construction workers and physical laborers

350: **plumèd:** feathered, as on parade

352: **trump:** trumpet

353: **fife:** a type of flute

355: **circumstance:** ceremony

356: **mortal engines:** machines that cause death (i.e., cannons)

357: **Jove:** from mythology, the supreme god, a.k.a. Jupiter, also the god of thunder and weather

357: **dread clamours:** i.e., thunderclaps

357: **counterfeit:** copy, imitate

358: **Othello's occupation's gone:** 1) Othello has lost all pleasure in his work, and 2) Othello has lost his ability to concentrate.

361: **give me the ocular proof:** Some editors add a stage direction here for Othello to take Iago by the throat; that he turns violently on Iago is implied by his upcoming words.

366: **probation:** proof

IAGO
    I am sorry to hear this.   345

OTHELLO
    I had been happy if the general camp,
    Pioneers and all, had tasted her sweet body,
    So I had nothing known. O now forever
    Farewell the tranquil mind, farewell content!
    Farewell the plumèd troops and the big wars,   350
    That makes ambition virtue! O farewell,
    Farewell the neighing steed and the shrill trump,
    The spirit-stirring drum, th' ear-piercing fife,
    The royal banner, and all quality,
    Pride, pomp and circumstance of glorious war!   355
    And, O you mortal engines, whose rude throats
    Th' immortal Jove's dread clamours counterfeit,
    Farewell! Othello's occupation's gone.

IAGO
    Is 't possible, my lord?

OTHELLO
    Villain, be sure thou prove my love a whore!   360
    Be sure of it; give me the ocular proof;
    Or by the worth of mine eternal soul,
    Thou hadst been better have been born a dog
    Than answer my waked wrath!

IAGO
                    Is 't come to this?

OTHELLO
    Make me to see 't, or, at the least, so prove it   365
    That the probation bear no hinge nor loop
    To hang a doubt on, or woe upon thy life!

IAGO
    My noble lord—

373: damnation: either Othello's damnation for taking his revenge or Iago's damnation for inflicting suffering on Othello

376: God buy you: i.e. Goodbye, I'm finished with you.

376: mine office: my resignation

377: vice: sin

380: profit: good lesson

381: sith: since

386: just: honest, truthful

387: Her name: This is the Second Quarto reading, though some editors prefer the First Folio reading, "My name". The First Quarto omits lines 426-433.

387-388: fresh as Dian's visage: clear and pure as the (full) moon

388: Dian: Diana, Roman goddess of the moon and of chastity

391: were satisfied: i.e., knew one way or the other

OTHELLO
    If thou dost slander her and torture me,
    Never pray more; abandon all remorse,   370
    On horror's head horrors accumulate;
    Do deeds to make heaven weep, all earth amazed;
    For nothing canst thou to damnation add
    Greater than that.

IAGO
                O grace! O heaven, forgive me!
    Are you a man? Have you a soul or sense?   375
    God buy you; take mine office. O wretched fool
    That lov'st to make thine honesty a vice!
    O monstrous world! Take note, take note, O world,
    To be direct and honest is not safe.
    I thank you for this profit, and from hence   380
    I'll love no friend, sith love breeds such offense.

OTHELLO
    Nay, stay. Thou shouldst be honest.

IAGO
    I should be wise, for honesty's a fool
    And loses that it works for.

OTHELLO
                By the world,
    I think my wife be honest, and think she is not;   385
    I think that thou art just, and think thou art not.
    I'll have some proof. Her name that was as fresh
    As Dian's visage is now begrimed and black
    As mine own face. If there be cords, or knives,
    Poison, or fire, or suffocating streams,   390
    I'll not endure it. Would I were satisfied!

IAGO
    I see, sir, you are eaten up with passion.
    I do repent me that I put it to you.
    You would be satisfied?

396: **supervisor:** observer

396: **grossly gape:** stare with mouth open

397: **topped:** literally under a man (engaging in sexual intercourse)

399: **prospect:** sight

400: **bolster:** cushion each other (with their bodies)

404: **prime:** in heat

405: **salt:** lecherous

405: **in pride:** in heat

405: **gross:** dull, stupid

407: **imputation:** insinuation, strong implication

410: **living:** valid

411: **office:** task

413: **Pricked:** spurred on, incited

414: **lay:** slept (next to each other on the same bunk)

415: **raging tooth:** toothache

416-426: **There are...O monstrous, monstrous:** Both the First Quarto and the First Folio have difficulties with this speech over both words and lineation, and editors have offered different solutions. I largely follow the First Folio rather than the First Quarto.

417: **loose of soul:** unrestrained, uninhibited

OTHELLO
                Would? Nay, and I will!

IAGO
    And may, but, how? How satisfied, my lord?   395
    Would you, the supervisor, grossly gape on?
    Behold her, topped?

OTHELLO
                Death and damnation! O!

IAGO
    It were a tedious difficulty, I think,
    To bring them to that prospect. Damn them then,
    If ever mortal eyes do see them bolster   400
    More than their own. What then? How then?
    What shall I say? Where's satisfaction?
    It is impossible you should see this,
    Were they as prime as goats, as hot as monkeys,
    As salt as wolves in pride, and fools as gross   405
    As ignorance made drunk. But yet, I say,
    If imputation and strong circumstances
    Which lead directly to the door of truth
    Will give you satisfaction, you might have't.

OTHELLO
    Give me a living reason she's disloyal.   410

IAGO
    I do not like the office.
    But, sith I am entered in this cause so far,
    Pricked to 't by foolish honesty and love,
    I will go on. I lay with Cassio lately,
    And, being troubled with a raging tooth,   415
    I could not sleep. There are a kind of men
    So loose of soul that in their sleeps will mutter
    Their affairs; one of this kind is Cassio.
    In sleep I heard him say, "Sweet Desdemona,
    Let us be wary, let us hide our loves,"   420

421: **gripe:** grip, grasp

Line 426: "O monstrous, monstrous!": Bill McCallum as Iago and Lester Purry as Othello in the Guthrie Theater's 2003 production directed by Joe Dowling
Photo: T. Charles Erickson

428: **denoted:** indicated

428: **foregone:** previous

428: **conclusion:** experience

429: **'Tis a shrewd...dream:** The First Folio gives this line to Othello, but it fits better with Iago's speech, as in the First Quarto.

And then, sir, would he gripe and wring my hand,
Cry, "O sweet creature!" and then kiss me hard,
As if he plucked up kisses by the roots
That grew upon my lips, lay his leg o'er my thigh,
And sigh, and kiss; and then cry "Cursed fate   425
That gave thee to the Moor!"

OTHELLO

           O monstrous, monstrous!

IAGO

Nay, this was but his dream.

OTHELLO

But this denoted a foregone conclusion.

IAGO

'Tis a shrewd doubt, though it be but a dream.
And this may help to thicken other proofs   430
That do demonstrate thinly.

OTHELLO

          I'll tear her all to pieces!

IAGO

Nay, be wise; yet we see nothing done;
She may be honest yet. Tell me but this,
Have you not sometimes seen a handkerchief
Spotted with strawberries in your wife's hand?   435

OTHELLO

I gave her such a one, 'twas my first gift.

IAGO

I know not that, but such a handkerchief—
I am sure it was your wife's—did I today
See Cassio wipe his beard with.

442: **the slave:** i.e., Cassio

Lines 445–446: "All my fond love thus do I blow to heaven. / 'Tis gone. / Arise, black vengenance, from thy hollow hell!": André Braugher as Iago and Avery Brooks as Othello in The Shakespeare Theatre's 1990–1991 production directed by Harold Scott
Photo: Joan Marcus

446: **the hollow hell:** The First Folio has "the hollow hell" while the First Quarto has "thy hollow cell". Either reading is possible since they were similarly written.
447: **crown and hearted:** crown = sovereignty, hearted = based in the heart
448: **fraught:** load, contents
449: **aspics':** a venomous snake
452-459: **Iago...heaven:** This fragment from one of Othello's more famous speeches is omitted in the First Quarto.
452: **Pontic sea:** the Black sea
453: **compulsive:** forced, constrained
454: **retiring:** reverse flow or tide
455: **Propontic:** the sea of Marmora, which connects the Black Sea to the Mediterranean; **Hellespont:** the Dardanelles, a straight that links the Sea of Marmora to the Mediterranean
457: **humble:** kind, benevolent

OTHELLO
                If it be that—

IAGO
    If it be that, or any, it was hers.   440
    It speaks against her with the other proofs.

OTHELLO
    O, that the slave had forty thousand lives!
    One is too poor, too weak for my revenge.
    Now do I see 'tis true. Look here, Iago,
    All my fond love thus do I blow to heaven. 'Tis gone.   445
    Arise, black vengeance, from the hollow hell,
    Yield up, O love, thy crown and hearted throne
    To tyrannous hate! Swell, bosom, with thy fraught,
    For 'tis of aspics' tongues!

IAGO
                Yet be content.

OTHELLO
    O, blood, blood, blood!   450
                                                                    Kneels

IAGO
    Patience, I say; your mind perhaps may change.

OTHELLO
    Never, Iago. Like to the Pontic sea
    Whose icy current and compulsive course
    Ne'er feels retiring ebb but keeps due on
    To the Propontic and the Hellespont,   455
    Even so my bloody thoughts with violent pace
    Shall ne'er look back, ne'er ebb to humble love,
    Till that a capable and wide revenge
    Swallow them up. Now, by yond marble heaven,
    In the due reverence of a sacred vow   460
    I here engage my words.

463: **clip us round about:** surround us

465: **execution:** action

468: **What bloody business ever:** no matter how bloody the business is

470: **put thee to 't:** assign a task to him

474: **lewd minx:** lascivious, wanton woman

475: **withdraw:** go inside

476: **furnish me:** equip me

477: **fair devil:** i.e., Desdemona

IAGO

Do not rise yet.

Kneels

Witness, you ever-burning lights above,
You elements that clip us round about,
Witness that here, Iago doth give up
The execution of his wit, hands, heart,   465
To wronged Othello's service. Let him command,
And to obey shall be in me remorse,
What bloody business ever.

[They rise]

OTHELLO

I greet thy love
Not with vain thanks, but with acceptance bounteous,
And will upon the instant put thee to 't.   470
Within these three days let me hear thee say
That Cassio's not alive.

IAGO

My friend is dead.
'Tis done at your request. But let her live.

OTHELLO

Damn her, lewd minx! O, damn her, damn her!
Come, go with me apart; I will withdraw   475
To furnish me with some swift means of death
For the fair devil. Now art thou my lieutenant.

IAGO

I am your own forever.

Exeunt

1: **lies:** sleeps, lodges

2: **lies:** a pun meaning "sleeps" as well as "be dishonest"

4: **stabbing:** 1) kill with a weapon, 2) betray (stab in the back)

5: **go to:** an interjection

6: **where I lie:** 1) where I lodge, and 2) where I tell lies

8: **devise:** make up

11: **inquire him out:** ask about

12: **catechize:** instruct by questions and appropriate answers

Act 3, Scene 4]

Enter DESDEMONA, EMILIA, and Clown

DESDEMONA
Do you know, sirrah, where Lieutenant Cassio lies?

Clown
I dare not say he lies anywhere.

DESDEMONA
Why, man?

Clown
He's a soldier, and for me to say a soldier lies, 'tis stabbing.

DESDEMONA
Go to. Where lodges he?   5

Clown
To tell you where he lodges is to tell you where I lie.

DESDEMONA
Can anything be made of this?

Clown
I know not where he lodges, and for me to devise a
lodging and say he lies here, or he lies there, were
to lie in mine own throat.   10

DESDEMONA
Can you inquire him out, and be edified by report?

Clown
I will catechize the world for him; that is, make
questions, and by them answer.

15: **moved:** applied to

16: **compass:** scope, range

16: **wit:** intellect

18: **should:** did

21: **crusadoes:** Portuguese coins

21: **but:** though

22: **baseness:** meanness, ill thought

26: **humors:** moods

DESDEMONA
Seek him; bid him come hither; tell him I have
moved my lord on his behalf and hope all will be well.   15

Clown
To do this is within the compass of man's wit, and
therefore I will attempt the doing it.

Exit

DESDEMONA
Where should I lose that handkerchief, Emilia?

EMILIA
I know not, madam.

DESDEMONA
Believe me, I had rather have lost my purse   20
Full of crusadoes. And but my noble Moor
Is true of mind and made of no such baseness
As jealous creatures are, it were enough
To put him to ill thinking.

EMILIA
                    Is he not jealous?

DESDEMONA
Who, he? I think the sun where he was born   25
Drew all such humors from him.

EMILIA
                    Look where he comes.

Enter OTHELLO

DESDEMONA
I will not leave him now till Cassio
Be called to him. How is 't with you, my lord?

29: **hardness:** difficulty

29: **dissemble:** give false appearance (i.e., not show his real mood)

35: **sequester:** separation, a retreat

39: **frank:** liberal

44: **chuck:** a term of endearment (an indication that in spite of his doubts, Othello still feels affection for her)

OTHELLO
  Well, my good lady. [*Aside*] O, hardness to dissemble!—
  How do you, Desdemona?

DESDEMONA
                              Well, my good lord.   30

OTHELLO
  Give me your hand. This hand is moist, my lady.

DESDEMONA
  It yet hath felt no age nor known no sorrow.

OTHELLO
  This argues fruitfulness and liberal heart:
  Hot, hot, and moist. This hand of yours requires
  A sequester from liberty, fasting and prayer,   35
  Much castigation, exercise devout;
  For here's a young and sweating devil here,
  That commonly rebels. 'Tis a good hand,
  A frank one.

DESDEMONA
                              You may, indeed, say so,
  For 'twas that hand that gave away my heart.   40

OTHELLO
  A liberal hand. The hearts of old gave hands.
  But our new heraldry is hands, not hearts.

DESDEMONA
  I cannot speak of this. Come now, your promise.

OTHELLO
  What promise, chuck?

DESDEMONA
  I have sent to bid Cassio come speak with you.   45

46: **salt:** bitter

46: **sorry:** painful

46: **rheum:** runny, stuffy nose

46: **offends:** bothers

57: **fancies:** sexual interests

59: **take heed on 't:** take care of it

60: **darling:** favorite

61: **perdition:** devastation

OTHELLO
> I have a salt and sorry rheum offends me;
> Lend me thy handkerchief.

DESDEMONA
> Here, my lord.

OTHELLO
> That which I gave you.

DESDEMONA
> I have it not about me.

OTHELLO
> Not?

DESDEMONA
> No, faith, my lord.

OTHELLO
> That's a fault. That handkerchief
> Did an Egyptian to my mother give. 50
> She was a charmer, and could almost read
> The thoughts of people. She told her, while she kept it
> 'Twould make her amiable and subdue my father
> Entirely to her love; but if she lost it
> Or made gift of it, my father's eye 55
> Should hold her loathèd, and his spirits should hunt
> After new fancies. She, dying, gave it me
> And bid me, when my fate would have me wived,
> To give it her. I did so, and, take heed on 't,
> Make it a darling like your precious eye. 60
> To lose 't or give 't away were such perdition
> As nothing else could match.

DESDEMONA
> Is 't possible?

64: sibyl: chief prophetess at any of the oracles, temples dedicated to the gods in ancient Greece

64-65: A sibyl...compasses: This is usually taken to mean that the sibyl is 200 years old, though Honigmann (following Dr Johnson) takes "course" to mean "run"; i.e., the sibyl prophesied that the world would end in 200 years.

67: hallowed: holy

68: mummy: a preparation for magical purposes, made from dead bodies

72: Wherefore: why

OTHELLO
'Tis true; there's magic in the web of it.
A sibyl that had numbered in the world
The sun to course two hundred compasses,   65
In her prophetic fury sewed the work;
The worms were hallowed that did breed the silk,
And it was dyed in mummy which the skillful
Conserved of maidens' hearts.

DESDEMONA
                    I' faith, is 't true?

OTHELLO
Most veritable; therefore look to 't well.   70

DESDEMONA
Then would to God that I had never seen 't!

OTHELLO
Ha? Wherefore?

DESDEMONA
Why do you speak so startingly and rash?

OTHELLO
Is 't lost? Is 't gone? Speak, is 't out o' th' way?

DESDEMONA
Heaven bless us!   75

OTHELLO
Say you?

DESDEMONA
It is not lost, but what an if it were?

OTHELLO
How?

81: **put me from my suit:** distract her from her petition (on Cassio's behalf)

83: **misgives:** has a presentiment of evil

84: **sufficient:** adequate, capable

87: **founded:** built, based

DESDEMONA
  I say it is not lost.

OTHELLO
                    Fetch 't, let me see 't.

DESDEMONA
  Why, so I can, sir; but I will not now.   80
  This is a trick to put me from my suit.
  Pray you, let Cassio be received again.

OTHELLO
  Fetch me the handkerchief; my mind misgives.

DESDEMONA
  Come, come. You'll never meet a more sufficient man.

OTHELLO
  The handkerchief!

DESDEMONA
                    I pray, talk me of Cassio.   85

OTHELLO
  The handkerchief!

DESDEMONA
                    A man that all his time
  Hath founded his good fortunes on your love,
  Shared dangers with you,—

OTHELLO
  The handkerchief!

DESDEMONA
  I'faith, you are to blame.   90

OTHELLO
  Zounds!

                                        Exit

93: **wonder:** miracle

95: **shows us a man:** shows us a man's true nature

96: **all but:** nothing but

100: **importune:** urge

104: **exist:** be, live (in Othello's good graces)

105: **office:** duty

107: **mortal:** fatal

109: **purposed:** intended

109: **futurity:** the future

110: **ransom:** return, deliver

112: **clothe me...content:** appear contended

113: **shut myself up:** i.e., follow

115: **advocation:** pleading

115: **in tune:** appropriate to the time and mood

EMILIA
Is not this man jealous?

DESDEMONA
                    I ne'er saw this before.
Sure, there's some wonder in this handkerchief;
I am most unhappy in the loss of it.

EMILIA
'Tis not a year or two shows us a man.   95
They are all but stomachs, and we all but food;
They eat us hungerly, and when they are full
They belch us.
                                    [Enter CASSIO and IAGO]
                    Look you, Cassio and my husband.

IAGO
There is no other way. 'Tis she must do 't.
And, lo, the happiness! Go and importune her.   100

DESDEMONA
How now, good Cassio, what's the news with you?

CASSIO
Madam, my former suit. I do beseech you
That, by your virtuous means, I may again
Exist and be a member of his love,
Whom I with all the office of my heart   105
Entirely honor. I would not be delayed.
If my offense be of such mortal kind
That nor my service past nor present sorrows
Nor purposed merit in futurity
Can ransom me into his love again,   110
But to know so must be my benefit;
So shall I clothe me in a forced content
And shut myself up in some other course
To fortune's alms.

DESDEMONA
                    Alas, thrice-gentle Cassio,
My advocation is not now in tune;   115
My lord is not my lord, nor should I know him,

117: **favor:** outward appearance

120: **blank:** the aim, the center (as in the center of a target or a rifle scope)

125: **unquietness:** agitation

127: **ranks:** soldiers under his command

129: **puffed:** blew up

130: **of moment:** momentary, fleeting

131: **matter in 't:** substance, serious meaning

132: **state:** relating to government

133: **unhatched:** unknown

133: **practice:** custom

135: **puddled:** made cloudy, darkened

136–137: **Men...object:** men become preoccupied with trivial matters, though the true causes of their discontent are major

138: **indues:** endows

141: **observancy:** reverential attention

142: **bridal:** nuptial festival

142: **beshrew me:** woe to me (mild oath)

143: **unhandsome:** incompetent

143: **warrior:** (because she is fighting for Cassio's cause)

144: **arraigning:** summoning before a court

145: **suborned:** corrupted

Were he in favor as in humor altered.
So help me every spirit sanctified,
As I have spoken for you all my best
And stood within the blank of his displeasure   120
For my free speech. You must awhile be patient;
What I can do I will; and more I will
Than for myself I dare. Let that suffice you.

IAGO
Is my lord angry?

EMILIA
                                   He went hence but now,
And certainly in strange unquietness.   125

IAGO
Can he be angry? I have seen the cannon
When it hath blown his ranks into the air,
And, like the devil, from his very arm
Puffed his own brother—and is he angry?
Something of moment then. I will go meet him.   130
There's matter in 't indeed, if he be angry.

DESDEMONA
I prithee, do so.
                                                                              Exit [IAGO]
                                   Something sure of state,
Either from Venice, or some unhatched practice
Made demonstrable here in Cyprus to him,
Hath puddled his clear spirit; and in such cases   135
Men's natures wrangle with inferior things,
Though great ones are their object. 'Tis even so,
For let our finger ache, and it indues
Our other healthful members even to a sense
Of pain. Nay, we must think men are not gods,   140
Nor of them look for such observancy
As fits the bridal. Beshrew me much, Emilia,
I was, unhandsome warrior as I am,
Arraigning his unkindness with my soul;
But now I find I had suborned the witness,   145
And he's indicted falsely.

147: **conception** : evil thought

148: **toy:** folly

153: **begot...on itself:** i.e., jealousy feeds on itself

157: **fit:** in a suitable mood

157: **move your suit:** plead your case

Lines 161-162: "How is it with you, my most fair Bianca? / I' faith, sweet love, I was coming to your house": Neil McCarthy as Cassio and Gaynor Young as Bianca in The Market Theater's 1987 production directed by Janet Suzman
Photo: Ruphin Coudyzer

EMILIA

                Pray heaven it be
State matters, as you think, and no conception
Nor no jealous toy concerning you.

DESDEMONA

  Alas the day, I never gave him cause.

EMILIA

  But jealous souls will not be answered so;   150
  They are not ever jealous for the cause,
  But jealous for they're jealous. It is a monster
  Begot upon itself, born on itself.

DESDEMONA

  Heaven keep the monster from Othello's mind!

EMILIA

  Lady, amen.   155

DESDEMONA

  I will go seek him. Cassio, walk hereabout,
  If I do find him fit, I'll move your suit
  And seek to effect it to my uttermost.

CASSIO

  I humbly thank your ladyship.

                   Exeunt DESDEMONA and EMILIA
                               Enter BIANCA

BIANCA

  Save you, friend Cassio!

CASSIO

                What make you from home?   160
  How is it with you, my most fair Bianca?
  I' faith, sweet love, I was coming to your house.

165: **Eight score eight hours:** score = 20, thus 8(20) + 8 = 168 hours

168: **leaden:** heavy

169: **in a more continuate time:** in a time unbroken by other business

173: **feel a cause:** see a reason

175: **Throw...teeth:** (and not in mine)

183: **Wherefore:** why

BIANCA

And I was going to your lodging, Cassio.
What, keep a week away? Seven days and nights?
Eight score eight hours? And lovers' absent hours,   165
More tedious than the dial eight score times?
O weary reckoning!

CASSIO

                    Pardon me, Bianca.
I have this while with leaden thoughts been pressed,
But I shall in a more continuate time
Strike off this score of absence. Sweet Bianca,   170
                    [Giving her DESDEMONA's handkerchief]
Take me this work out.

BIANCA

                    O Cassio, whence came this?
This is some token from a newer friend.
To the felt absence now I feel a cause—
Is 't come to this? Well, well.

CASSIO

                    Go to, woman.
Throw your vile guesses in the devil's teeth   175
From whence you have them. You are jealous now
That this is from some mistress some remembrance.
No, by my faith, Bianca.

BIANCA

                    Why, whose is it?

CASSIO

I know not, neither. I found it in my chamber.
I like the work well, ere it be demanded,   180
As like enough it will, I would have it copied.
Take it, and do 't, and leave me for this time.

BIANCA

Leave you? Wherefore?

184: **attend here on:** wait here for

185: **no addition:** not honorable

186: **womaned:** in the company of a woman

189: **bring:** come with

193: **circumstanced:** submit to circumstances

CASSIO
  I do attend here on the general
  And think it no addition, nor my wish,   185
  To have him see me womaned.

BIANCA
                          Why, I pray you?

CASSIO
  Not that I love you not.

BIANCA
  But that you do not love me.
  I pray you, bring me on the way a little,
  And say if I shall see you soon at night?   190

CASSIO
  'Tis but a little way that I can bring you,
  For I attend here, but I'll see you soon.

BIANCA
  'Tis very good. I must be circumstanced.

                                        Exeunt

[Othello

Act 4

2: **unauthorized:** unjustifiable

6: **hypocrisy...devil:** i.e., hypocritical in the face of evil to appear bad while actually meaning no harm

8: **tempt:** test

9: **venial slip:** In the Roman Catholic Church, a "venial sin" is a minor infraction, committed without knowledge or deliberate intent; a "slip" is even less serious

13: **bestow 't:** contraction for "bestow it"

Act 4, Scene 1]

Enter OTHELLO and IAGO

IAGO
   Will you think so?

OTHELLO
                    Think so, Iago?

IAGO
                              What,
   To kiss in private?

OTHELLO
                    An unauthorized kiss!

IAGO
   Or to be naked with her friend in bed
   An hour or more, not meaning any harm?

OTHELLO
   Naked in bed, Iago, and not mean harm?   5
   It is hypocrisy against the devil.
   They that mean virtuously, and yet do so,
   The devil their virtue tempts, and they tempt heaven.

IAGO
   If they do nothing, 'tis a venial slip;
   But if I give my wife a handkerchief, —   10

OTHELLO
   What then?

IAGO
   Why then 'tis hers, my lord, and being hers,
   She may, I think, bestow 't on any man.

14: **honor:** can also mean chastity

16: **essence...not seen:** i.e., it is an abstract aspect of the spirit

17: **They have it...not:** i.e., people who seem honorable often are not

21: **raven:** a traditional omen of bad luck; **infectious:** (from the First Folio; the First Quarto has "infected") infected with disease

22: **boding:** foreboding or foreshadowing bad luck

Lines 20–22: "it comes o'er my memory, / As doth the raven o'er the infected house, / Boding to all — he had my handkerchief": Ron Canada as Iago and Patrick Stewart as Othello in The Shakespeare Theatre's 1997–1998 production directed by Jude Kelly
Photo: Carol Rosegg

25-29: **Or heard him...must blab:** i.e., knaves who have dallied with women, either by seducing them or giving in to their seductions, can't help but brag about it

26: **importunate :** urgent, pressing

27: **dotage:** excessive fondness

28: **cannot choose:** have no choice

31: **unswear:** swear it is not true

OTHELLO
     She is protectress of her honor too.
     May she give that?   15

IAGO
     Her honor is an essence that's not seen,
     They have it very oft that have it not.
     But, for the handkerchief—

OTHELLO
     By heaven, I would most gladly have forgot it.
     Thou said'st—O it comes o'er my memory,   20
     As doth the raven o'er the infectious house,
     Boding to all—he had my handkerchief.

IAGO
     Ay, what of that?

OTHELLO
                         That's not so good now.

IAGO
                         What
     If I had said I had seen him do you wrong?
     Or heard him say—as knaves be such abroad,   25
     Who, having by their own importunate suit
     Or voluntary dotage of some mistress
     Convincèd or supplied them, cannot choose
     But they must blab—

OTHELLO
                         Hath he said any thing?

IAGO
     He hath, my lord, but be you well assured,   30
     No more than he'll unswear.

OTHELLO
                         What hath he said?

32: **I know not what he did:** This is the reading in both the First Quarto and the First Folio; Honigmann suggests punctuating "I know not what. He did –", giving another pause and another unfinished sentence, left to Othello's imagination.

34: **lie:** (Iago leaves this word hanging with deliberate ambiguity)

34: **on her:** (tell lies) about her, but can also be taken in a more literal sense to mean lie on top of her

34–45:
Hugh Quarshie as Othello, Anton Lesser as Iago
Paul Robeson as Othello, Jose Ferrer as Iago

tracks 26-28

35: **We say...belie her:** i.e., we say "lie on her" when they (people) tell lies about her

36: **fulsome:** disgusting

37-41: **To confess...O devil:** omitted in the First Quarto

37: **be hanged:** popular expression meaning "be damned" in a general sense

37-38: **First, to be...confess:** Othello reverses the proverb, "Confess and be hanged."

39: **shadowing:** full of shapes and images

40: **Pish:** interjection of contempt or disgust

Lines 42-43: "Work on, / My medicine, work!": Patrick Stewart as Othello and Ron Canada as Iago in The Shakespeare Theatre's 1997–1998 production directed by Jude Kelly
Photo: Carol Rosegg

45: **reproach:** disgrace, infamy

48: **epilepsy:** a brain disorder causing strange sensations, convulsions, muscle spasms, and loss of consciousness

IAGO
'Faith, that he did—I know not what he did.

OTHELLO
What? What?

IAGO
Lie.

OTHELLO
     With her?

IAGO
       With her, on her, what you will.

OTHELLO
Lie with her? Lie on her? We say "lie on her" when they belie her. 35
Lie with her? Zounds, that's fulsome! Handkerchief—confessions—
handkerchief! To confess and be hanged for his labor. First, to be
hanged, and then to confess! I tremble at it. Nature would not invest
herself in such shadowing passion without some instruction. It is not
words that shakes me thus. Pish! Noses, ears, and lips! Is 't possible? 40
Confess! handkerchief!—O devil!

                  Falls in a trance

IAGO
Work on,
My medicine, work! Thus credulous fools are caught,
And many worthy and chaste dames even thus,
All guiltless, meet reproach.—What ho! My lord!   45
My lord, I say! Othello!

               Enter CASSIO

    How now, Cassio?

CASSIO
What's the matter?

IAGO
My lord is fall'n into an epilepsy;
This is his second fit, he had one yesterday.

50: **Rub...temples:** Cassio inadvertently reinforces Iago's plot by pointing out Othello's temples, the place where a cuckold's horns are said to grow.

50: **forbear:** hold off

51: **his** : its

58: **I mock you not, by heaven:** This is the First Folio reading; the First Quarto has "I mock you? No, by heaven", an alternative sometimes preferred.

60: **hornèd:** i.e., a cuckold

60: **monster:** an unnatural creature

60: **beast:** a wild or domesticated animal

62: **civil:** decent, well-mannered (with a linguistic quibble or pun on "of the city," or "civilized")

64: **yoked:** married

65: **May draw:** is in the same situation

66: **unproper:** 1) not one's own, and 2) indecent

67: **peculiar:** exclusively one's own

68: **arch-mock:** main jest

69: **lip:** kiss

69: **secure:** (apparently) carefree and unsuspecting

69: **couch:** bed

CASSIO
    Rub him about the temples.

IAGO
                    No, forbear;   50
    The lethargy must have his quiet course;
    If not, he foams at mouth and by and by
    Breaks out to savage madness. Look, he stirs;
    Do you withdraw yourself a little while,
    He will recover straight. When he is gone,   55
    I would on great occasion speak with you.
                                        [Exit CASSIO]

    How is it, general? Have you not hurt your head?

OTHELLO
    Dost thou mock me?

IAGO
                    I mock you not, by heaven.
    Would you would bear your fortune like a man!

OTHELLO
    A hornèd man's a monster and a beast.   60

IAGO
    There's many a beast then in a populous city,
    And many a civil monster.

OTHELLO
    Did he confess it?

IAGO
                    Good sir, be a man,
    Think every bearded fellow that's but yoked
    May draw with you. There's millions now alive   65
    That nightly lie in those unproper beds
    Which they dare swear peculiar. Your case is better.
    O, 'tis the spite of hell, the fiend's arch-mock,
    To lip a wanton in a secure couch
    And to suppose her chaste. No, let me know,   70
    And knowing what I am, I know what she shall be.

73: **patient list:** within the bounds of patience (list = boundary, limit)

77: **'scuse:** excuse

77: **ecstasy:** fainting fit, a swoon

78: **anon:** soon

79: **encave:** hide

80: **fleers:** sneers

84: **cope:** meet (in this instance, for the purposes of having sex)

85: **mark:** observe

85: **marry:** exclamation

86: **in spleen:** in a fit of passion

90: Stage Direction: ***OTHELLO retires:*** The stage directions for Othello to retire and to come forward again at line 157 are not in the First Quarto or the First Folio. At the Globe he may merely have hidden himself behind one of the stage pillars (so visible to the audience)

92: **housewife:** a light woman, nearer in meaning to the modern "hussy"; sometimes spelled "huswife" and pronounced perhaps "hussif"

92: **selling her desires:** i.e., selling her body

93: **It:** she

94: **strumpet:** wanton woman

94: **plague:** curse

OTHELLO
  O, thou art wise, 'tis certain.

IAGO
                Stand you a while apart,
  Confine yourself but in a patient list.
  Whilst you were here o'erwhelmed with your grief—
  A passion most unsuiting such a man—   75
  Cassio came hither. I shifted him away
  And laid good 'scuse upon your ecstasy,
  Bade him anon return and here speak with me,
  The which he promised. Do but encave yourself
  And mark the fleers, the gibes, and notable scorns   80
  That dwell in every region of his face.
  For I will make him tell the tale anew:
  Where, how, how oft, how long ago, and when
  He hath, and is again to cope your wife.
  I say, but mark his gesture—marry, patience!   85
  Or I shall say you 're all in all in spleen
  And nothing of a man.

OTHELLO
                Dost thou hear, Iago?
  I will be found most cunning in my patience,
  But—dost thou hear?—most bloody.

IAGO
                That's not amiss,
  But yet keep time in all. Will you withdraw?   90

                                        OTHELLO retires

  Now will I question Cassio of Bianca,
  A housewife that by selling her desires
  Buys herself bread and clothes. It is a creature
  That dotes on Cassio—as 'tis the strumpet's plague
  To beguile many and be beguiled by one.   95
  He, when he hears of her, cannot refrain
  From the excess of laughter. Here he comes.

                                        Enter CASSIO

Line 98: "As he shall smile, Othello shall go mad": Orson Welles' sketch of "Second Jealousy" from the 1951 staging at St. James Theatre

Rare Book and Special Collections Library, University of Illinois at Urbana-Champaign

99: **unbookish:** unsophisticated, ignorant
102: **addition:** title (i.e., lieutenant)
103: **want:** lack, absence

tracks 29-30

105–150:
Anton Lesser as Iago, Roger May as Cassio, Hugh Quarshie as Othello, Allison Pettit as Bianca

106: **speed:** be successful
106: **caitiff:** wretch
109: **rogue:** rascal (unusual usage, usually refers to a man)
110: **faintly:** without zeal or conviction
111: **importunes:** urges, solicits
112: **o'er:** over
112: **go to:** a general expression meaning "get on with it"
113: **gives it out:** announces, publicly declares

As he shall smile, Othello shall go mad,
And his unbookish jealousy must construe
Poor Cassio's smiles, gestures, and light behaviors   100
Quite in the wrong. – How do you now, lieutenant?

CASSIO
The worser that you give me the addition
Whose want even kills me.

IAGO
Ply Desdemona well, and you are sure on 't.

[Speaking lower]

Now, if this suit lay in Bianca's power,   105
How quickly should you speed!

CASSIO
                    Alas, poor caitiff!

OTHELLO
Look, how he laughs already!

IAGO
I never knew a woman love man so.

CASSIO
Alas, poor rogue, I think i' faith she loves me.

OTHELLO
Now he denies it faintly, and laughs it out.   110

IAGO
Do you hear, Cassio?

OTHELLO
                    Now he importunes him
To tell it o'er; go to, well said, well said.

IAGO
She gives it out that you shall marry her.
Do you intend it?

tracks 29-30

105–150:
Anton Lesser as Iago, Roger May as Cassio, Hugh Quarshie as Othello,
Allison Pettit as Bianca

116: **triumph:** exult

117: **customer:** Cassio is referring to himself as being a customer of Bianca's sexual services (see lines 91-93)

118: **unwholesome:** morally tainted

120: **cry:** gossip

123: **scored:** marked, branded

124: **monkey:** i.e., Bianca

125: **flattery:** delusion

128: **sea-bank:** seashore

129: **thither:** there

129: **bauble:** trinket, plaything (i.e., Bianca)

129: **by this hand:** exclamation "I swear"

131: **imports:** conveys, shows

CASSIO

Ha, ha, ha!   115

OTHELLO

Do you triumph, Roman? Do you triumph?

CASSIO

I marry her? What, a customer? Prithee, bear some charity to my wit, do not think it so unwholesome. Ha, ha, ha!

OTHELLO

So, so, so, so; they laugh that win.

IAGO

'Faith, the cry goes that you shall marry her.   120

CASSIO

Prithee, say true!

IAGO

I am a very villain else.

OTHELLO

Have you scored me? Well.

CASSIO

This is the monkey's own giving out; she is persuaded I will marry her out of her own love and flattery, not out of my promise.   125

OTHELLO

Iago beckons me; now he begins the story.

CASSIO

She was here even now; she haunts me in every place. I was the other day talking on the sea-bank with certain Venetians, and thither comes the bauble, and, by this hand, she falls me thus about my neck—   130

OTHELLO

Crying, "O dear Cassio!" as it were; his gesture imports it.

tracks 29-30

105–150:
*Anton Lesser as Iago, Roger May as Cassio, Hugh Quarshie as Othello,
Allison Pettit as Bianca*

132: **lolls:** leans to one side

134: **plucked:** took

135: **nose:** possibly also a euphemism for penis

138: **fitchew:** polecat (reputed to be very amorous and lecherous), thus meaning lascivious woman

138: **marry:** indeed

140: **dam:** mother

142: **take out:** copy

142: **work:** design

142: **piece of work:** story

144: **minx:** a pert and wanton woman

144: **token:** gift

145: **hobbyhorse:** term of contempt for a loose person

148: **should be:** appears to be

150: **when you are next prepared for:** i.e., when next I am ready for you (which may be never)

CASSIO

So hangs, and lolls, and weeps upon me, so shakes, and pulls me.
Ha, ha, ha!

OTHELLO

Now he tells how she plucked him to my chamber. O, I see that
nose of yours, but not that dog I shall throw it to.   135

CASSIO

Well, I must leave her company.

IAGO

Before me, look where she comes!

Enter BIANCA

CASSIO

'Tis such another fitchew; marry, a perfumed one!
What do you mean by this haunting of me?

BIANCA

Let the devil and his dam haunt you! What did you mean by that   140
same handkerchief you gave me even now? I was a fine fool to
take it. I must take out the work? A likely piece of work that you
should find it in your chamber and not know who left it there!
This is some minx's token, and I must take out the work? There,
give it your hobbyhorse, wheresoever you had it, I'll take out no   145
work on 't.

CASSIO

How now, my sweet Bianca? How now? How now?

OTHELLO

By heaven, that should be my handkerchief!

BIANCA

If you'll come to supper tonight, you may. If you will not, come
when you are next prepared for.   150

Exit

152: **rail:** revile, scold

155: **fain:** willingly, gladly

159: **vice:** transgression, sin

163: **prizes:** values

IAGO
>   After her, after her!

CASSIO
>   'Faith, I must, she'll rail in the streets else.

IAGO
>   Will you sup there?

CASSIO
>   'Faith, I intend so.

IAGO
>   Well, I may chance to see you, for I would very fain speak with you.   155

CASSIO
>   Prithee come, will you?

IAGO
>   Go to; say no more.

Exit CASSIO

OTHELLO

[Advancing]

>   How shall I murder him, Iago?

IAGO
>   Did you perceive how he laughed at his vice?

OTHELLO
>   O, Iago!   160

IAGO
>   And did you see the handkerchief?

OTHELLO
>   Was that mine?

IAGO
>   Yours by this hand! And to see how he prizes the foolish woman,
>   your wife—she gave it him, and he hath giv'n it his whore.

165: **nine years a-killing:** take nine years to kill him i.e., have him die a slow death

165: **fair:** beautiful or honorable

169: **it:** i.e., his chest

170-171: **she might...tasks:** i.e., she would have power even over an emperor (an interesting inversion of the precepts of courtly love, where a woman's power over a man was strongest before he was granted unlimited access to her)

175: **plenteous:** copious

177: **condition:** disposition

181: **over:** of

181: **iniquity:** sin

Lines 179–180: "O, Iago, the pity of it, Iago!": Raul Julia as Othello and Richard Dreyfuss as Iago in the Public Theater's 1978–1979 production directed by Wilford Leach
Photo: George E. Joseph

181: **patent:** permission

183: **messes:** small pieces

OTHELLO
  I would have him nine years a-killing. A fine woman, a fair woman,   165
  a sweet woman!

IAGO
  Nay, you must forget that.

OTHELLO
  Ay, let her rot and perish and be damned tonight, for she shall not
  live. No, my heart is turned to stone; I strike it, and it hurts my
  hand. O, the world hath not a sweeter creature; she might lie by   170
  an emperor's side and command him tasks.

IAGO
  Nay, that's not your way.

OTHELLO
  Hang her, I do but say what she is: so delicate with her needle, an
  admirable musician. O, she will sing the savageness out of a bear!
  Of so high and plenteous wit and invention!   175

IAGO
  She's the worse for all this.

OTHELLO
  O, a thousand, thousand times; and then, of so gentle a condition!

IAGO
  Ay, too gentle.

OTHELLO
  Nay, that's certain—but yet the pity of it, Iago! O Iago, the pity of
  it, Iago!   180

IAGO
  If you are so fond over her iniquity, give her patent to offend, for
  if it touch not you, it comes near nobody.

OTHELLO
  I will chop her into messes! Cuckold me?

187: **expostulate:** remonstrate

188: **unprovide my mind:** weaken my resolve

Lines 187-189: "I'll not expostulate her, lest her body and beauty unprovide my mind again. This night, Iago.": Raul Julia as Othello and Christopher Walken as Iago in the Public Theater's 1991 production directed by Joe Dowling
Photo: George E. Joseph

193: **undertaker:** a pun meaning a) undertake the task of killing him and b) become the undertaker, i.e., the one who buries him

IAGO
O, 'tis foul in her.

OTHELLO
With mine officer!   185

IAGO
That's fouler.

OTHELLO
Get me some poison, Iago; this night. I'll not expostulate with her,
lest her body and beauty unprovide my mind again. This night,
Iago.

IAGO
Do it not with poison, strangle her in her bed, even the bed she   190
hath contaminated.

OTHELLO
Good, good. The justice of it pleases; very good.

IAGO
And for Cassio, let me be his undertaker. You shall hear more by
midnight.

OTHELLO
Excellent good.

                                                              A trumpet [within]
                                  What trumpet is that same?   195

IAGO
I warrant something from Venice.
                              Enter LODOVICO, DESDEMONA, and Attendants
'Tis Lodovico, this, comes from the Duke.
See, your wife's with him.

LODOVICO
God save you, worthy general!

202: **instrument of their pleasures:** i.e., the letter that conveys the orders (pleasures) of the duke and senators

209: **unkind:** ungentle, hard-hearted

213: **call:** speak

213: **paper:** i.e., the letter

OTHELLO
   With all my heart, sir.   200

LODOVICO
   The Duke and senators of Venice greet you.

                                                    [Gives him a letter]

OTHELLO
   I kiss the instrument of their pleasures.

                                              [Opens the letter, and reads]

DESDEMONA
   And what's the news, good cousin Lodovico?

IAGO
   I am very glad to see you, signior.
   Welcome to Cyprus.   205

LODOVICO
   I thank you. How does Lieutenant Cassio?

IAGO
   Lives, sir.

DESDEMONA
   Cousin, there's fall'n between him and my lord
   An unkind breach; but you shall make all well.

OTHELLO
   Are you sure of that?   210

DESDEMONA
   My lord?

OTHELLO
                                                                [Reads]

   "This fail you not to do, as you will —"

LODOVICO
   He did not call; he's busy in the paper.
   Is there division 'twixt my lord and Cassio?

216: **atone:** reconcile

216: **love:** affection

221: **troth:** truth

221: **glad on 't:** i.e., glad they are going home and glad for Cassio

Stage direction: Striking her: Laurence Olivier as Othello and Maggie Smith
as Desdemona in Stuart Burge's 1965 movie production
Courtesy: Douglas Lanier

222: Stage Direction: ***Striking her***: There is no stage direction in either the First
Quarto or the First Folio but the text implies that Othello strikes Desdemona (see
Lodovico's comment at line 257) and it is usual in productions for him to do so.

DESDEMONA
   A most unhappy one; I would do much   215
   T' atone them for the love I bear to Cassio.

OTHELLO
   Fire and brimstone!

DESDEMONA
           My lord?

OTHELLO
               Are you wise?

DESDEMONA
   What, is he angry?

LODOVICO
           May be the letter moved him;
   For, as I think, they do command him home,
   Deputing Cassio in his government.   220

DESDEMONA
   By my troth, I am glad on 't.

OTHELLO
          Indeed?

DESDEMONA
           My lord?

OTHELLO
   I am glad to see you mad.

DESDEMONA
         Why, sweet Othello, —

OTHELLO
                            [Striking her]

   Devil!

226: **very much:** it is a major occurrence, a terrible thing

227: **Make her amends:** apologize to her

229: **crocodile:** the crocodile was thought to be a deceptive creature; "crocodile tears"

238: **turn and turn:** i.e., she is changeable, deceptive

241: **Proceed you...tears:** (spoken to Desdemona)

DESDEMONA

    I have not deserved this.

LODOVICO

    My lord, this would not be believed in Venice,   225
    Though I should swear I saw 't. 'Tis very much,
    Make her amends; she weeps.

OTHELLO

                O devil, devil!
    If that the earth could teem with woman's tears,
    Each drop she falls would prove a crocodile:
    Out of my sight!   230

DESDEMONA

    I will not stay to offend you.

                            [Going]

LODOVICO

    Truly, an obedient lady.
    I do beseech your lordship call her back.

OTHELLO

    Mistress!

DESDEMONA

    My lord?   235

OTHELLO

    What would you with her, sir?

LODOVICO

                Who, I, my lord?

OTHELLO

    Ay; you did wish that I would make her turn.
    Sir, she can turn and turn, and yet go on
    And turn again; and she can weep, sir, weep;
    And she's obedient, as you say, obedient,   240
    Very obedient.—Proceed you in your tears?—

242: **well-painted:** well-painted like a prostitute or well-painted in deception

242: **O well-painted passion:** (spoken to Desdemona)

244: **mandate:** government order

248: **goats and monkeys:** Othello is still obsessing over Iago's words. See 3.3.404.

250: **sufficient:** capable

250–251: **the nature Whom:** i.e., the one whose nature

252: **shot of...chance:** war images reflecting Othello's former reputation as a great general

254: **safe:** sound, intact

254: **light of brain:** insane

255: **He's that he is:** Iago leaves this ambiguous to allow Lodovico's imagination to assume the worst

255: **censure:** judgment, opinion

256–257: **if what he might...he were:** i.e., if he is not, in fact, insane, I wish he were (for that would at least explain his actions)

258: **not so well:** not good, not appropriate

258–259: **yet I...the worst:** i.e., I wish I knew this was the worst of his abuses

259: **use:** habit, custom

260: **work upon his blood:** enrage him

Concerning this, sir—O well-painted passion!—
I am commanded home.—Get you away;
I'll send for you anon.—Sir, I obey the mandate
And will return to Venice.—Hence, avaunt!   245

[Exit DESDEMONA]

Cassio shall have my place. And, sir, tonight,
I do entreat that we may sup together.
You are welcome, sir, to Cyprus.—Goats and monkeys!

Exit

LODOVICO
Is this the noble Moor whom our full senate
Call all in all sufficient? Is this the nature   250
Whom passion could not shake? Whose solid virtue
The shot of accident nor dart of chance
Could neither graze nor pierce?

IAGO
                    He is much changed.

LODOVICO
Are his wits safe? Is he not light of brain?

IAGO
He's that he is. I may not breathe my censure   255
What he might be; if what he might, he is not,
I would to heaven he were!

LODOVICO
                    What? strike his wife?

IAGO
'Faith, that was not so well; yet would I knew
That stroke would prove the worst!

LODOVICO
                    Is it his use?
Or did the letters work upon his blood   260
And new-create this fault?

262: **honesty in me:** decent or honorable for me

264: **courses:** actions, conduct

264: **denote:** indicate (his character)

IAGO
> Alas, alas!
It is not honesty in me to speak
What I have seen and known. You shall observe him,
And his own courses will denote him so
That I may save my speech. Do but go after,   265
And mark how he continues.

LODOVICO
I am sorry that I am deceived in him.

Exeunt

5: **Each syllable...them:** i.e., every word they exchanged

8: **mask:** part of a woman's attire at that time

Act 4, Scene 2]

OTHELLO
You have seen nothing then?

EMILIA
Nor ever heard, nor ever did suspect.

OTHELLO
Yes, you have seen Cassio and she together.

EMILIA
But then I saw no harm, and then I heard
Each syllable that breath made up between them.   5

OTHELLO
What? Did they never whisper?

EMILIA
                        Never, my lord.

OTHELLO
Nor send you out o' th' way?

EMILIA
                        Never.

OTHELLO
To fetch her fan, her gloves, her mask, nor nothing?

EMILIA
Never, my lord.

OTHELLO
                        That's strange.

10: **durst:** would dare

12: **remove your thought:** forget the idea

12: **bosom:** heart

14: **serpent's curse:** a biblical reference to the story of Adam and Eve, in which they are banished from paradise

18: **bawd:** procuress, a pimp

19: **a subtle whore:** i.e., Desdemona

20: **A closet lock and key:** i.e., a locked closet or chamber (filled with villainous secrets)

21: **do 't:** do it (i.e., pray)

22: **chuck:** Othello still refers to her with an affectionate pet name

25: **function:** job, duties

26: **procreants:** ones who procreate (i.e., husbands and wives)

28: **mystery:** calling, occupation (i.e., as a procuress)

28: **dispatch:** make haste

EMILIA

    I durst, my lord, to wager she is honest,   10
    Lay down my soul at stake. If you think other,
    Remove your thought; it doth abuse your bosom.
    If any wretch have put this in your head,
    Let heaven requite it with the serpent's curse,
    For if she be not honest, chaste, and true,   15
    There's no man happy; the purest of their wives
    Is foul as slander.

OTHELLO

                 Bid her come hither—go.

                                  Exit EMILIA

    She says enough; yet she's a simple bawd
    That cannot say as much. This is a subtle whore,
    A closet lock and key of villainous secrets;   20
    And yet she'll kneel and pray, I have seen her do 't.

                  Enter DESDEMONA with EMILIA

DESDEMONA

    My lord, what is your will?

OTHELLO

                 Pray you, chuck, come hither.

DESDEMONA

    What is your pleasure?

OTHELLO

                 Let me see your eyes—
    Look in my face.

DESDEMONA

                 What horrible fancy's this?

OTHELLO

    [*To EMILIA*] Some of your function, mistress,   25
    Leave procreants alone and shut the door,
    Cough or cry "hem" if anybody come.
    Your mystery, your mystery—nay, dispatch!

                                    Exit EMILIA

29: **Upon my knee...import:** Desdemona is clearly kneeling at this point; she usually rises again at line 39.

29: **import:** mean

35: **like one of heaven:** i.e., like an angel

36: **be double-damned:** i.e., damned not only for lying, but also for committing adultery

37: **honest:** faithful

41: **heavy:** sad, full of sorrow

43: **haply:** by chance

43-44: **if haply...calling back:** if you suspect my father was instrumental in commanding you back home

DESDEMONA
    Upon my knee, what doth your speech import?
    I understand a fury in your words,   30
    But not the words.

OTHELLO
    Why? What art thou?

DESDEMONA
    Your wife, my lord, your true and loyal wife.

OTHELLO
    Come, swear it, damn thyself,
    Lest, being like one of heaven, the devils themselves   35
    Should fear to seize thee. Therefore, be double-damned—
    Swear thou art honest.

DESDEMONA
                Heaven doth truly know it.

OTHELLO
    Heaven truly knows that thou art false as hell.

DESDEMONA
    To whom, my lord? With whom? How am I false?

OTHELLO
    Ah Desdemon, away, away, away!   40

DESDEMONA
    Alas the heavy day! Why do you weep?
    Am I the motive of these tears, my lord?
    If haply you my father do suspect
    An instrument of this your calling back,
    Lay not your blame on me; if you have lost him,   45
    I have lost him too.

46: **heaven** and 47 **they:** Dr Johnson amended the First Quarto and the First Folio's "heaven" to "heavens", but the First Quarto's reading "he" for "they" in line 47 may suggest that "heaven" was originally "God" and that this is another profanity removed.

50: **Given...hopes:** i.e., enslaved him and his deepest desires

53: **fixed:** permanent, like a statue or shrine

53: **for the time of scorn:** i.e., to be ridiculed and scorned for all time

56: **garnered:** collected and stowed away like a treasure

57: **bear no life:** an echo of line 55: ("bear that too"); die, and possibly also by extension, have no children

58: **current:** life force, energy

60: **cistern:** receptacle of water

61: **knot:** copulate (used for toads)

61: **gender:** engender, breed

61: **complexion:** face

63: **grim:** terrifying

64: **esteems:** holds, considers

65: **shambles:** slaughterhouses, butchers' shops

66: **quicken:** enliven, come to life, become pregnant

66: **blowing:** i.e., of the wind

68: **That the sense...been born:** Honigmann suggests that this is an almost regular line if we elide "thou'dst" (from "thou hadst").

69: **ignorant:** i.e., committed in ignorance, unintentional

70: **paper:** (metaphorically) skin

70: **book:** (metaphorically) Desdemona's skin or face

71: **What committed:** what sin have you committed

72: **Committed:** perpetrated, also sometimes used to mean surrender (as in her fidelity)

72: **public commoner:** whore

73: **forges:** blacksmith's fires, therefore red hot with anger

OTHELLO
                   Had it pleased heaven
To try me with affliction, had they rained
All kind of sores and shames on my bare head,
Steeped me in poverty to the very lips,
Given to captivity me and my utmost hopes,   50
I should have found in some place of my soul
A drop of patience; but, alas, to make me
The fixèd figure for the time of scorn
To point his slow and moving finger at!
Yet could I bear that too, well, very well,   55
But there, where I have garnered up my heart,
Where either I must live or bear no life,
The fountain from the which my current runs
Or else dries up—to be discarded thence!
Or keep it as a cistern for foul toads   60
To knot and gender in! Turn thy complexion there,
Patience, thou young and rose-lipped cherubin,
Ay, here look grim as hell!

DESDEMONA
I hope my noble lord esteems me honest.

OTHELLO
O, ay, as summer flies are in the shambles,   65
That quicken even with blowing. O thou weed
Who art so lovely fair and smell'st so sweet
That the sense aches at thee, would thou hadst ne'er been born!

DESDEMONA
Alas, what ignorant sin have I committed?

OTHELLO
Was this fair paper, this most goodly book,   70
Made to write "whore" upon? What committed?
Committed! O thou public commoner!
I should make very forges of my cheeks
That would to cinders burn up modesty

76: stops the nose at it: plugs its nose

76: moon winks: the moon goes dark, turns away. (Diana, the goddess of the moon, is also the goddess of chastity)

77: bawdy: unchaste

80: strumpet: prostitute

82: vessel: i.e., her body

83: unlawful: i.e., touch by anyone other than her lawful husband

85: saved: go to heaven

87: I cry you mercy: I pray for God's mercy on you

88: took: mistook, thought you to be

89: Stage Direction: *Enter Emilia*: The First Folio marks Emilia's entry here, but Michael Neill notes that in lines 114 and 119 Emilia knows that Othello has called Desdemona "whore" and suggests she enters earlier, at line 87. The First Quarto marks her entry at line 85, but the First Quarto's stage directions usually anticipate, suggesting that they derive from a playhouse manuscript where actors would be warned to get ready, shortly before they appear.

90: office: duty

90: Saint Peter: biblical saint who guards heaven's gates

91: keeps: guards

Did I but speak thy deeds. What committed?   75
Heaven stops the nose at it, and the moon winks;
The bawdy wind that kisses all it meets
Is hushed within the hollow mine of earth
And will not hear 't. What committed?
Impudent strumpet!

DESDEMONA
            By heaven, you do me wrong.   80

OTHELLO
Are you not a strumpet?

DESDEMONA
            No, as I am a Christian.
If to preserve this vessel for my lord
From any other foul unlawful touch
Be not to be a strumpet, I am none.

OTHELLO
What, not a whore?

DESDEMONA
            No, as I shall be saved.   85

OTHELLO
Is 't possible?

DESDEMONA
O, heaven forgive us!

OTHELLO
            I cry you mercy, then.
I took you for that cunning whore of Venice
That married with Othello.

Enter Emilia

            You, mistress,
That have the office opposite to Saint Peter   90
And keeps the gate of hell, you, you, ay, you!

92: **course:** business

93: **counsel:** secret

94: **conceive:** think

96: **half asleep:** senseless, numb

Lines 101–102: "I have none; do not talk to me, Emilia. / I cannot weep, nor answer have I none": Franchelle Stewart Dorn as Emilia and Patrice Johnson as Desdemona in The Shakespeare Theatre's 1997–1998 production directed by Jude Kelly
Photo: Carol Rosegg

103: **water:** tears

103: **prithee:** please

We have done our course; there's money for your pains;
I pray you, turn the key and keep our counsel.

Exit

EMILIA
Alas, what does this gentleman conceive?
How do you, madam? How do you, my good lady?   95

DESDEMONA
'Faith, half asleep.

EMILIA
Good madam, what's the matter with my lord?

DESDEMONA
With who?

EMILIA
Why, with my lord, madam.

DESDEMONA
Who is thy lord?

EMILIA
                    He that is yours, sweet lady.   100

DESDEMONA
I have none; do not talk to me, Emilia.
I cannot weep, nor answers have I none
But what should go by water. Prithee, tonight
Lay on my bed my wedding sheets, remember,
And call thy husband hither.

EMILIA
                    Here's a change indeed.   105
                                        Exit

106: **meet:** fitting, appropriate

106: **used:** treated

107: **I been behaved:** I behaved

107–108: **How have...misuse:** i.e., How have I behaved that he might criticize me so harshly for the smallest transgression?

108: **least misuse:** This is the First Folio reading; the First Quarto has "greatest abuse". Honigmann amends to "greatest misuse".

112: **chid:** scolded

113: **a child to chiding:** unused to being scolded

114: **bewhored:** called her a whore

115: **despite:** malice, contemptuous hate

115: **heavy terms:** severe expressions of hate

119: **in his drink:** drunk

120: **laid such terms:** applied such words

120: **callet:** woman of ill repute

DESDEMONA

'Tis meet I should be used so, very meet.
How have I been behaved, that he might stick
The small'st opinion on my least misuse?

Enter EMILIA with IAGO

IAGO

What is your pleasure, madam? How is 't with you?

DESDEMONA

I cannot tell. Those that do teach young babes   110
Do it with gentle means and easy tasks.
He might have chid me so; for in good faith,
I am a child to chiding.

IAGO

What is the matter, lady?

EMILIA

Alas, Iago, my lord hath so bewhored her,
Thrown such despite and heavy terms upon her   115
That true hearts cannot bear it.

DESDEMONA

Am I that name, Iago?

IAGO

What name, fair lady?

DESDEMONA

Such as she said my lord did say I was.

EMILIA

He called her whore. A beggar in his drink
Could not have laid such terms upon his callet.   120

IAGO

Why did he so?

127: **Beshrew:** curse

128: **trick:** vicious or foolish action

129: **eternal:** damned, abhorrent

130: **busy and insinuating:** meddling and ingratiating

131: **cogging:** deceiving

131: **cozening:** cheating

131: **office:** position, rank

135: **halter:** hangman's noose

138: **abused:** deceived

139: **base:** not noble, common, cheap

139: **scurvy:** vile, contemptible

DESDEMONA

I do not know; I am sure I am none such.

IAGO

Do not weep, do not weep—alas the day!

EMILIA

Hath she forsook so many noble matches,
Her father, and her country, and her friends,   125
To be called whore? Would it not make one weep?

DESDEMONA

It is my wretched fortune.

IAGO

                        Beshrew him for 't!
How comes this trick upon him?

DESDEMONA

                        Nay, heaven doth know.

EMILIA

I will be hanged if some eternal villain,
Some busy and insinuating rogue,   130
Some cogging, cozening slave, to get some office,
Have not devised this slander. I'll be hanged else.

IAGO

Fie, there is no such man, it is impossible.

DESDEMONA

If any such there be, heaven pardon him.

EMILIA

A halter pardon him, and hell gnaw his bones!   135
Why should he call her whore? Who keeps her company?
What place? What time? What form? What likelihood?
The Moor's abused by some most villainous knave,
Some base notorious knave, some scurvy fellow.

140: **companions:** i.e., dishonorable men
140: **thou'dst:** you should
140: **unfold:** be revealed or discovered
143: **within door:** softly, so no one outside can hear
145: **turned...without:** turned your way of thinking inside out
146: **made you to suspect me:** i.e., Iago once suspected Emilia had an affair with Othello

Lines 147–148: "O God, Iago, / What shall I do to win my lord again?": Joyce Redman as Emilia, Maggie Smith as Desdemona, and Frank Finlay as Iago in Stuart Burge's 1965 movie production
Courtesy: Douglas Lanier

150-163: **Here I kneel...could make me:** One of the longer passages in this scene is omitted in the First Quarto.
151: **will:** intentions
152: **discourse of thought:** in her thoughts
154: **them:** themselves (i.e., her eyes, ears and senses)
157: **beggarly divorcement:** penniless divorce
158: **Comfort forswear me:** I renounce all comforts
162: **addition:** title, rank
163: **world's mass of vanity:** all the vanity in the world
165: **does him offense:** upsets him
166: **chide with you:** take it out on you

O heaven, that such companions thou'dst unfold,   140
And put in every honest hand a whip
To lash the rascals naked through the world
Even from the east to th' west!

IAGO

                    Speak within door.

EMILIA

O, fie upon them! Some such squire he was
That turned your wit the seamy side without   145
And made you to suspect me with the Moor.

IAGO

You are a fool—go to.

DESDEMONA

                    O God, Iago,
What shall I do to win my lord again?
Good friend, go to him, for by this light of heaven,
I know not how I lost him. Here I kneel;   150
If e'er my will did trespass 'gainst his love,
Either in discourse of thought or actual deed,
Or that mine eyes, mine ears, or any sense
Delighted them in any other form,
Or that I do not yet, and ever did,   155
And ever will—though he do shake me off
To beggarly divorcement—love him dearly,
Comfort forswear me! Unkindness may do much,
And his unkindness may defeat my life
But never taint my love. I cannot say, "whore."   160
It does abhor me now I speak the word,
To do the act that might the addition earn
Not the world's mass of vanity could make me.

IAGO

I pray you, be content, 'tis but his humor;
The business of the state does him offense,   165
And he does chide with you.

167: **warrant:** swear

169: **stays the meat:** wait for food

173: **What in the contrary:** i.e., how is that not true

174: **daff'st me:** puts me aside, evades me; the First Quarto has "doff'st", an alternative form with the same meaning

174: **device:** trick

175-6: **keep'st from me...of hope:** i.e., keep opportunities away from me, yet keep me interested with a small amount of hope

175: **conveniency:** advantage, opportunity

175: **than:** rather than

176: **least advantage:** least occasion

181: **no kin together:** unrelated

DESDEMONA
If 'twere no other—

IAGO

It is but so, I warrant.

[Trumpets within]

Hark, how these instruments summon to supper—
The messengers of Venice stays the meat.
Go in, and weep not; all things shall be well.   170

Exeunt DESDEMONA and EMILIA
Enter RODERIGO

How now, Roderigo?

RODERIGO
I do not find that thou deal'st justly with me.

IAGO
What in the contrary?

RODERIGO
Every day thou daff'st me with some device, Iago, and rather, as
it seems to me now, keep'st from me all conveniency than suppli-   175
est me with the least advantage of hope. I will indeed no longer
endure it, nor am I yet persuaded to put up in peace what already
I have foolishly suffered.

IAGO
Will you hear me, Roderigo?

RODERIGO
'Faith, I have heard too much; for your words and performances   180
are no kin together.

IAGO
You charge me most unjustly.

183: **naught:** nothing

183: **wasted myself...means:** wasted all of my money and resources

185: **votarist:** an acolyte or devotee of the church

188: **go to:** expression of dismissal

189: **go to:** a quibble on the meaning of "go to"; Iago means it as a casual dismissal, while Roderigo takes it to mean "go to" Desdemona (for an extramarital affair)

190: **scurvy:** contemptible

190: **fobbed:** tricked, deluded

193: **make myself known:** speak to her directly and explain my situation

194: **give over:** give up

196: **satisfaction of:** amends from

197: **You have said now:** i.e., you have said your piece

198: **intendment:** intention

199: **mettle:** fighting spirit

201–202: **exception:** objection

202: **directly:** openly, honestly

RODERIGO

With naught but truth. I have wasted myself out of my means.
The jewels you have had from me to deliver to Desdemona would
half have corrupted a votarist. You have told me she hath   185
received them, and returned me expectations and comforts of sudden respect and acquaintance, but I find none.

IAGO

Well, go to; very well.

RODERIGO

"Very well", " Go to"? I cannot go to, man, nor 'tis not very well!
By this hand, I think it is scurvy and begin to find myself fopped   190
in it.

IAGO

Very well.

RODERIGO

I tell you 'tis not very well! I will make myself known to
Desdemona: if she will return me my jewels, I will give over my
suit and repent my unlawful solicitation. If not, assure yourself, I   195
will seek satisfaction of you.

IAGO

You have said now.

RODERIGO

Ay, and said nothing but what I protest intendment of doing.

IAGO

Why, now I see there's mettle in thee, and even from this instant
do build on thee a better opinion than ever before. Give me thy   200
hand, Roderigo. Thou hast taken against me a most just exception, but yet I protest I have dealt most directly in thy affair.

RODERIGO

It hath not appeared.

209: **engines:** instruments of torture, deadly plots

210: **compass:** reach

211: **depute:** substitute

211–212: **depute Cassio in Othello's place:** i.e., promote Cassio to Othello's current position

215: **Mauritania:** a country in Northern Africa

216: **abode:** stay

216: **lingered:** protracted, extended

217: **determinate:** decisive, certain

IAGO
> I grant indeed it hath not appeared, and your suspicion is not
> without wit and judgment. But, Roderigo, if thou hast that in   205
> thee indeed, which I have greater reason to believe now than
> ever—I mean purpose, courage and valour—this night show it. If
> thou the next night following enjoy not Desdemona, take me
> from this world with treachery and devise engines for my life.

RODERIGO
> Well, what is it? Is it within reason and compass?   210

IAGO
> Sir, there is especial commission come from Venice to depute
> Cassio in Othello's place.

RODERIGO
> Is that true? Why, then Othello and Desdemona return again to
> Venice.

IAGO
> O, no. He goes into Mauritania and taketh away with him the fair   215
> Desdemona, unless his abode be lingered here by some accident—
> wherein none can be so determinate as the removing of Cassio.

RODERIGO
> How do you mean, "removing" of him?

IAGO
> Why, by making him uncapable of Othello's place: knocking out
> his brains.   220

RODERIGO
> And that you would have me to do?

222: **profit:** benefit

223: **harlotry:** harlot, prostitute

224: **honorable fortune:** i.e., his promotion

224: **thence:** from that place

225: **fashion:** contrive

225: **fall out:** occur

226: **second:** back up

227: **between us:** with both our efforts

229: **bound:** obligated

229: **put it on:** inflict it on

229: **high:** well into

IAGO

Ay, if you dare do yourself a profit and a right. He sups tonight
with a harlotry, and thither will I go to him. He knows not yet of
his honorable fortune. If you will watch his going thence—which
I will fashion to fall out between twelve and one—you may take   225
him at your pleasure. I will be near to second your attempt, and
he shall fall between us. Come, stand not amazed at it, but go
along with me—I will show you such a necessity in his death
that you shall think yourself bound to put it on him. It is now high
supper time, and the night grows to waste. About it!   230

RODERIGO

I will hear further reason for this.

IAGO

And you shall be satisfied.

Exeunt

Set rendering of "Willow Scene" from the 1951 staging by Orson Welles at St. James Theatre

Rare Book and Special Collections Library, University of Illinois at Urbana-Champaign

0: **Scene:** In the First Quarto this is a continuation of the previous scene.

6: **be returned:** return to you

6: **forthwith:** shortly

Act 4, Scene 3]

Enter OTHELLO, LODOVICO, DESDEMONA,
EMILIA and Attendants

LODOVICO
I do beseech you, sir, trouble yourself no further.

OTHELLO
O, pardon me, 'twill do me good to walk.

LODOVICO
Madam, good night: I humbly thank your ladyship.

DESDEMONA
Your honor is most welcome.

OTHELLO
                        Will you walk, sir?
O, Desdemona—

DESDEMONA
                My lord?

OTHELLO
                        Get thee to bed   5
On th' instant, I will be returned forthwith.
Dismiss your attendant there: look't be done.
                Exeunt [OTHELLO, LODOVICO, and Attendants]

DESDEMONA
I will, my lord.

EMILIA
How goes it now? He looks gentler than he did.

10: **incontinent:** immediately

12: **dismiss:** send (Emilia) away for the night

14: **nightly wearing:** nightclothes

16: **Ay. Would you have never seen him:** After "Ay.", the First Quarto has "I would", the First Folio has "I, would", the Second Quarto has "Would". "Ay" was regularly written as "I" at the time, so both the First Quarto reading "I would you had never seen him" and the First Folio reading "Ay. Would you have never seen him" are possible.

17: **approve:** adore

18: **checks:** rebukes

21: **All's one:** all's the same

22: **shroud:** wrap in cloth in preparation for burial

24–54:
Emma Fielding as Desdemona, Patience Tomlinson as Emilia

27: **an old thing:** i.e., the song

27: **fortune:** (bad) luck

29-59: **I have much...no question:** The First Quarto has a number of omissions in this scene, the most striking being the whole Willow Song section (lines 29-49, 51-53, and 56-59). Rather than the First Folio text being a revision, it seems more likely that the First Quarto text was cut [see Honigmann, Texts p. 11]. Some scholars speculate that the boy playing Desdemona in a revival of the play either could not sing or found his voice breaking.

30: **hang...one side:** over to one side (like a sad or insane person)

DESDEMONA
He says he will return incontinent,   10
And hath commanded me to go to bed,
And bid me to dismiss you.

EMILIA
                    Dismiss me?

DESDEMONA
It was his bidding; therefore, good Emilia,
Give me my nightly wearing and adieu.
We must not now displease him.   15

EMILIA
Ay. Would you had never seen him!

DESDEMONA
So would not I; my love doth so approve him
That even his stubbornness, his checks, his frowns—
Prithee, unpin me,—have grace and favor.

EMILIA
I have laid those sheets you bade me on the bed.   20

DESDEMONA
All's one. Good faith, how foolish are our minds!
If I do die before thee, prithee, shroud me
In one of these same sheets.

EMILIA
                    Come, come, you talk.

DESDEMONA
My mother had a maid called Barbary,
She was in love, and he she loved proved mad   25
And did forsake her. She had a song of "willow,"
An old thing 'twas, but it expressed her fortune,
And she died singing it. That song tonight
Will not go from my mind. I have much to do,
But to go hang my head all at one side   30
And sing it like poor Barbary. Prithee, dispatch.

24–54:
Emma Fielding as Desdemona, Patience Tomlinson as Emilia

33: This Lodovico is a proper man: Following Ridley, Honigmann suggests that this line (only in the First Folio) is spoken by Emilia rather than Desdemona and that the speech prefix has become displaced.

36: nether: lower, bottom

Line 40: *"Sing willow, willow, willow"*: Dorothy Gould as Emilia and Joanna Weinberg as Desdemona in The Market Theater's 1987 production directed by Janet Suzman

Photo: Ruphin Coudyzer

44: Lay by these: lay these (items) here

48: let nobody...approve: In her distraction, Desdemona confuses her own feeling and those of the song

EMILIA
Shall I go fetch your nightgown?

DESDEMONA
                    No, unpin me here.
This Lodovico is a proper man.

EMILIA
A very handsome man.

DESDEMONA
                    He speaks well.

EMILIA
I know a lady in Venice would have walked barefoot   35
to Palestine for a touch of his nether lip.

DESDEMONA
                                        [Singing]

The poor soul sat sighing by a sycamore tree,
Sing all a green willow.
Her hand on her bosom, her head on her knee,
Sing willow, willow, willow.   40
The fresh streams ran by her, and murmured her moans;
Sing willow, willow, willow;
Her salt tears fell from her, and softened the stones; —
Lay by these.—

                                        [Singing]
Sing willow, willow, willow;   45
Prithee, hie thee. He'll come anon.—

                                        [Singing]
Sing all a green willow must be my garland.
Let nobody blame him; his scorn I approve, —
Nay, that's not next.—Hark! Who is 't that knocks?

EMILIA
It's the wind.   50

tracks 31-32

24–54:
Emma Fielding as Desdemona, Patience Tomlinson as Emilia

53: **court:** seek favor from

53: **moe:** more

53: **couch:** lie in bed with

tracks 33-35

57–101:
Uta Hagen as Desdemona, Edith King as Emilia
Joanna Weinberg as Desdemona, Dorothy Gould as Emilia

59: **gross:** shocking, unseemly

60: **such a deed:** i.e., abuse your husband by being unfaithful

61: **by this heavenly light:** an oath meaning "no, by heaven"

62: **by this heavenly light:** by this actual source of light (i.e., Emilia would not be unfaithful where she can be seen)

63: **do 't:** do it (i.e., be unfaithful)

DESDEMONA

[Singing]

> *I called my love false love; but what said he then?*
> *Sing willow, willow, willow.*
> *If I court moe women, you'll couch with moe men.—*
So get thee gone, good night. Mine eyes do itch;
Doth that bode weeping?

EMILIA

'Tis neither here nor there.   55

DESDEMONA

I have heard it said so. O, these men, these men!
Dost thou in conscience think—tell me Emilia—
That there be women do abuse their husbands
In such gross kind?

EMILIA

There be some such, no question.

DESDEMONA

Wouldst thou do such a deed for all the world?   60

EMILIA

Why, would not you?

DESDEMONA

No, by this heavenly light!

EMILIA

Nor I neither, by this heavenly light;
I might do 't as well i' the dark.

DESDEMONA

Wouldst thou do such a deed for all the world?

EMILIA

The world's a huge thing; it is a great price   65
For a small vice.

tracks 33-35

57–101:
Uta Hagen as Desdemona, Edith King as Emilia
Joanna Weinberg as Desdemona, Dorothy Gould as Emilia

67: In troth: in truth. This is the First Folio reading; the First Quarto has "Good troth". Neill suggests that the First Folio has removed another profanity and that the original reading was "God's troth".

69: joint-ring: a ring with joints in it, thus consisting of two halves making a whole like a husband and wife

69-70: measures of lawn: lengths of fine cloth

70: petty: small

70-71: exhibition: allowance

71: Ud's pity: God's pity

73: purgatory: a biblical place of atonement between heaven and hell

74: beshrew: curse

75: for the whole world: Desdemona continues to mean "not for anything, not ever" while Emilia takes a more literal meaning

76: i' th' world: i.e., in this world (the real one)

77: for your labor: i.e., as a reward for your infidelity

80-81: Yes...played for: This sentence is apparently prose in both the First Quarto and the First Folio, but the rest of the speech (which appears only in the First Folio) is in verse. Neill prints it as verse, breaking the line after "vantage".

80: to th' vantage: in addition

81: store: populate

81: played for: i.e., traded their bodies for

82-99: But I do think...instruct us so: This large section is not in the First Quarto.

83: do fall: (morally)

84: our treasures: jewels and/or sexual favors

86: restraint: restrictions

87: scant: limit, reduce

87: former having: previous allowance, pin-money

87: in despite: for spite

88: galls: resentment

88: grace: virtue

93: change us for others: i.e., have sex with other women

DESDEMONA
In troth, I think thou wouldst not.

EMILIA
By my troth, I think I should and undo't when I had done. Marry,
I would not do such a thing for a joint-ring, nor for measures of
lawn, nor for gowns, petticoats, nor caps, nor any petty exhibi-   70
tion. But for all the whole world? Ud's pity, who would not make
her husband a cuckold to make him a monarch? I should venture
purgatory for 't.

DESDEMONA
Beshrew me, if I would do such a wrong
For the whole world.   75

EMILIA
Why the wrong is but a wrong i' th' world; and having the world
for your labor, 'tis a wrong in your own world, and you might
quickly make it right.

DESDEMONA
I do not think there is any such woman.

EMILIA
Yes, a dozen, and as many to th' vantage as would   80
store the world they played for.
But I do think it is their husbands' faults
If wives do fall: say that they slack their duties,
And pour our treasures into foreign laps,
Or else break out in peevish jealousies,   85
Throwing restraint upon us; or say they strike us,
Or scant our former having in despite—
Why, we have galls, and though we have some grace,
Yet have we some revenge. Let husbands know
Their wives have sense like them; they see and smell,   90
And have their palates both for sweet and sour
As husbands have. What is it that they do
When they change us for others? Is it sport?

57–101:
Uta Hagen as Desdemona, Edith King as Emilia
Joanna Weinberg as Desdemona, Dorothy Gould as Emilia

94: **affection:** disposition

98: **use us:** behave well toward us

99: **ills:** evils

100: **uses:** habits, behavior

101: **pick bad from bad:** copy or follow bad behavior

101: **by bad mend:** i.e., by recognizing it, be able to learn from it

I think it is. And doth affection breed it?
I think it doth. Is 't frailty that thus errs?   95
It is so too. And have not we affections,
Desires for sport, and frailty, as men have?
Then let them use us well, else let them know,
The ills we do, their ills instruct us so.

DESDEMONA

Good night, good night. God me such uses send,   100
Not to pick bad from bad, but by bad mend!

Exeunt

[*Othello*

Act 5

0: Scene: This is another street scene of darkness and confusion, offering many opportunities for stage business with both Cassio and Roderigo being wounded and crying for help. It should not be so dark that the audience cannot see what is happening. Iago is in his element here, wounding Cassio in the leg (line 27) and going out and coming in again (line 45) after a quick change of costume to make it look as if he's just been disturbed. In some productions, he makes as if to finish off Cassio but is prevented by the appearance of Lodovico and Gratiano (line 59) and stabs Roderigo instead (line 62).

1: **bulk:** The First Folio has "Barke"; the First Quarto has "bulk". Most scholars think the word is either "bulk", the jutting portion of a building, or "balk", a timber beam (which could also be spelled "baulk" or "bulk" at the time) and that the First Folio's "Barke" is a misreading. On stage, this could either be one of the pillars on the stage, or some form of framework, perhaps, as Neill suggests, used again to curtain off Desdemona's bed in the following scene.; **straight:** immediately

2: **rapier:** a type of two-edged sword; **bare:** unsheathed; **home:** to the target (i.e., his heart)

4: **makes:** makes our fortunes

6: **miscarry:** fail, be unsuccessful

7: **take thy stand:** position oneself in preparation of a fight

11: **quat:** pimple, postule; **to the sense:** to the quick

14: **makes my gain:** is to my advantage; **live Roderigo:** if Roderigo lives

15: **calls me:** will demand of me

16: **bobbed:** filched

19–20: **a daily...ugly:** Iago indicates his jealousy of Cassio, but whether "a daily beauty" means that Cassio is physically better looking than Iago or that Cassio's life is more upstanding and pure is a matter of debate

21: **unfold:** reveal

Act 5, Scene 1]

IAGO
Here, stand behind this bulk, straight will he come.
Wear thy good rapier bare, and put it home;
Quick, quick, fear nothing; I'll be at thy elbow.
It makes us, or it mars us, think on that,
And fix most firm thy resolution.   5

RODERIGO
Be near at hand, I may miscarry in 't.

IAGO
Here, at thy hand: be bold, and take thy stand.

[Retires]

RODERIGO
I have no great devotion to the deed,
And yet he hath given me satisfying reasons:
'Tis but a man gone. Forth my sword: he dies!   10

IAGO
I have rubbed this young quat almost to the sense,
And he grows angry. Now, whether he kill Cassio,
Or Cassio him, or each do kill the other,
Every way makes my gain. Live Roderigo,
He calls me to a restitution large   15
Of gold and jewels that I bobbed from him
As gifts to Desdemona.
It must not be. If Cassio do remain,
He hath a daily beauty in his life
That makes me ugly; and besides, the Moor   20
May unfold me to him: there stand I in much peril—
No, he must die. But so, I hear him coming.

Enter CASSIO

25: **coat:** might also refer to protective clothing (armor) or even undergarments

26: **make proof:** test (the integrity)

27: **Enter OTHELLO:** Othello's entrance is usually on the upper part of the stage or balcony, and his words are asides.

33: **Minion:** darling (used pejoratively here), i.e., Desdemona; **your dear:** i.e., Cassio

34: **unblest:** unblessed, cursed; **hies:** makes haste, hurries closer; **strumpet:** i.e., Desdemona

35: **Forth of:** from

Set rendering of "Street" from the 1951 staging by Orson Welles at St. James Theatre

Rare Book and Special Collections Library, University of Illinois at Urbana-Champaign

RODERIGO
I know his gait, 'tis he. Villain, thou diest!

[Makes a pass at CASSIO]

CASSIO
That thrust had been mine enemy indeed
But that my coat is better than thou know'st—   25
I will make proof of thine.

[Draws, and wounds RODERIGO]

RODERIGO
                    O, I am slain!

*[IAGO from behind wounds CASSIO
in the leg, and exit]*

CASSIO
I am maimed for ever. Help, ho! Murder! Murder!

Enter OTHELLO

OTHELLO
The voice of Cassio. Iago keeps his word.

RODERIGO
O, villain that I am!

OTHELLO
                    It is even so.

CASSIO
O, help, ho! Light! A surgeon!   30

OTHELLO
'Tis he—O brave Iago, honest and just,
That hast such noble sense of thy friend's wrong,
Thou teachest me. Minion, your dear lies dead,
And your unblest fate hies; strumpet, I come.
Forth of my heart, those charms, thine eyes, are blotted.   35
Thy bed, lust-stained, shall with lust's blood be spotted.

Exit
Enter LODOVICO and GRATIANO

37: **watch:** night guard

37: **passage:** pedestrians

38: **mischance:** misfortune

38: **direful:** dreadful, dismal

41: **villain:** (Roderigo is referring to himself)

42: **heavy:** dark and dismal

43: **counterfeits:** false cries (designed to trick or lure passersby)

47: **shirt:** without coat, vest or armour

CASSIO
What ho! No watch? No passage? Murder, murder!

GRATIANO
'Tis some mischance; the voice is very direful.

CASSIO
O, help!

LODOVICO
Hark!   40

RODERIGO
O wretched villain!

LODOVICO
Two or three groan. It is a heavy night.
These may be counterfeits, let's think 't unsafe
To come in to the cry without more help.

RODERIGO
Nobody come? Then shall I bleed to death.   45
                                            Enter IAGO with a light

LODOVICO
Hark!

GRATIANO
Here's one comes in his shirt, with light and weapons.

IAGO
Who's there? Whose noise is this that cries on murder?

LODOVICO
We do not know.

IAGO
                        Do not you hear a cry?

51: **ancient:** next in command under lieutenant

54: **spoiled:** destroyed

56: **lieutenant:** Iago flatters by using Cassio's former rank of lieutenant.

58: **make away:** escape

59: **What:** who (what person)

63: **O...inhuman dog:** The First Quarto adds "O, O, O" to Roderigo's speech, perhaps an indication that the actor continued to make groaning noises.

CASSIO
Here, here! For heaven's sake, help me!

IAGO
What's the matter? 50

GRATIANO
This is Othello's ancient, as I take it.

LODOVICO
The same indeed, a very valiant fellow.

IAGO
What are you here that cry so grievously?

CASSIO
Iago? O, I am spoiled, undone by villains!
Give me some help. 55

IAGO
O me, lieutenant! What villains have done this?

CASSIO
I think that one of them is hereabout,
And cannot make away.

IAGO
O treacherous villains!
[To LODOVICO and GRATIANO] What are you there? Come in, and
give some help. 60

RODERIGO
O, help me there!

CASSIO
That's one of them.

IAGO
O murd'rous slave! O villain!
[Stabs RODERIGO]

67: **prove us:** ascertain our value to be

67: **praise us:** give us our due praise

72: **cut in two:** deeply cut

RODERIGO
O damned Iago! O inhuman dog!

IAGO
Kill men i' th' dark? Where be these bloody thieves?
How silent is this town! Ho, murder, murder!   65
What may you be? Are you of good or evil?

LODOVICO
As you shall prove us, praise us.

IAGO
Signior Lodovico?

LODOVICO
He, sir.

IAGO
I cry you mercy—here's Cassio, hurt by villains.

GRATIANO
Cassio?   70

IAGO
How is 't, brother?

CASSIO
My leg is cut in two.

IAGO
Marry, heaven forbid!
Light, gentlemen, I'll bind it with my shirt.

Enter BIANCA

BIANCA
What is the matter, ho? Who is 't that cried?

IAGO
Who is 't that cried?

77: **notable:** infamous

81: **garter:** a string or fabric band used to keep stockings from falling down (Iago wants it to bind Cassio's leg)

81: **chair:** stretcher

84: **trash:** i.e., Bianca

91: **Even he:** i.e., that same man

BIANCA
O my dear Cassio!

My sweet Cassio, O Cassio, Cassio, Cassio! 75

IAGO
O notable strumpet! Cassio, may you suspect
Who they should be that have thus mangled you?

CASSIO
No.

GRATIANO
I am sorry to find you thus; I have been to seek you. 80

IAGO
Lend me a garter. So.—O for a chair
To bear him easily hence!

BIANCA
Alas, he faints! O Cassio, Cassio, Cassio!

IAGO
Gentlemen all, I do suspect this trash
To be a party in this injury. 85
Patience awhile, good Cassio. Come, come;
Lend me a light. Know we this face or no?
Alas my friend and my dear countryman,
Roderigo? No—Yes, sure!—O heaven, Roderigo!

GRATIANO
What, of Venice? 90

IAGO
Even he, sir. Did you know him?

GRATIANO
Know him? Ay!

93: **accidents:** events

94: **neglected you:** i.e., failed you (by not issuing proper greetings)

99: **For you:** as for you

100: **labor:** efforts

100: **He that lies slain:** (spoken to Cassio)

101: **dear friend:** i.e., Roderigo

103: **out o' the air:** i.e., indoors

105: **gastness:** ghastliness, haggard look

106: **anon:** shortly, soon

108: **guiltiness will speak:** i.e., her guilt will show in her face

109: **'Las:** alas

IAGO
>Signior Gratiano? I cry your gentle pardon;
>These bloody accidents must excuse my manners
>That so neglected you.

GRATIANO
>   I am glad to see you.

IAGO
>How do you, Cassio? O, a chair, a chair!   95

GRATIANO
>Roderigo?

IAGO
>He, he, 'tis he. [*A chair is brought in*] O, that's well said, the chair.
>Some good man bear him carefully from hence,
>I'll fetch the general's surgeon. [*To BIANCA*] For you, mistress,
>Save you your labor. He that lies slain here, Cassio,   100
>Was my dear friend. What malice was between you?

CASSIO
>None in the world, nor do I know the man.

IAGO
>[*To BIANCA*] What? Look you pale?—O, bear him out o' the air.
>   [*CASSIO and RODERIGO are borne off*]
>Stay you, good gentlemen.—Look you pale, mistress?—
>Do you perceive the gastness of her eye?—   105
>Nay, if you stare, we shall hear more anon.—
>Behold her well. I pray you, look upon her.
>Do you see, gentlemen? Nay, guiltiness will speak,
>Though tongues were out of use.
>   [*Enter EMILIA*]

EMILIA
>   'Las, what's the matter?
>What is the matter, husband?   110

112: **scaped:** escaped

116: **supped:** had supper

117: **shake :** tremble

118: **therefore shake not:** i.e., do not tremble for that reason

119: **fie:** expression of distain

121: **of life:** in life

122: **Foh:** an expression of disgust

123: **dressed:** his wounds cleaned and bandaged

124: **tell 's:** tell us

126: **happ'd:** happened

128: **makes me:** makes his fortunes

128: **fordoes:** destroys

IAGO

    Cassio hath here been set on in the dark
    By Roderigo and fellows that are scaped.
    He's almost slain, and Roderigo quite dead.

EMILIA

    Alas, good gentleman! Alas, good Cassio!

IAGO

    This is the fruits of whoring. Prithee Emilia,   115
    Go know of Cassio where he supped tonight.
    [*To BIANCA*] What, do you shake at that?

BIANCA

    He supped at my house, but I therefore shake not.

IAGO

    O, did he so? I charge you, go with me.

EMILIA

    O, fie upon thee, strumpet!

BIANCA

                  I am no strumpet,   120
    But of life as honest as you that thus
    Abuse me.

EMILIA

             As I? Foh! Fie upon thee!

IAGO

    Kind gentlemen, let's go see poor Cassio dressed.
    Come, mistress, you must tell 's another tale.
    Emilia run you to the citadel   125
    And tell my lord and lady what hath happ'd.
    Will you go on afore? [*Aside*] This is the night
    That either makes me or fordoes me quite.

                                           Exeunt

1-22:
Paul Scofield as Othello
Hugh Quarshie as Othello

0: Scene: There has been much discussion of how this scene was originally staged. The First Quarto stage direction is "Enter Othello with a light", while the First Folio has "Enter Othello, and Desdemona in her bed". There clearly needs to be a bed, with curtains to be closed (line 105) and opened (line 120), and a door, locked at Othello's entrance and opened to admit Emilia (line 106). If the inner stage is used for the bed, the audience need to be able to see what is happening. Some scholars think that a curtained structure used for the "bulk" in 5.1 (see note for 5.1.1) became the bed in this scene.

5: **monumental:** used to make statues and monuments; **alabaster:** a type of marble

7: **put out the light:** i.e., extinguish the light of the candle; **then put out the light:** i.e., extinguish her life

8: **flaming minister:** i.e., burning torch

9: **restore:** relight (if he puts out a candle, he can relight its flame)

10: **should I repent me:** if I regret my actions; **put out thy light:** i.e., end Desdemona's life

11: **cunning'st:** skillful; **pattern:** example; **excelling:** sublime

12: **Promethean:** related to Prometheus, the titan in Greek mythology responsible for defying the Gods in order to bring fire to humankind

13: **relume:** relight

14: **give it vital growth:** i.e., bring it back to life

15-19: Scene: Othello's speech implies that he may kiss Desdemona several times (at lines 15, 17, 19) before she wakes, though the First Quarto places the stage direction (which is not in the First Folio) at line 19 so Othello may merely smell Desdemona's fragrance at the earlier points in the speech and kiss her at line 19.

15: **needs must:** will, by necessity,

17: **Justice:** Justice is often depicted in early imagery as a blindfolded woman holding scales and a sword; **break her sword:** give up retribution or punishment

21: **this sorrow's heavenly:** (proverbial) like God's love

Act 5, Scene 2]

Enter OTHELLO with a light and DESDEMONA in her bed [asleep]

OTHELLO

It is the cause, it is the cause, my soul.
Let me not name it to you, you chaste stars.
It is the cause. Yet I'll not shed her blood,
Nor scar that whiter skin of hers than snow
And smooth as monumental alabaster.   5
Yet she must die, else she'll betray more men.
Put out the light, and then put out the light.
If I quench thee, thou flaming minister,
I can again thy former light restore
Should I repent me. But once put out thy light,   10
Thou cunning'st pattern of excelling nature,
I know not where is that Promethean heat
That can thy light relume. When I have plucked the rose,
I cannot give it vital growth again.
It needs must wither. I'll smell thee on the tree.   15
Oh balmy breath, that dost almost persuade
Justice to break her sword! One more, one more.
Be thus when thou art dead, and I will kill thee
And love thee after. One more, and that's the last.

He kisses her

So sweet was ne'er so fatal. I must weep,   20
But they are cruel tears. This sorrow's heavenly;
It strikes where it doth love. She wakes.

DESDEMONA

Who's there? Othello?

OTHELLO

Ay, Desdemona.

DESDEMONA

Will you come to bed, my lord?

Patrick Stewart as Othello and Patrice Johnson as Desdemona in The Shakespeare Theatre's 1997–1998 production directed by Jude Kelly

Photo: Carol Rosegg

26: **bethink:** can think

27: **Unreconciled:** not yet confessed

28: **Solicit:** pray

28: **straight:** immediately

30: **walk by:** be nearby

32: **forefend:** forbid

32: **kill thy soul:** Within a Christian worldview, one must confess all one's sins before death in order to be accepted into heaven

OTHELLO
Have you prayed tonight, Desdemon?

DESDEMONA
     Ay, my lord.   25

OTHELLO
If you bethink yourself of any crime
Unreconciled as yet to heaven and grace,
Solicit for it straight.

DESDEMONA
Alack, my lord, what may you mean by that?

OTHELLO
Well, do it, and be brief. I will walk by—   30
I would not kill thy unprepared spirit.
No, heaven forfend, I would not kill thy soul.

DESDEMONA
Talk you of killing?

OTHELLO
     Ay, I do.

DESDEMONA
       Then heaven
Have mercy on me!

OTHELLO
       Amen, with all my heart.

DESDEMONA
If you say so, I hope you will not kill me.   35

OTHELLO
Hum!

DESDEMONA
And yet I fear you, for you're fatal then
When your eyes roll so. Why I should fear I know not,
Since guiltiness I know not; but yet I feel I fear.

Line 40: "Think on thy sins": Jordan Baker as Desdemona and Avery Brooks
as Othello in The Shakespeare Theatre's 1990–1991 production,
directed by Harold Scott
Photo: Joan Marcus

40: **loves I bear to you:** i.e., her sin is that she loves him too much

42: **unnatural:** inhuman in the highest degree

43: **nether:** lower

44: **passion:** strong emotion

44: **frame:** i.e., body, skeleton

45: **portents:** bad omens

46: **point on me:** point toward me

OTHELLO
   Think on thy sins.

DESDEMONA
                    They are loves I bear to you.   40

OTHELLO
   Ay, and for that thou diest.

DESDEMONA
   That death's unnatural that kills for loving.
   Alas, why gnaw you so your nether lip?
   Some bloody passion shakes your very frame,
   These are portents, but yet I hope, I hope,   45
   They do not point on me.

OTHELLO
                    Peace, and be still!

DESDEMONA
   I will so. What's the matter?

OTHELLO
   That handkerchief which I so loved and gave thee,
   Thou gav'st to Cassio.

DESDEMONA
                    No, by my life and soul—
   Send for the man, and ask him.

OTHELLO
                    Sweet soul, take heed,   50
   Take heed of perjury. Thou art on thy death-bed.

DESDEMONA
   Ay, but not yet to die.

53: **freely:** without inhibitions or concerns

54: **article:** item of sin

55: **conception:** idea

60: **warranty:** permission, allowance

62: **in's:** in his

63: **stone:** harden

68: **confessed:** sworn it (the accusation) is true

70: **'ud's death:** by God's death

OTHELLO
                    Yes, presently.
Therefore confess thee freely of thy sin,
For to deny each article with oath
Cannot remove nor choke the strong conception   55
That I do groan withal. Thou art to die.

DESDEMONA
  Then Lord have mercy on me!

OTHELLO
                    I say, amen.

DESDEMONA
  And have you mercy too. I never did
  Offend you in my life; never loved Cassio
  But with such general warranty of heaven   60
  As I might love. I never gave him token.

OTHELLO
  By heaven, I saw my handkerchief in's hand.
  O perjured woman! Thou dost stone my heart,
  And makes me call what I intend to do
  A murder, which I thought a sacrifice.   65
  I saw the handkerchief.

DESDEMONA
                    He found it then,
  I never gave it him. Send for him hither,
  Let him confess a truth.

OTHELLO
                    He hath confessed.

DESDEMONA
  What, my lord?

OTHELLO
  That he hath—'ud's death!—used thee.   70

Orson Welles's sketch of "Bedroom" from the 1951 staging at St. James Theatre
Rare Book and Special Collections Library, University of Illinois at Urbana-Champaign

73: **ta'en order for 't:** i.e., ensured it

74: **interprets:** deciphers, conjectures

82-84: **Nay...too late:** Othello's words imply that he is forcibly restraining her. In some productions she tries to escape through the door, which is locked.

82: **strive:** resist

83: **But:** only

DESDEMONA
How? Unlawfully?

OTHELLO
                    Ay.

DESDEMONA
                              He will not say so.

OTHELLO
No, his mouth is stopped.
Honest Iago hath ta'en order for 't.

DESDEMONA
O, my fear interprets! What, is he dead?

OTHELLO
Had all his hairs been lives, my great revenge   75
Had stomach for them all.

DESDEMONA
Alas, he is betrayed, and I undone.

OTHELLO
Out, strumpet! Weep'st thou for him to my face?

DESDEMONA
O, banish me, my lord, but kill me not!

OTHELLO
Down, strumpet!   80

DESDEMONA
Kill me tomorrow, let me live tonight!

OTHELLO
Nay, if you strive—

DESDEMONA
But half an hour!

83: Being done: i.e., having been decided, being inevitable

85: Stage Direction: *He smothers her*: The First Quarto has "stifles", while the First Folio has "smothers", both meaning death by suffocation. Othello usually accomplishes this either with some of the bedclothes or by strangling her with his hands round her throat. His attempt doesn't succeed immediately (see lines 87-90), and Desdemona is still able to speak to Emilia (lines 118-125) before finally dying at line 125. In nineteenth century productions it became common for Othello to finish Desdemona off with a knife or dagger (as Olivier does in the film) though this runs contrary to Othello's statement (line 3) that he will "not shed her blood".

92: By and by: in a moment, soon

92: she's dead: referring to Desdemona

93: she: referring to Emilia

Line 95: "Still as the grave": John Kani as Othello and Joanna Weinberg as Desdemona in The Market Theater's 1987 production directed by Janet Suzman

Photo: Ruphin Coudyzer

95: Shall she: referring to Emilia

96: she stirs: referring to Desdemona

97: If she come: referring to Emilia

OTHELLO
                    Being done, there is no pause.

DESDEMONA
    But while I say one prayer!

OTHELLO
                    It is too late.

DESDEMONA
    O Lord, Lord, Lord!   85

                                                    He smothers her

EMILIA *[within]*
    My lord, my lord! What ho! My lord, my lord!

OTHELLO
    What noise is this? Not dead? Not yet quite dead?
    I that am cruel am yet merciful,
    I would not have thee linger in thy pain.
    So, so.

EMILIA
                                                    [Within]
                    What ho! My lord, my lord!

OTHELLO
                    Who's there?   90

EMILIA
                                                    [Within]
    O, good my lord, I'd speak a word with you.

OTHELLO
    Yes, 'tis Emilia. [to EMILIA] By and by!—she's dead.
    'Tis like she comes to speak of Cassio's death;
    The noise was high. Ha! No more moving?
    Still as the grave. Shall she come in? Were't good?   95
    I think she stirs again. No. What's best to do?
    If she come in, she'll sure speak to my wife.
    My wife, my wife! What wife? I have no wife.

99 **insupportable:** intolerable

99: **heavy:** dismal, grim

Line 99: "O insupportable! O heavy hour!": Raul Julia as Othello and
Kathryn Meisle as Desdemona in the Public Theater's 1991 production directed
by Joe Dowling.
Photo: George E. Joseph

101: **affrighted globe:** frightened earth

102: **yawn:** gape in fear

102: **alteration:** momentous change (because Desdemona is now dead)

105: **Soft:** hush

111: **She comes:** referring to the moon

111: **wont:** accustomed

112: **makes men mad:** (madness was thought to be caused by increased proximity
of the moon)

O insupportable! O heavy hour!
Methinks it should be now a huge eclipse   100
Of sun and moon, and that th' affrighted globe
Should yawn at alteration.

EMILIA

[Within]

              I do beseech you
That I may speak with you! O, good my lord!

OTHELLO
I had forgot thee. O, come in, Emilia.
Soft, by and by. Let me the curtains draw.   105
Where art thou?

[Unlocks the door]
Enter EMILIA

         What's the matter with thee now?

EMILIA
O, my good lord, yonder's foul murders done!

OTHELLO
What? Now?

EMILIA
But now, my lord.

OTHELLO
It is the very error of the moon.   110
She comes more nearer earth than she was wont
And makes men mad.

EMILIA
          Cassio, my lord, hath killed
A young Venetian called Roderigo.

OTHELLO
Roderigo killed? And Cassio killed?

117: **sweet revenge:** (the music of) sweet revenge

118: **falsely:** wrongly

Lines 121–122: "O lady, speak again! / Sweet Desdemona! O sweet mistress, speak!":
Sada Thompson as Emilia, Julienne Marie as Desdemona, and
James Earl Jones as Othello in the Public Theater's 1964 production directed
by Gladys Vaughan
Photo: George E. Joseph

EMILIA
  No, Cassio is not killed.   115

OTHELLO
  Not Cassio killed! Then murder's out of tune,
  And sweet revenge grows harsh.

DESDEMONA
  O, falsely, falsely murdered!

EMILIA
  Alas, what cry is that?

OTHELLO
                    That? What?

EMILIA
  Out, and alas! That was my lady's voice.   120
                    [She opens the bed curtains]
  Help! Help, ho! Help! O lady, speak again!
  Sweet Desdemona, O sweet mistress, speak!

DESDEMONA
  A guiltless death I die.

EMILIA
                    O, who hath done this deed?

DESDEMONA
  Nobody. I myself. Farewell
  Commend me to my kind lord. O, farewell!   125
                                                                Dies

OTHELLO
  Why, how should she be murdered?

EMILIA
                    Alas, who knows?

OTHELLO
  You heard her say herself it was not I.

131: **blacker:** darker, more evil (with a racist slur on his color)

132: **folly:** wantonness

133: **belie:** tell lies about her

134: **false as water:** i.e., water goes wherever it can flow

134–165:
Patience Tomlinson as Emilia, Hugh Quarshie as Othello
Dorothy Gould as Emilia, John Kani as Othello

135: **true:** faithful

136: **top:** have sexual intercourse with

136: **else:** otherwise

137: **all depth in hell:** the lowest regions of hell

138: **But:** except

138: **just:** justifiable

139: **extremity:** extreme action

140: **false to wedlock:** unfaithful

EMILIA
She said so; I must needs report the truth.

OTHELLO
She's like a liar, gone to burning hell—
'Twas I that killed her.

EMILIA
                        O, the more angel she,   130
And you the blacker devil!

OTHELLO
She turned to folly, and she was a whore.

EMILIA
Thou dost belie her, and thou art a devil.

OTHELLO
She was false as water.

EMILIA
                    Thou art rash as fire to say
That she was false. O, she was heavenly true!   135

OTHELLO
Cassio did top her; ask thy husband else.
O, I were damned beneath all depth in hell
But that I did proceed upon just grounds
To this extremity. Thy husband knew it all.

EMILIA
My husband?

OTHELLO
                 Thy husband.

EMILIA
                    That she was false to wedlock?   140

tracks 39-41

134–165:
Patience Tomlinson as Emilia, Hugh Quarshie as Othello
Dorothy Gould as Emilia, John Kani as Othello

143: **chrysolite:** a green precious stone

148: **iterance:** repetition

149: **mocks:** mockery, fools

153: **pernicious:** wicked

154: **Rot half a grain a day:** i.e., die a slow, torturous death

155: **filthy bargain:** i.e., marrying Othello (filthy = a continued slur, as in line 131)

OTHELLO
    Ay, with Cassio. Nay, had she been true,
    If heaven would make me such another world
    Of one entire and perfect chrysolite,
    I'd not have sold her for it.

EMILIA
                    My husband?

OTHELLO
    Ay, 'twas he that told me on her first.   145
    An honest man he is, and hates the slime
    That sticks on filthy deeds.

EMILIA
                    My husband?

OTHELLO
    What needs this iterance, woman? I say, thy husband.

EMILIA
    O, mistress, villainy hath made mocks with love:
    My husband say she was false?

OTHELLO
                    He, woman;   150
    I say, thy husband—dost understand the word?
    My friend, thy husband; honest, honest Iago.

EMILIA
    If he say so, may his pernicious soul
    Rot half a grain a day! He lies to th' heart.
    She was too fond of her most filthy bargain.   155

OTHELLO
    Ha?

tracks 39-41

134–165:
Patience Tomlinson as Emilia, Hugh Quarshie as Othello
Dorothy Gould as Emilia, John Kani as Othello

158: **worthy heaven** : worthy of heaven

159: **worthy her:** worthy of her

159: **you were best:** i.e., be quiet

160–161: **Thou hast...to be hurt:** you can't harm me half as much as I can tolerate

161: **gull:** fool, dupe

162: **ignorant as dirt:** continued slur (see lines 131 and 155)

163: **make thee known:** i.e., tell the authorities about you

168: **lay:** justify

170: **Disprove:** prove him false

173: **full:** heavy (with sorrow)

175: **apt:** plausible

EMILIA
Do thy worst;
This deed of thine is no more worthy heaven
Than thou wast worthy her.

OTHELLO
Peace, you were best.

EMILIA
Thou hast not half that power to do me harm   160
As I have to be hurt. O gull, O dolt,
As ignorant as dirt, thou hast done a deed—
I care not for thy sword, I'll make thee known,
Though I lost twenty lives. Help, help, ho help!
The Moor hath killed my mistress! Murder, murder!   165
Enter MONTANO, GRATIANO, and IAGO

MONTANO
What is the matter? How now, general!

EMILIA
O, are you come, Iago? You have done well,
That men must lay their murders on your neck.

GRATIANO
What is the matter?

EMILIA
Disprove this villain, if thou be'st a man;   170
He says thou told'st him that his wife was false;
I know thou didst not, thou'rt not such a villain.
Speak, for my heart is full.

IAGO
I told him what I thought, and told no more
Than what he found himself was apt and true.   175

EMILIA
But did you ever tell him she was false?

181: **charm your tongue:** be silent

182: **bound:** obliged

183-191: **My mistress here...villainy, villainy:** omitted in the First Quarto

184: **forfend:** prevent

185: **set the murder on:** instigated the murder

187: **strange:** extraordinary

192: **charge:** order

IAGO
I did.

EMILIA
You told a lie, an odious, damnèd lie!
Upon my soul, a lie, a wicked lie!
She false with Cassio? Did you say with Cassio?   180

IAGO
With Cassio, mistress. Go to, charm your tongue.

EMILIA
I will not charm my tongue. I am bound to speak:
My mistress here lies murdered in her bed.

All
O heavens forfend!

EMILIA
And your reports have set the murder on.   185

OTHELLO
Nay, stare not, masters, it is true indeed.

GRATIANO
'Tis a strange truth.

MONTANO
O monstrous act!

EMILIA
                      Villainy, villainy, villainy!
I think upon 't, I think—I smell 't. O villainy!
I thought so then. I'll kill myself for grief.   190
O villainy, villainy!

IAGO
What, are you mad? I charge you, get you home.

194: **'Tis proper I obey him:** compare line 3.3.301: "I nothing but to please his fantasy"

198: **e'er:** ever

198: **lift up eye:** looked up (from a position of humility)

199: **uncle:** referring to Gratiano

201: **shows:** appears

203: **match:** marriage

203: **mortal:** fatal

204: **shore:** cut

204: **his old thread:** his life. According to Greek Mythology, each life is a thread spun by the Fates, and death occurs whenever a thread is cut

204: **in twain:** in two

205: **turn:** act

206: **his better angel:** his conscience

207: **reprobance:** depravity, eternal damnation

211: **gratify:** reward

211: **works:** efforts

212: **recognizance:** token, gift

EMILIA

    Good gentlemen, let me have leave to speak.
    'Tis proper I obey him, but not now.
    Perchance, Iago, I will ne'er go home.   195

OTHELLO

    O, O, O!

                                    He falls on the bed

EMILIA

                Nay, lay thee down and roar.
    For thou hast killed the sweetest innocent
    That e'er did lift up eye.

OTHELLO

                                [Rising]
               O, she was foul!
    I scarce did know you, uncle; there lies your niece,
    Whose breath, indeed, these hands have newly stopped;   200
    I know this act shows horrible and grim.

GRATIANO

    Poor Desdemon, I am glad thy father's dead,
    Thy match was mortal to him, and pure grief
    Shore his old thread in twain. Did he live now,
    This sight would make him do a desperate turn,   205
    Yea, curse his better angel from his side
    And fall to reprobance.

OTHELLO

    'Tis pitiful; but yet Iago knows
    That she with Cassio hath the act of shame
    A thousand times committed. Cassio confessed it,   210
    And she did gratify his amorous works
    With that recognizance and pledge of love
    Which I first gave her. I saw it in his hand—
    It was a handkerchief, an antique token
    My father gave my mother.   215

217: **'Twill out:** It will be out, it will be said

218: **liberal as the north:** freely as the north (wind)

222: Stage direction: **offers:** attempts

224: **by fortune:** by chance, luck

EMILIA
O God! O heavenly God!

IAGO
Zounds, hold your peace.

EMILIA
'Twill out, 'twill out! I peace?
No, I will speak as liberal as the north;
Let heaven and men and devils, let them all,
All, all, cry shame against me, yet I'll speak.   220

IAGO
Be wise, and get you home.

EMILIA
I will not.

[IAGO offers to stab EMILIA]

GRATIANO
Fie, your sword upon a woman?

EMILIA
O thou dull Moor, that handkerchief thou speak'st of
I found by fortune and did give my husband,
For often, with a solemn earnestness,   225
More than indeed belonged to such a trifle,
He begged of me to steal 't.

IAGO
Villainous whore!

EMILIA
She give it Cassio? No, alas! I found it,
And I did give 't my husband.

IAGO
Filth, thou liest!

231: coxcomb: fool

231-232: what...good a wife: i.e., why should such a fool have so good a wife

232: do with: want to do (such horrible things)

232: stones: thunderbolts

239: without: from outside

240: rather: instead (if he tries to pass)

240: villain: Iago

241: 'tis: he is

241: not valiant neither: a double negative used for emphasis

242: whipster: insignificant or contemptible fellow

244-247: What did...willow: omitted in the First Quarto

245: play the swan: the swan is said to sing a mournful song before it dies, hence the expression "swan song"

EMILIA
   By heaven, I do not, I do not, gentlemen: 230
   O murderous coxcomb, what should such a fool
   Do with so good a wife?

OTHELLO
                 Are there no stones in heaven
  But what serves for the thunder?—Precious villain!
               [He] runs at IAGO; IAGO stabs his wife

GRATIANO
   The woman falls, sure he hath killed his wife.
                              Exit IAGO

EMILIA
   Ay, ay. O lay me by my mistress' side.   235

GRATIANO
   He's gone, but his wife's killed.

MONTANO
   'Tis a notorious villain. Take you this weapon
   Which I have here recovered from the Moor:
   Come, guard the door without, let him not pass,
   But kill him rather. I'll after that same villain,   240
   For 'tis a damnèd slave.
               Ex[eunt] MONTANO and GRATIANO

OTHELLO
             I am not valiant neither, .
  But every puny whipster gets my sword.
  But why should honor outlive honesty?
  Let it go all.

EMILIA
            What did thy song bode, lady?
  Hark, canst thou hear me? I will play the swan,   245
  And die in music.
                           [Singing]

        Willow, willow, willow,—

252: **ice-brook's temper:** a Spanish sword-making technique made by plunging hot steel into a cold river

255: **perforce:** necessarily

257: **naked:** without a sword or weapon

259: **a better:** i.e., weapon

259: **sustain:** maintain a place

261: **little:** insignificant, not powerful

263: **twenty times:** twenty times greater than

263: **stop:** obstacle, block

265-271: **Be not afraid....ill-starred wench:** omitted in the First Quarto

266: **butt:** goal

267: **sea-mark:** navigational reference point at sea

268: **go back:** step back

269: **Man but a rush:** i.e., just use a reed

270: **retires:** retreats/dies

271: **ill-starred:** ill-fated, cursed

272: **compt:** judgment day

Moor, she was chaste, she loved thee, cruel Moor,
So come my soul to bliss, as I speak true!
So speaking as I think, alas, I die.   250

She dies

OTHELLO
I have another weapon in this chamber,
It is a sword of Spain, the ice-brook's temper;
O, here it is—uncle, I must come forth.

GRATIANO

[Within]

If thou attempt it, it will cost thee dear;
Thou hast no weapon, and perforce must suffer.   255

OTHELLO
Look in upon me then and speak with me,
Or, naked as I am, I will assault thee.

[Enter GRATIANO]

GRATIANO
What is the matter?

OTHELLO
                    Behold, I have a weapon,
A better never did itself sustain
Upon a soldier's thigh. I have seen the day   260
That, with this little arm and this good sword,
I have made my way through more impediments
Than twenty times your stop. But, O vain boast,
Who can control his fate? 'Tis not so now.
Be not afraid, though you do see me weaponed;   265
Here is my journey's end, here is my butt
And very sea-mark of my utmost sail.
Do you go back dismayed? 'Tis a lost fear;
Man but a rush against Othello's breast,
And he retires. Where should Othello go?   270
Now, how dost thou look now? O ill-starred wench,
Pale as thy smock, when we shall meet at compt,

278: **sulphur:** brimstone, the material which feeds the fires of hell

279: **steep-down:** precipitous

283: **viper:** poisonous snake, i.e., Iago

284: **I look...feet:** to see if they are cloven, like the Devil

285: **If that thou be'st:** If you are

Stage direction: Wounds IAGO: Ensemble in Stuart Burge's 1965 movie production
Courtesy: Douglas Lanier

288: **in my sense:** in my state

This look of thine will hurl my soul from heaven,
And fiends will snatch at it. Cold, cold, my girl?
Even like thy chastity. O cursèd, cursèd slave!   275
Whip me, ye devils,
From the possession of this heavenly sight!
Blow me about in winds, roast me in sulphur,
Wash me in steep-down gulfs of liquid fire!
O Desdemon! Dead Desdemon. Dead! O, O!   280

Enter LODOVICO, CASSIO, MONTANO,
and IAGO, and Officers, Cassio in a chair

LODOVICO
Where is this rash and most unfortunate man?

OTHELLO
That's he that was Othello; here I am.

LODOVICO
Where is that viper? Bring the villain forth.

[IAGO is brought forth]

OTHELLO
I look down towards his feet, but that's a fable.
If that thou be'st a devil, I cannot kill thee.   285

[Wounds IAGO]

LODOVICO
Wrench his sword from him.

IAGO
                    I bleed, sir, but not killed.

OTHELLO
I am not sorry neither. I'd have thee live,
For in my sense 'tis happiness to die.

LODOVICO
O thou Othello, that was once so good,
Fall'n in the practice of a cursèd slave,   290
What shall be said to thee?

292: **honorable murderer:** Othello is making a distinction between one who kills with malice and one who kills for honor

294: **part:** partly

295: **consent:** agree (to murder), collude

303: **Torments:** torture

303: **ope:** open

305: **understand:** learn

308: **imports:** signifies, explains

OTHELLO
                    Why, anything:
    An honorable murderer, if you will;
    For nought I did in hate, but all in honor.

LODOVICO
    This wretch hath part confessed his villainy:
    Did you and he consent in Cassio's death?   295

OTHELLO
    Ay.

CASSIO
    Dear general, I never gave you cause.

OTHELLO
    I do believe it, and I ask your pardon.
    Will you, I pray, demand that demi-devil
    Why he hath thus ensnared my soul and body?   300

IAGO
    Demand me nothing—what you know, you know.
    From this time forth, I never will speak word.

LODOVICO
    What, not to pray?

GRATIANO
                    Torments will ope your lips.

OTHELLO
    Well, thou dost best.

LODOVICO
    Sir, you shall understand what hath befallen,   305
    Which, as I think, you know not. Here is a letter
    Found in the pocket of the slain Roderigo,
    And here another—the one of them imports
    The death of Cassio to be undertook
    By Roderigo.   310

311: **heathenish:** savage

311: **gross:** shocking

312: **discontented paper:** letter filled with dissatisfaction

314: **this damnèd villain:** Othello

315: **belike:** apparently

315: **in the nick:** at the critical moment

316: **satisfied:** gratified

316: **pernicious caitiff:** malicious wretch

321: **wrought:** came to fulfill

323: **upbraids:** reproaches, accuses

324: **Brave me:** attack

325: **cast:** thrown (i.e., drawn into)

325: **spake:** spoke

328: **forsake:** abandon, leave

329: **taken off:** relieved of duty

330: **this slave:** Iago

331: **cunning cruelty:** ingenious torture

OTHELLO
   O villain!

CASSIO
               Most heathenish and most gross!

LODOVICO
   Now here's another discontented paper,
   Found in his pocket too, and this, it seems,
   Roderigo meant t' have sent this damnèd villain,
   But that belike Iago in the nick   315
   Came in and satisfied him.

OTHELLO
                     O thou pernicious caitiff!
   How came you, Cassio, by that handkerchief
   That was my wife's?

CASSIO
                     I found it in my chamber;
   And he himself confessed but even now
   That there he dropped it for a special purpose   320
   Which wrought to his desire.

OTHELLO
                     O fool, fool, fool!

CASSIO
   There is besides in Roderigo's letter
   How he upbraids Iago, that he made him
   Brave me upon the watch, whereon it came
   That I was cast; and even but now he spake,   325
   After long seeming dead, Iago hurt him,
   Iago set him on.

LODOVICO
   You must forsake this room, and go with us.
   Your power and your command is taken off,
   And Cassio rules in Cyprus. For this slave,   330
   If there be any cunning cruelty

333: **close prisoner rest:** remain a closely watched prisoner

336–357:
Paul Robeson as Othello
John Kani as Othello

340: **extenuate:** soften, lessen in severity

341: **aught:** anything

344: **perplexed:** confounded, confused, bewildered

345: **base :** unsophisticated, primitive

345: **Indian:** The First Quarto reads "Indian"; the First Folio "Iudean" (i.e., Judean, referring to Judas). This is probably the most famous crux in the play and has been much debated. Either reading is possible since they could be confused in handwriting. Most modern editors prefer "Indian".

347: **melting:** softening, i.e., peace time

349: **medicinable:** with healing properties (four syllables in pronunciation: med'cinable)

350: **Aleppo:** a city in Syria once famous as a commercial center

351: **malignant:** disaffected, rebellious

352: **traduced:** defamed

354: **smote:** killed

355: **period:** ending, conclusion; **is marred:** i.e., has been spoken in vain

356: **ere:** before

That can torment him much and hold him long,
It shall be his. You shall close prisoner rest,
Till that the nature of your fault be known
To the Venetian state. Come, bring away.   335

OTHELLO
Soft you, a word or two before you go.
I have done the state some service, and they know 't.
No more of that. I pray you, in your letters,
When you shall these unlucky deeds relate,
Speak of me as I am. Nothing extenuate,   340
Nor set down aught in malice. Then must you speak
Of one that loved not wisely but too well;
Of one not easily jealous, but, being wrought,
Perplexed in the extreme; of one whose hand,
Like the base Indian, threw a pearl away   345
Richer than all his tribe; of one whose subdued eyes,
Albeit unusèd to the melting mood,
Drops tears as fast as the Arabian trees
Their medicinable gum. Set you down this,
And say besides that in Aleppo once,   350
Where a malignant and a turbaned Turk
Beat a Venetian and traduced the state,
I took by th' throat the circumcisèd dog
And smote him, thus.

                                                    He stabs himself

LODOVICO
O bloody period!

GRATIANO
                    All that's spoke is marred.   355

OTHELLO
I kissed thee, ere I killed thee—no way but this,
Killing myself, to die upon a kiss.

                                    [Falls on the bed, and] dies

359: **great of heart:** passionate, proud

360: **fell:** cruel

361: **loading:** burden (of corpses)

364: **seize upon:** claim

365: **succeed:** i.e., Gratiano inherits Othello's fortunes

John Kani as Othello and Joanna Weinberg as Desdemona in The Market Theater's 1987 production directed by Janet Suzman

Photo: Ruphin Coudyzer

CASSIO

    This did I fear, but thought he had no weapon,
    For he was great of heart.

LODOVICO

              [*To IAGO*] O Spartan dog,
    More fell than anguish, hunger, or the sea,   360
    Look on the tragic loading of this bed;
    This is thy work. The object poisons sight,
    Let it be hid. Gratiano, keep the house,
    And seize upon the fortunes of the Moor,
    For they succeed on you. To you, lord governor,   365
    Remains the censure of this hellish villain:
    The time, the place, the torture; O, enforce it!
    Myself will straight aboard, and to the state
    This heavy act with heavy heart relate.

                                          Exeunt

The Cast Speaks

Marie Macaisa

In the text of the play, directors, actors, and other interpreters of Shakespeare's work find a wealth of information. A hallmark of Shakespeare's writing is to tell us more than we need to know about a particular character, more than is needed to understand the plot. For example, in Iago, we are presented with a myriad of motivations for him to destroy Othello and Desdemona's marriage. Janet Suzman, director of the acclaimed 1987 Johannesburg *Othello*, offers the following: "he's jealous of Cassio's advancement; he's suspicious that the Moor has had a fling with his wife Emilia; he despises Othello because he's black or because he's credulous; he's disgusted with Desdemona for breaking the rules of white Venice." Yet, despite the spate of reasons, we remain very much uncertain of his primary motivation, an uncertainty that Shakespeare reinforces with Iago's response to Othello's direct question: "Demand me nothing: what you know, you know: / From this time forth I never will speak word."

While providing extra information, Shakespeare (like all playwrights and unlike novelists) also leaves gaps. We are thus coaxed to fill in the missing information ourselves, either through reasonable surmises (we can guess that Gertrude and Claudius were attracted to each other before Old Hamlet died) or through back stories we supply on our own (the idea that Mercutio was disappointed in love, not present in the text, to explain his attitude). This mix, simultaneously knowing too much and not enough about the characters, enables us to paint vivid, varied interpretations of the same play.

In staging a play, directors create a vision for their production starting from the text but also moving beyond that, by making decisions on what *isn't* in the text. In collaboration with actors, they flesh out the characters: they discuss what they might be like, they create stories that explain their actions, they determine motivations, and they speculate on the nature of their relationships. In Shakespeare they have a rich text to draw on and hundreds of years of performances for inspiration. Thus we, the audience, can experience a play anew each time we see a different production: perhaps it is in an unfamiliar setting, perhaps it is in a scene or characterization we hadn't noticed in the past, perhaps it is in the realization that we somehow sympathize with different characters now (for example, the parents Lord and Lady Capulet instead of the teenage lovers Romeo and Juliet). Whatever the case, a closer look into one cast's interpretation creates an opportunity for us to make up our own minds about their stories and in the process, gain new insights not just into a play hundreds of years old but, quite possibly, ourselves.

ACTORS FROM THE LONDON STAGE, 2005

Now in its thirtieth year, Actors From The London Stage (AFTLS) is one of the oldest established touring Shakespeare theater companies in the world. Their approach to performance is a unique one: in each tour, five classically trained actors, working without a director and guided only by the text, work through the staging of the play by themselves. Each actor plays multiple roles, using only simple props and costumes along with their voice and bearing, to delineate the characters from each other. The sets are minimal. Through it all, their emphasis is on Shakespeare's words. According to Professor Peter Holland, their current academic director, "The aim is to make Shakespeare's words exert their magic and their power in performance. The actors ask the audience to perform that same kind of imaginative engagement that Shakespeare was thinking about when, in the Prologue to *Henry V*, he instructed his spectators:

> Think, when we talk of horses, that you see them,
> Printing their proud hoofs i' th' receiving earth
> For 'tis your thoughts that now must deck our kings."

The following actors were interviewed in February, 2005, in the middle of their tour of *Othello*:

Andrew Dennis (Othello, Clown, Gentleman)

Gemma Larke (Desdemona, Bianca, Montano, Second Senator, Officer)

George May (Cassio, Brabantio, Lodovico, Officer)

Paul McCleary (Iago, Duke)

Julia Watson (Emilia, Roderigo, Gratiano, First Senator)

A group discussion was held, and they were asked about their characters, their main relationships, and scenes in the play. In many cases, because the group had worked on the scenes together, the actors had a lot to contribute about characters not their own. Keep in mind that their thoughts and ideas represent but one interpretation of the play. You may be surprised, you may agree or disagree strongly with some of their choices. That is exactly the point.

APPROACHING THE PLAY

Working without a director provides challenges but also opportunities for the actors. The actors elaborate on their approach to the play and what the absence of a director means for the production.

Paul McCleary: Part of the way this happens is that we end up working from within the play. We're not trying to put a gloss on it or an interpretation that is for now, or tomorrow, or the future sometime. We have to come to the characters and find their interrelationships all within the play.

Julia Watson: The director feels an obligation to have some kind of view on the play, but from where we're coming, all we have are the words. We have no set, very few costumes, hardly any props; so really, we can only let the play speak for itself. And if any of us have views on the play, they have to be filtered through four other people.

George May: When you work with a director, you're often trying to fit into his plan.

Paul McCleary: And he's hired you with a plan in mind.

George May: With this approach, you can't just sit there and wait for someone to tell you what to do. You've got to volunteer and say, "I think this is what happens." You've much more at stake in a personal way, because you really have to make the decisions yourself.

In fact, the actors are responsible for everything you see on stage: the sets, costumes, and props, in addition to the performance. Serendipity played a role in their costume design.

Paul McCleary: Sometimes things just happened accidentally. Gemma, Julia, and I were walking along Oxford Street in London, and I noticed a shop and said, "Let's go have a look in here." We found some things we thought we could use as uniforms that suggested a military tone. These things can be dressed very blankly, these tours—almost like rehearsal clothes. We decided we wanted to give the play a military feel. The fact that it happens to a soldier and it involves a group of people on a military campaign is important to the play, we felt.

Julia Watson: We found jackets, desert combats but with a sort of a World War II style, and paratrooper berets. It's a great mixture. We didn't want it to look American, and we didn't want it to look British. We wanted to give a suggestion. As women we ran into problems because we're both playing men, we're both playing soldiers. Yet we're also playing women, so we had to have costumes that would fit in all of those as much as we could. Because there are no combats for girls, we tried on the men's combats and looked ridiculous in them because they're cut so differently. It's quite difficult.

For the set and the props, the actors settled on nine chairs and a briefcase of goodies including cups, wine bottles, and torches. They have had to be creative with the staging of key scenes. For one of the final scenes, they cut out the character of Cassio entirely. They used army blankets stuffed with pillows to suggest extra bodies. And, lacking a bed, the murder of Desdemona happens in full view of the audience.

Andrew Dennis: We don't have a bed or curtains, so Othello and Desdemona fight standing up. I strangle Desdemona standing up and she fights for her life. It's horrible, and the audience witnesses it all.

THE CHARACTERS AND THEIR RELATIONSHIPS
While each actor is responsible for his or her own character, the group collaborates on the interpretation. In a sense, they are all directors for one another.

DESDEMONA
Gemma Larke: Desdemona is the daughter of Brabantio. She's had a sheltered upbringing with no mother figure, so I see her as having lived a very sheltered life. As she got older, she kind of looked after her father too. In the play they talked about dinners that Othello would attend. She'd be eavesdropping on the conversations but also being a part of it, and then she would get called on to serve as well. Brabantio never saw any relationship between them. She fell in love with his words and that is the witchcraft and the magic of Othello, I think. It's his language.

She saw beneath color; it wasn't an obstacle. She saw the foppishness of Roderigo and all these other suitors and that wasn't good enough for her. That's the strength of this character; she didn't accept what she didn't feel was right and I think she has a lot of grace and dignity because of that. And strength.

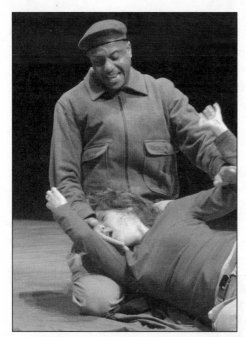

Andrew Dennis as Othello and Gemma Larke as Desdemona

Julia Watson: Something interesting you might want to talk about is the scene where they first arrive in Cyprus. Iago talks quite raunchily, talks about sex, in fact, in front of Desdemona, who is still a virgin at this point. You might want to talk about the fact that she's not cowed by that at all, although she's been incredibly protected by her father, partly because she's a commodity to him. Who he marries his daughter to was very important for his status.

George May: The dowry as well.

Gemma Larke: Othello is off at sea and the stakes are high. He hasn't landed yet, and there's a terrible storm. We don't know where Othello is; Cyprus is completely alien to her and she's with people she doesn't know, and Iago is being quite rude in front of her. She's trying to fit in, but she does say that her outside shows that she's laughing and joking but really it's a façade.

> I am not merry; but I do beguile
> The thing I am, by seeming otherwise.

Julia Watson: It does show her feistiness and her ability to be in control because she takes Iago on.

Gemma Larke: Yes, she really does. She really trusts Iago, I think. Well, she takes the trust that Othello has for him. She goes to him and asks for his help and she wants him to talk to Othello. She doesn't see the bad in Iago.

Desdemona's great trust and faith in Othello leave her vulnerable to the consequences of Iago's manipulation. She's puzzled by the change in Othello's behavior but attributes it to matters of state because she knows she's given him no reason to be jealous or upset with her. She tries very hard to understand, asking Emilia and even approaching Iago, who malevolently affirms her mistaken guess. She pleads her case to the very end.

Gemma Larke: In rehearsals I was playing it as if she was shocked by the change in him and kind of went against it, getting a bit angry. That turned out to be the wrong choice. She is a very active person and she would have

Gemma Larke as Desdemona

tried to understand what was wrong with Othello and talk to him, because I think they really communicate well with each other. But it's also early in their relationship; I don't feel that they know each other particularly well, but that's exciting because they've got a whole life together, and it turns so, so terribly. That's the shock. She never gave up, and to her death, she pleads her innocence. And she lays no blame on Othello whatsoever, to the very end. Which is an amazing, amazing thing to do.

DESDEMONA AND EMILIA

Gemma Larke: We played that Emilia doesn't think much of Desdemona in the beginning.

Julia Watson: There's not much detail in this part of the play, when Othello asks Iago for his wife, look after Desdemona. Emilia is a soldier's wife and there's no suggestion that she's ever been a servant. So we understand from looking at the text, although it's not written explicitly, that Emilia doesn't normally wait on other women. She's used to being a soldier's wife and trekking around behind Iago, or staying at home while he goes off to campaigns. Presumably, they can live on his soldier's pay; he's doing quite well as a soldier. So I think she's fairly fed up that she's being dragged to Cyprus on this long voyage to look after this chit of a girl, really.

I think Emilia is pretty racist. And the way I'm playing it, I think there's something faintly disgusting about this relationship. In fact, when they kiss, I turn away, because I don't want to see it. For me, I think Emilia grows to respect Desdemona and by the willow scene is desperate for this very young girl, who she can see is just spiraling out of control. Yet, one has to remember that she has taken the handkerchief.

Stealing that handkerchief, that seems to me most bizarre. Why does she do this when she knows what weight it has to Desdemona? She doesn't know that the Moor thinks it's magical. Whether she believes that or not, and whether he's telling Desdemona a lie when he says there's magic in the web of it, we don't know. Maybe he's making up a story to give it more weight. Yet she takes it. She knows that Desdemona reserves it "evermore about her/ to kiss and talk to." Othello "conjured her she should ever keep it." She knows this is terribly important. But she does say, what I'm going to do is I'm going to have it copied and then I'll give it to Iago. So I'll stick it back and I'll cover myself.

Julia Watson as Emilia

George May: That line, "I'll have the work ta'en out" (meaning copied), is so often lost.

Gemma Larke: In the willow scene I think Desdemona wants comfort from Emilia. It's the first time she actually asks anything of Emilia in the script, for her to stay. She also asks her, "Wouldst thou do such a deed for all the world?" (i.e., cheat on your husband) because she's trying to understand. Before, she had always gone to Othello to discuss problems and this time—

Julia Watson: Well, she is in a bizarre situation. She's suddenly being completely uprooted from her home and she's with a man she doesn't really know very well. They've fallen in love in secret and they've eloped. So how long is this relationship going to last?

EMILIA AND IAGO

Julia Watson: By contrast, Emilia and Iago have been married a long time. I think if you look in terms of women's status in that world, she was owned by

Iago. When she married him, what tiny bit of wealth she might have had would have gone to him as her husband. She owns nothing. So if she leaves him, she has nothing and nowhere to go; he is her provider. I think we see from the text, although it's very underwritten, that it's an abusive relationship.

Who knows if they were ever in love? Presumably there was some kind of sexual relationship in the beginning. I'm assuming there isn't one now, because he goes on about housewives in your beds. Obviously, she pleads a headache quite a lot. The way he puts her down in front of the entire company, you don't feel that there's a great deal of love lost between them. I think he's a bully. He verbally abuses her in that first scene, but there's a suggestion that he may do other things too. She certainly understands the Moor's behavior. She recognizes his bullying tactics and has a lot to say about men and their attitude toward women. So one feels this comes from a wealth of experience. I think she's deeply unhappy, I think he (Iago) is a violent and abusive husband and she's scared of him. In the final scene she says:

> Good gentlemen, let me have leave to speak:
> 'Tis proper I obey him, but not now.
> Perchance, Iago, I will ne'er go home.

Iago and Emilia only have one scene together, the one in which she gives him the handkerchief. We play it that she's scared of him. She said that she's going to have the handkerchief copied, but within two lines, she's offering it to him. As an actress, I had to decide why she suddenly changed her mind. Certainly in Act 4 she gets a voice, and I think in that scene she speaks for women who've been abused. In the willow scene (Act 4, Scene 3) she and Desdemona come to have a sort of a mother-daughter relationship and the killing of the child (Desdemona) releases in her the mother tiger. We don't know if they had children. The suggestion, I suppose, is that they don't.

BIANCA

In addition to Desdemona and Emilia, there is one other female character in the play, Bianca. She's quite different from both of them. In contrast to Emilia, she's not married and seems to have a fine relationship with her partner. In contrast to Desdemona, she's definitely not a virgin. There's a question as to whether she's a Cypriot or whether she came with the women on the boat.

Gemma Larke: Well, Bianca is this, well, kind of a—

Paul McCleary: Nymphomaniac!

Gemma Larke: I come off the stage as Desdemona and come on as Bianca. And the contrast between the two characters is very great and it's really, really fun to play. She's out for what she can get. She does hassle Cassio terribly, and I think she's out for money. I don't think there's any love in her, really. She knows how to manipulate men and she's very canny. I don't know if that's right, or what. It's a sexual thing, and she knows how to get men. She's not after Cassio to marry her though, although Iago says that.

Julia Watson: "She gives it out that you shall marry her"…I think that's Iago baiting.

Gemma Larke: I think she knows there is no chance of that. But from her point of view it would be very good for her if she did get him to marry her.

Gemma Larke as Bianca and George May as Cassio

Julia Watson: Do we know if she has come from Venice with Cassio or if she's a Cypriot?

Gemma Larke: It doesn't say, but that's just the choice I've made—that he met her in Cyprus. Were we ever agreed on that?

Paul McCleary: Well, I've always thought you were on the boat with the wives coming out after him. You just follow the soldiers.

Gemma Larke: Oh my gosh, we're playing different things.

George May: You've turned up, and you're kind of the surprise. Cassio does take his job very seriously, but he's also a jolly chap. He's very fond of her, and I think he likes her when he's ready for her. Otherwise, he likes to get on with his job.

Gemma Larke: I think she breaks down his barriers in some ways because she goes straight for him.

Julia Watson: It's the perfect relationship because he doesn't have to marry her but he gets great sex. In a sense it's the only male-female relationship in the play.

Andrew Dennis: It's really unfortunate, because we've cut this quite heavily, and one that's cut is a huge chunk of Bianca in the night action scene where Cassio gets wounded (5.1). You really see her treated so inhumanly by the men in that scene. But all of that's gone, it's a shame because then it's not just a piece about racism, it's a play too about men's behavior towards women.

Despite suggestions that Bianca is a prostitute, she may have had the best relationship in the play. Of the three men who are romantically attached, her partner, Cassio, is the only one who doesn't murder his mate.

CASSIO

George May: I don't think I've totally decided on one way of playing him. Sometimes he's naive; sometimes he's the joke of the party. The text suggests he's a Florentine, so he's not part of Venetian society. Perhaps that allows him to be a mercenary solider like Othello is. He might have been able to be promoted since he's not a Venetian; they wouldn't have wanted a Venetian to be too powerful. I think he's intensely loyal and I think he also admires Othello enormously. I don't think he sees anything odd in the relationship between Desdemona and Othello; he sees it purely as true love. In my mind, there's nothing in the text to suggest that he finds the relationship disgusting or anything. I think he's very fond of Desdemona. He's obviously gone between the two of them many times and there's a suggestion that when they've fallen out or had some kind of argument or Desdemona's cross with Othello, he's often been the one that patched up the differences. He's sort of stuck his neck out a little for Othello, but at the same time he's been rewarded: Othello has promoted him.

He's also very fond of Iago. I think he sees Iago as a very efficient, very good solider. He enjoys his company. I think on occasion he finds him a bit bawdy and sometimes he kind of goes along with that.

I think he has quite a strong quality of naiveté. He thinks the best of people and sadly that does get him into trouble. He's not a strong-willed man. The whole drinking scene, he could have said no and walked away from it. But he wants to try and please everyone and ends up going along with it and drinking. Then he gets drunk very quickly and reacts very aggressively once he's drunk, which is Shakespeare's device that we just have to play along with though I'm sure it does happen. He quickly degenerates into a very aggressive character. He knows this about himself and that's why he doesn't like to drink. It's not in the text, but there is a fight and we've chosen to make that fight quite brutal. And that's his downfall.

I think the whole life of a soldier is very important to him and it's what he feels comfortable doing; it gives him the support that he needs. When that is taken away from him he feels quite lost. Then Iago comes along and says, "Look, I know how you can get it back." So he confides completely in Iago, and from then on, interestingly enough, his character says very little. It's almost like he sold his soul to the devil; he becomes a pawn in Iago's game. All he wants to do is see Othello, and he never does for the rest of the play. He sees Desdemona and then is seen by Othello, but Iago manages to manipulate things so that he doesn't see Othello, except when [Othello] is having a fit. He doesn't get a chance to talk to him or look him in the eye. They just keep missing.

Julia Watson: Except for the last scene [in the text]. But in our production, we had to cut Cassio from the last act because we just ran out of people.

Andrew Dennis: We ran out of bodies. We've included a device to bring a couple of people back on, but we just didn't have enough bodies. We didn't have enough army blankets to stuff to make into bodies.

Julia Watson: It's interesting that Cassio often is played as rather feckless because of his relationship with Bianca: another man with a bad relationship with a woman in the play. But the way you play him, he comes across as so

Julia Watson as Roderigo and Paul McCleary as Iago

charming and trying to please everybody, including Bianca. He doesn't want anyone not to like him. So all of us do end up liking him.

On the other hand, Roderigo, apparently a Venetian gentleman, is nevertheless spurned by Desdemona and Brabantio (initially). Yet, as a character, Roderigo plays an important role, as the actors point out.

RODERIGO

Julia Watson: I think he's in the line of Shakespeare's characters from Sir Andrew Aguecheek. He is one of those city gentlemen. Why is Roderigo in the play apart from some light relief? He's a dupe for Iago, an easy dupe.

Paul McCleary: It shows that Iago is keeping all these different balls up in the air. He goes from Cassio to Roderigo to Othello. He manipulated all these people. It adds to the complexity of that.

Julia Watson: I think he's light [comic] relief. From the text, Iago suggests that he go and follow the army in disguise with a usurped beard. We decided a beard might be a bit much, so I just wear a mustache.

George May: He's the guy, in Brabantio's mind, whom Desdemona should have married.

Julia Watson: Except Brabantio didn't want it. Brabantio never wanted him around. In the first scene, Roderigo oddly seems more upset that Iago has gone to work for Othello and that Othello has taken Desdemona than he is concerned for Desdemona. I think Roderigo saw Desdemona as a commodity; she would have had a great dowry. He does say once that he's going to kill himself for love, but I never saw him as being desperately in love with this woman.

Gemma Larke: He hardly knows her.

Paul McCleary: He's the only Venetian male that we get to see—the most developed character of the Venetians throughout the play.

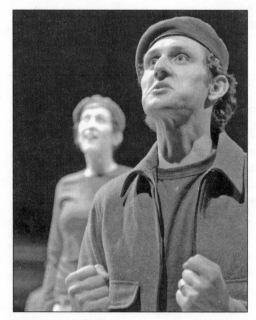

George May as Brabantio

Julia Watson: He's the prime example of a Venetian gentleman.

Paul McCleary: It helps to give a fabric to the play for when I turn around to Othello and say I know our country disposition well. If it was full of Roderigo's, god help us all. He's selfish. He thinks he can buy this woman's body and affections.

Julia Watson: I think he sees her as a commodity, as a prize. He's not in love with her for her—he hasn't gotten to know her. He may well be gay. It's just that he needs to secure his position within Venetian society.

Andrew Dennis: Speaking structurally as well, it helps us be amused by Iago. If Roderigo were a sound, solid, heartbroken chap who's been jilted by this woman, then the way Iago treats him wouldn't be so amusing; but because he's such a fool we laugh at that. It's a very clever way that Shakespeare does it because he gets us to laugh along—yeah, these people are fools aren't they?

BRABANTIO

Paul McCleary: Brabantio is clearly racist. He's happy to have the Moor there telling stories but when he runs off with his daughter—

George May: I think that is what is so shocking to Brabantio, because in a sense, he never before saw Othello as a threat to his daughter. It was inconceivable. Young men he probably wouldn't have allowed in the house but Othello, he just never thought that it would be an issue so he allowed this man in and entertained him.

Julia Watson: But also, [Othello] was the sideshow at dinner parties.

George May: He was an entertainer, an exotic outsider you brought in. Presumably Othello was a unique character in this society, so if you had him coming to your house every night, it was a certain kind of status symbol.

Julia Watson: He was highly prized, wasn't he, by the Venetian state because apparently they always had outsiders as generals, mercenaries as generals of their army. It would mean that if you had an outsider paid by the state, he couldn't turn on the state (a bit like the Vatican city having Swiss guards). Mercenaries would be less likely to usurp power and—

George May: seek it for themselves.

Andrew Dennis: The amazing thing about Brabantio is how quickly he turns around. When Roderigo identifies himself to Brabantio, Brabantio says "The worser welcome: / I have charged thee not to haunt about my doors."

Within a page or two, he says to Roderigo, "O, would you had had her!" It's amazing how quickly the transformation happened—just the speed of it.

Julia Watson: Yes. It's not that he's worried about her going off to war with Othello or marrying a soldier or being in danger. It's purely about class and race.

Paul McCleary: "To fall in love with what she fear'd to look on!" There's another line somewhere else: "Run from her guardage to the sooty bosom / Of such a thing as thou, to fear, not to delight."

OTHELLO AND IAGO

Andrew Dennis: I was probably off track a bit, and I said to Paul one day during rehearsals, "I think that Othello just knows that Iago is there and that's why he overlooks his transformation." Othello needs Iago by his side because he doesn't have the time nor does he want to forge a new relationship as close as what he has with Iago. Iago is just my right-hand man. If I want something done and I say I want it done by eight o'clock, I know it'll be done. If I drop something, metaphorically or physically speaking, I know it'll be picked up. He's not my crutch, but he's just there and I know he will always be there. So, maybe Othello's biggest downfall is he never promoted Iago, never gave Iago the position he wanted, and he kept him there because that's where he needed him to be.

Paul and I were discovering that, particularly in the two bits towards the end of that interval, in the famous "indeed scene" between Iago and Othello (3.3). It's not that Othello doesn't care, but he's in love, he's gone to Cyprus, he's had to stand up before the senate and the duke to plead his case. Iago's there—my honest and my ancient. It's always a case of how he may benefit me, not necessarily how I may benefit him. Once Paul and I sat down one morning, and we agreed there is an element of that in their relationship, it became, not necessarily easy to play, but it put me on a road. Iago's there, he's my right-hand man. Not knowing that these demons are working overtime triple time within him.

Paul McCleary: I don't know what Iago thinks of all this. That's sort of at the heart of what I've tried to do in the play. I think Iago is psychopathic. He's very arrogant in the way that a psychopath might be. In terms of Othello, he doesn't think anybody's better than himself. I felt, working through the play, that it's wrong to look for motives for Iago and that his

Andrew Dennis as Othello and Paul McCleary as Iago

apparent search in the soliloquies for motives often don't add up. He's fascinated with the human condition, which he doesn't understand. He's unsocialized, he doesn't understand emotions, and he thinks that any grand emotions, grand feelings, are hypocrisy because he doesn't get them. I think he probably got on well with Othello when Othello was just a soldier because a soldier at heart has to be a machine and doesn't have to have emotions. As soon as he gets emotions, I suppose that belittles Othello in Iago's eyes. It's vaguely offensive seeing him falling all over Desdemona when they arrive in Cyprus. And I don't think Iago likes company of women much at all.

George May: Do you think he's gay?

Paul McCleary: One feels, when I do have him under my thumb, there is a physical fascination there, but whether that's a sexual fantasy...I won't exclude it, but I don't think it's driving him. I don't think he's jealous of Desdemona in that respect. He's jealous of everybody because he thinks he can do anything that anyone else can do. I think he just despises the human race really.

George May: When he says, "From hence I will not speak another word," he conveys very little respect for anyone.

Julia Watson: He has been a victim of this world. It is a class-ridden society. He's not from the officer class, and however talented he is as a solider, however much he has put into the work, he's not going to get ahead. He's done all those campaigns, but when Othello is a general and needs a right hand man, he picks a darling of the state, Cassio, one who has never fought. Iago is in a menial role, and he had hoped to better himself. [*To Paul*] The way you play the moment when he gets told to disembark the coffers, you made a choice. You have the attitude, "Oh great. It's up to me, is it?" You don't say, "Yes, sir,"

IAGO

George May: It's interesting that the play could have been called Iago, instead of Othello. For whatever reason Shakespeare doesn't make Iago's motives clear. It all has to do with the story; it's about Othello. Iago disappears from the action once he's spun his web. Do you think Shakespeare's less interested in Iago's motivation?

Paul McCleary: Shakespeare's very clever with manipulating his audience. He knows where the story lies. I think he doesn't want the audience to get emotionally involved with Iago because then they don't have room for the tragedy, and it's a tragedy. It's about grand human beings. In a way, it's a great part to play, because any part where you get to talk to the audience a lot is great. They sort of always like you when you talk to them...The funny thing is, he's always trying to make people laugh, he's trying to amuse people, but it's almost because he doesn't understand how all of that stuff works. In the beginning of the drunk scene (2.3) I say, "There's Desdemona," and I do it in a really lewd way. But Cassio doesn't bite, so I just switch and do something else.

Julia Watson: You're much wittier with the audience in your soliloquies. It's odd that his humor doesn't always pay off with the characters in the play. I always think Iago finds a voice in the soliloquies with the audience, which he never finds with the interaction other characters on stage. Well, that's not true; he has it with Othello.

OTHELLO

Andrew Dennis: Othello falls for all this, possibly because of his honesty and trust. Plus he's had no reason in the past to doubt any of Iago's concerns. He's caught up in the whirlwind of love and romance. Within the excitement of that, Iago plants seeds of doubt. "She could have had anyone, but she chose you. Look how she spun her father around to make him think that you actually poisoned her with drugs and so forth." And Othello knows from past experience that Iago doesn't vocalize anything unless he's thought through it. Then Iago says, "I know how these people behave. You don't. I know how they behave. They'd rather hide certain things than let them be known." He now has a persistent outside voice saying, "Look, I'm watching your back, just be careful." This from someone who's always had his back in the past. His ancient. There is no reason not to believe him. These droplets of information make him start to think.

Paul McCleary: Everything I say seems to come true.

Andrew Dennis: Once the seeds are planted that's all he can then see. Desdemona may be talking about Othello, but as soon as she says the word Cassio, I'm like, "Oh God, it's true!" And again, again, and you brought him up again. Iago does a good job on him.

WHAT IF?

The lack of clear motivation for Iago fascinates the cast and they continue to explore his character and what would have happened had his plot succeeded.

Paul McCleary: If you're playing a part, you have to play him as a human being. There are signs of hypocrisy, of arrogance in all of us, isn't there? And bitterness? It's a very childlike thing. You see kids pulling legs off insects or worse. It's sort of what he does, just to see what happens.

Julia Watson: One moment in the play that always affects me, when I'm sitting off stage watching it, is when Desdemona comes to Iago after Othello has slapped her. I find it such a shocking moment that Iago, seeing the slap, seeing Desdemona, this child in such distress, still pursues that line [*4.2, assuring her it is the business of the state that has Othello so upset*]. It's a moment in our production that stands out to me as a very shocking moment. Having witnessed all that, he still pursues. To what end, I don't know, because by the second half, he in a sense has no hope of success. There is no way there will be a good outcome for him. He tells Othello to kill her, but once Othello kills her, the Venetian state is going to come down on Othello. Iago is stuck every which way.

George May: The biggest misfortune for him is that he doesn't kill Cassio. If Cassio had died and couldn't talk, he might have gotten away with it.

Julia Watson: Othello wouldn't have gotten away with. What would've happened to Iago? He wouldn't have been promoted. He wouldn't have been made general. There would be no monetary advantage.

Paul McCleary: I think it's just seeing people suffer, isn't it?

Julia Watson: That, at the end of the day, is what is so malevolent about him. If he had a goal, if he thought he could become a lieutenant and really achieve success within the army, one might find some understanding of his actions, but—

Paul McCleary: Can you honestly never admit to ever, ever being glad that...if you're not going to have something, no one should have it.

Andrew Dennis: Before 5.2 he says, "This is the night / that either makes me or fordoes me quite." So he knows he's stirred things enough. I don't know why he doesn't make sure to kill Cassio; he only wounds him. He doesn't make sure of it, even when Cassio's down.

George May: I think possibly he's going to go back to try and kill him but Lodovico and Montano are there. He's quite a coward, really, isn't he?

Andrew Dennis: Yes, he attacks Cassio from behind.

George May: He kills his wife to try and shut her up.

Julia Watson: What I find fascinating is he's never done this before. He's not a man of the first flush of youth. His wife knows he's a nasty piece of work, but she's never known he was this nasty until—

Paul McCleary: I think it has something to do with us all being in Cyprus. That's what I've always thought: that in Venice it wouldn't be like this. It's like we've all got a blank canvas, because we're all stuck there in Cyprus where we haven't got homes to go to.

Andrew Dennis: He even said in the beginning in Venice, "I am not what I am."

Despite their interesting conjectures, the cast, as with actors and scholars before them, make no definitive conclusions. The final words from one who can settle the issue is this are as follows:

IAGO
Demand me nothing. What you know, you know.
From this time forth, I never will speak word.

A Voice Coach's Perspective on Speaking Shakespeare

KEEPING SHAKESPEARE PRACTICAL

Andrew Wade

tracks 45-46

Introduction to Speaking Shakespeare: Derek Jacobi
Speaking Shakespeare: Andrew Wade with Bill McCallum

Why, you might be wondering, is it so important to keep Shakespeare practical? What do I mean by practical? Why is this the way to discover how to speak the text and understand it?

Plays themselves are not simply literary events—they demand interpreters in the deepest sense of the word, and the language of Shakespeare requires, therefore, not a vocal demonstration of writing techniques but an imaginative response to that writing. The key word here is imagination. The task of the voice coach is to offer relevant choices to the actor so that the actor's imagination is titillated, excited by the language, which he or she can then share with an audience, playing on that audience's imagination. Take the word "IF"—it is only composed of two letters when written, but if you say it aloud and listen to what it implies, then your reaction, the way the word plays through you, can change the perception of meaning. "Iffffffff"… you might hear and feel it implying "possibilities," "choices," "questioning," "trying to work something out." The saying of this word provokes active investigation of thought. What an apt word to launch a play: "If music be the food of love, play on" (Act 1, Scene 1 in *Twelfth Night, or What You Will*). How this word engages the listener and immediately sets up an involvement is about more than audibility.

How we verbalize sounds has a direct link to meaning and understanding. In the words of Touchstone in *As You Like It*, "Much virtue in if."

I was working with a company in Vancouver on *Macbeth,* and at the end of the first week's rehearsal—after having explored our voices and opening out different pieces of text to hear the possibilities of the rhythm, feeling how the meter affects the thinking and feeling, looking at structure and form—one of the actors admitted he was also a writer of soap operas and that I had completely changed his way of writing. Specifically, in saying a line like, "The multitudinous seas incarnadine / Making the green one red" he heard the complexity of meaning revealed in the use of polysyllabic words becoming monosyllabic, layered upon the words' individual dictionary definitions. The writer was reminded that merely reproducing the speech of everyday life was nowhere near as powerful and effective as language that is shaped.

Do you think soap operas would benefit from rhyming couplets? Somehow this is difficult to imagine! But, the writer's comments set me thinking. As I am constantly trying to find ways of exploring the acting process, of opening out actors' connection with language that isn't their own, I thought it would be a good idea to involve writers and actors in some practical work on language. After talking to Cicely Berry (Voice Director, the Royal Shakespeare Company) and Colin Chambers (the then RSC Production Adviser), we put together a group of writers and actors who were interested in taking part. It was a fascinating experience all round, and it broke down barriers and misconceptions.

The actors discovered, for instance, that a writer is not coming from a very different place as they are in their creative search; that an idea or an image may result from a struggle to define a gut feeling and not from some crafted, well-formed idea in the head. The physical connection of language to the body was reaffirmed. After working with a group on Yeats' poem *Easter 1916*, Ann Devlin changed the title of the play she was writing for the Royal Shakespeare Company to *After Easter*. She had experienced the poem read aloud by a circle of participants, each voice becoming a realization of the shape of the writing. Thus it made a much fuller impact on her and caused her thinking to shift. Such practical exchanges, through language work and voice, feed and stimulate my work to go beyond making sure the actors' voices are technically sound.

It is, of course, no different when we work on a Shakespeare play. A similar connection with the language is crucial. Playing Shakespeare, in many ways, is crafted instinct. The task is thus to find the best way to tap into someone's imagination. As Peter Brook put it: "People forget that a text is dumb. To make it speak, one must create a communication machine. A living network, like a nervous system, must be made if a text which comes from far away is to touch the sensibility of the present."

This journey is never to be taken for granted. It is the process that every text must undergo every time it is staged. There is no definitive rehearsal that would solve problems or indicate ways of staging a given play. Again, this is where creative, practical work on voice can help forge new meaning by offering areas of exploration and challenge. The central idea behind my work comes back to posing the question, "How does meaning change by speaking out aloud?" It would be unwise to jump hastily to the end process for, as Peter Brook says, "Shakespeare's words are records of the words that he wanted spoken, words issuing from people's mouths, with pitch, pause and rhythm and gesture as part of their meaning. A word does not start as a word—it is the end product which begins as an impulse, stimulated by attitude and behavior which dictates the need for expression." (1)

PRACTICALLY SPEAKING

Something happens when we vocalize, when we isolate sounds, when we start to speak words aloud, when we put them to the test of our physicality, of our anatomy. We expose ourselves in a way that makes taking the language back more difficult. Our body begins a debate with itself, becomes alive with the vibrations of sound produced in the mouth or rooted deep in the muscles that aim at defining sound. In fact, the spoken words bring into play all the senses, before sense and another level of meaning are reached.

"How do I know what I think, until I see what I say," Oscar Wilde once said. A concrete illustration of this phrase was reported to me when I was leading a workshop recently. A grandmother said the work we had done that day reminded her of what her six-year-old grandson had said to his mother while they were driving through Wales: "Look, mummy, sheep! Sheep! Sheep!" "You don't have to keep telling us," the mother replied, but the boy said, "How do I know they're there, if I don't tell you?!"

Therefore, when we speak of ideas, of sense, we slightly take for granted those physical processes which affect and change their meaning. We tend to separate something that is an organic whole. In doing so, we become blind to the fact that it is precisely this physical connection to the words that enables the actors to make the language theirs.

The struggle for meaning is not just impressionistic theater mystique; it is an indispensable aspect of the rehearsal process and carries on during the life of every production. In this struggle, practical work on Shakespeare is vital and may help spark creativity and shed some light on the way meaning is born into language. After a performance of *More Words*, a show devised and directed by Cicely Berry and myself, Katie Mitchell (a former artistic director of The Other Place in Stratford-upon-Avon) gave me an essay by Ted Hughes that echoes with the piece. In it, Ted Hughes compares the writing of a poem—the coming into existence of words—to the capture of a wild animal. You will notice that in the following passage Hughes talks of "spirit" or "living parts" but never of "thought" or "sense." With great care and precaution, he advises, "It is better to call [the poem] an assembly of living parts moved by a single spirit. The living parts are the words, the images, the rhythms. The spirit is the life which inhabits them when they all work together. It is impossible to say which comes first, parts or spirit."

This is also true of life in words, as many are connected directly to one or several of our senses. Here Hughes talks revealingly of "the five senses," of "word," "action," and "muscle," all things which a practical approach to language is more likely to allow one to perceive and do justice to.

Words that live are those which we hear, like "click" or "chuckle," or which we see, like "freckled" or "veined," or which we taste, like "vinegar" or "sugar," or touch, like "prickle" or "oily," or smell, like "tar" or "onion," words which belong to one of the five senses. Or words that act and seem to use their muscles, like "flick" or "balance." (2)

In this way, practically working on Shakespeare to arrive at understanding lends itself rather well, I think, to what Adrian Noble (former artistic director of the RSC) calls "a theater of poetry," a form of art that, rooted deeply in its classical origins, would seek to awaken the imagination of its audiences through love and respect for words while satisfying our eternal craving for myths and twice-told tales.

This can only be achieved at some cost. There is indeed a difficult battle to fight and hopefully win "the battle of the word to survive." This phrase was coined by Michael Redgrave at the beginning of the 1950s, a period when theater began to be deeply influenced by more physical forms, such as mime. (3) Although the context is obviously different, the fight today is of the same nature.

LISTENING TO SHAKESPEARE

Because of the influence of television, our way of speaking as well as listening has changed. It is crucial to be aware of this. We can get fairly close to the way *Henry V* or *Hamlet* was staged in Shakespeare's time; we can try also to reconstruct the way English was spoken. But somehow, all these fall short of the real and most important goal: the Elizabethan ear. How did one "hear" a Shakespeare play? This is hardest to know. My personal view is that we will probably never know for sure. We are, even when we hear a Shakespeare play or a recording from the past, bound irrevocably to modernity. The Elizabethan ear was no doubt different from our own, as people were not spoken to or entertained in the same way. A modern voice has to engage us in a different way in order to make us truly listen in a society that seems to rely solely on the belief that image is truth, that it is more important to show than to tell.

Sometimes, we say that a speech in Shakespeare, or even an entire production, is not well-spoken, not up to standard. What do we mean by that? Evidently, there are a certain number of "guidelines" that any actor now has to know when working on a classical text. Yet, even when these are known, actors still have to make choices when they speak. A sound is not a sound without somebody to lend an ear to it: rhetoric is nothing without an audience.

There are a certain number of factors that affect the receiver's ear. These can be cultural factors such as the transition between different acting styles or the level of training that our contemporary ear has had. There are also personal and emotional factors. Often we feel the performance was not well-spoken because, somehow, it did not live up to our expectations of how we think it should have been performed. Is it that many of us have a self-conscious model, perhaps our own first experience of Shakespeare, that meant something to us and became our reference point for the future (some treasured performance kept under glass)? Nothing from then on can quite compare with that experience.

Most of the time, however, it is more complex than nostalgia. Take, for example, the thorny area of accent. I remind myself constantly that audibility is not embedded in Received Pronunciation or Standard American. The familiarity that those in power have with speech and the articulate confidence gained from coming from the right quarters can lead us all to hear certain types of voices as outshining others. But, to my mind, the role of theater is at least to question these assumptions so that we do not perpetuate those givens but work towards a broader tolerance.

In Canada on a production of *Twelfth Night*, I was working with an actor who was from Newfoundland. His own natural rhythms in speaking seemed completely at home with Shakespeare's. Is this because his root voice has direct links back to the voice of Shakespeare's time? It does seem that compared to British dialects, which are predominantly about pitch, many North American dialects have a wonderful respect and vibrancy in their use of vowels. Shakespeare's language seems to me very vowel-aware. How useful it is for an actor to isolate the vowels in the spoken words to hear the music they produce, the rich patterns, their direct connection to feelings. North Americans more easily respond to this and allow it to feed their speaking. I can only assume it is closer to how the Elizabethans spoke.

In *Othello* the very names of the characters have a direct connection to one vowel in particular. All the male names, except the Duke, end in the sound OH: Othello, Cassio, Iago, Brabantio, etc. Furthermore, the sound OH ripples through the play both consciously and unconsciously. "Oh" occurs repeatedly and, more interestingly, is contained within other words: "so," "soul," and "know." These words resonate throughout the play, reinforcing another level of meaning. The repeating of the same sounds affects us beyond what we can quite say.

Vowels come from deep within us, from our very core. We speak vowels before we speak consonants. They seem to reveal the feelings that require the consonants to give the shape to what we perceive as making sense.

Working with actors who are bilingual (or ones for whom English is not the native language) is fascinating because of the way it allows the actor to have an awareness of the cadence in Shakespeare. There seems to be an objective perception to the musical patterns in the text, and the use of alliteration and assonance are often more easily heard not just as literary devices, but also as means by which meaning is formed and revealed to an audience.

Every speech pattern (i.e., accent, rhythm) is capable of audibility. Each has its own music, each can become an accent when juxtaposed against another. The point at which a speech pattern becomes audible is in the dynamic of the physical making of those sounds. The speaker must have the desire to get through to a listener and must be confident that every speech pattern has a right to be heard.

SPEAKING SHAKESPEARE

So, the way to speak Shakespeare is not intrinsically tied to a particular sound; rather, it is how a speaker energetically connects to that language. Central to this is how we relate to the form of Shakespeare. Shakespeare employs verse, prose, and rhetorical devices to communicate meaning. For example, in *Romeo and Juliet*, the use of contrasts helps us to quantify Juliet's feelings: "And learn me how to lose a winning match," "Whiter than new snow upon a raven's back." These extreme opposites, "lose" and "winning," "new snow" and "raven's back," are her means to express and make sense of her feelings.

On a more personal note, I am often reminded how much, as an individual, I owe to Shakespeare's spoken word. The rather quiet and inarticulate schoolboy I once was found in the speaking and the acting of those words a means to quench his thirst for expression.

NOTES:

(1) Peter Brook, *The Empty Space* (Harmondsworth: Penguin, 1972)
(2) Ted Hughes, *Winter Pollen* (London: Faber and Faber, 1995)
(3) Michael Redgrave, *The Actor's Ways and Means*
   (London: Heinemann, 1951)

In the Age of Shakespeare

Thomas Garvey

One of the earliest published pictures of Shakespeare's birthplace, from an original watercolor by Phoebe Dighton (1834)

The works of William Shakespeare have won the love of millions since he first set pen to paper some four hundred years ago, but at first blush, his plays can seem difficult to understand, even willfully obscure. There are so many strange words: not fancy, exactly, but often only half-familiar. And the very fabric of the language seems to spring from a world of forgotten assumptions, a vast network of beliefs and superstitions that have long been dispelled from the modern mind.

In fact, when "Gulielmus filius Johannes Shakespeare" (Latin for "William, son of John Shakespeare") was baptized in Stratford-on-Avon in 1564, English itself was only just settling into its current form; no dictionary had yet been written, and Shakespeare coined hundreds of words himself. Astronomy and medicine were entangled with astrology and the occult arts; democracy was waiting to be reborn; and even educated people believed in witches and fairies, and that the sun revolved around the Earth. Yet somehow Shakespeare still speaks to us today, in a voice as fresh and direct as the day his lines were first spoken, and to better understand both their artistic depth and enduring power, we must first understand something of his age.

REVOLUTION AND RELIGION

Shakespeare was born into a nation on the verge of global power, yet torn by religious strife. Henry VIII, the much-married father of Elizabeth I, had

From *The Book of Martyrs* (1563), this woodcut shows the Archbishop of Canterbury being burned at the stake in March 1556

Map of London ca. 1625

defied the Pope by proclaiming a new national church, with himself as its head. After Henry's death, however, his daughter Mary reinstituted Catholicism via a murderous nationwide campaign, going so far as to burn the Archbishop of Canterbury at the stake. But after a mere five years, the childless Mary also died, and when her half-sister Elizabeth was crowned, she declared the Church of England again triumphant.

In the wake of so many religious reversals, it is impossible to know which form of faith lay closest to the English heart, and at first, Elizabeth was content with mere outward deference to the Anglican Church. Once the Pope hinted her assassination would not be a mortal sin, however, the suppression of Catholicism grew more savage, and many Catholics—including some known in Stratford—were hunted down and executed, which meant being hanged, disemboweled, and carved into quarters. Many scholars suspect that Shakespeare himself was raised a Catholic (his father's testament of faith was found hidden in his childhood home). We can speculate about the impact this religious tumult may have had on his plays. Indeed, while explicit Catholic themes, such as the description of Purgatory in *Hamlet*, are rare, the larger themes of disguise and double allegiance are prominent across the canon. Prince Hal offers false friendship to Falstaff in the histories, the heroines of the comedies are forced to disguise themselves as men, and the action of the tragedies is driven by double-dealing villains. "I am not what I am," Iago tells us (and himself) in *Othello*, summing up in a single stroke what may have been Shakespeare's formative social and spiritual experience.

If religious conflict rippled beneath the body politic like some ominous undertow, on its surface the tide of English power was clearly on the rise. The defeat of the Spanish Armada in 1588 had established Britain as a global power; by 1595 Sir Walter Raleigh had founded the colony of Virginia (named for the Virgin Queen), and discovered a new crop, tobacco, which would inspire a burgeoning international trade. After decades of strife and the threat of invasion, England enjoyed a welcome stability. As the national coffers grew, so did London; over the course of Elizabeth's reign, the city would nearly double in size to a population of some 200,000.

Hornbook from Shakespeare's lifetime

A 1639 engraving of a scene from a royal state visit of Marie de Medici depicts London's packed, closely crowded half-timbered houses.

FROM COUNTRY TO COURT

The urban boom brought a new dimension to British life—the mentality of the metropolis. By contrast, in Stratford-on-Avon, the rhythms of the rural world still held sway. Educated in the local grammar school, Shakespeare was taught to read and write by a schoolmaster called an "abecedarian", and as he grew older, he was introduced to logic, rhetoric, and Latin. Like most schoolboys of his time, he was familiar with Roman mythology and may have learned a little Greek, perhaps by translating passages of the New Testament. Thus while he never attended a university, Shakespeare could confidently refer in his plays to myths and legends that today we associate with the highly educated.

Beyond the classroom, however, he was immersed in the life of the countryside, and his writing all but revels in its flora and fauna, from the wounded deer of *As You Like It* to the herbs and flowers which Ophelia scatters in *Hamlet*. Pagan rituals abounded in the rural villages of Shakespeare's day, where residents danced around maypoles in spring, performed "mummers' plays" in winter, and recited rhymes year-round to ward off witches and fairies.

The custom most pertinent to Shakespeare's art was the medieval "mystery play," in which moral allegories were enacted in country homes and village squares by troupes of traveling actors. These strolling players—usually four men and two boys who played the women's roles—often lightened the moralizing with bawdy interludes in a mix of high and low feeling, which would become a defining feature of Shakespeare's art. Occasionally even a professional troupe, such as Lord Strange's Men, or the Queen's Men, would arrive in town, perhaps coming straight to Shakespeare's door (his father was the town's bailiff) for permission to perform.

Rarely, however, did such troupes stray far from their base in London, the nation's rapidly expanding capital and cultural center. The city itself had existed since the time of the Romans (who built the original London Bridge), but it was not until the Renaissance that its population spilled beyond its ancient walls and began to grow along (and across) the Thames, by whose banks the Tudors had built their glorious palaces. It was these two contradictory worlds—a modern metropolis cheek-by-jowl with a medieval court—that provided the two very different audiences who applauded Shakespeare's plays.

Londoners both high and low craved distraction. Elizabeth's court constantly celebrated her reign with dazzling pageants and performances that required a local pool of professional actors and musicians. Beyond the graceful landscape of the royal parks, however, the general populace was packed into little more than a square mile of cramped and crooked streets where theatrical entertainment was frowned upon as compromising public morals.

Just outside the jurisdiction of the city fathers, however, across the twenty arches of London Bridge on the south bank of the Thames, lay the wilder district of "Southwark." A grim reminder of royal power lay at the end of the bridge—the decapitated heads of traitors stared down from pikes at passersby. Once beyond their baleful gaze, people found the amusements they desired, and their growing numbers meant a market suddenly existed for daily entertainment. Bear-baiting and cockfighting flourished, along with taverns, brothels, and even the new institution of the theater.

Southwark, as depicted in Hollar's long view of London (1647). Blackfriars is on the top right and the labels of Bear-baiting and the Globe were inadvertently reversed.

THE ADVENT OF THE THEATRE

The first building in England designed for the performance of plays—called, straightforwardly enough, "The Theatre"—was built in London when Shakespeare was still a boy. It was owned by James Burbage, father of Richard Burbage, who would become Shakespeare's lead actor in the acting company The Lord Chamberlain's Men. "The Theatre," consciously or unconsciously, resembled the yards in which traveling players had long plied their trade—it was an open-air polygon, with three tiers of galleries surrounding a canopied stage in a flat central yard, which was ideal for the athletic competitions the building also hosted. The innovative arena must have found an appreciative audience, for it was soon joined by the Curtain, and then the Rose, which was the first theater to rise in Southwark among the brothels, bars, and bear-baiting pits.

Even as these new venues were being built, a revolution in the drama itself was taking place. Just as Renaissance artists turned to classical models for inspiration, so English writers looked to Roman verse as a prototype for the new national drama. "Blank verse," or iambic pentameter (that is, a poetic line with five alternating stressed and unstressed syllables), was an adaptation of Latin forms, and first appeared in England in a translation of Virgil's *Aeneid*. Blank verse was first spoken on stage in 1561, in the now-forgotten *Gorboduc*, but it was not until the brilliant Christopher Marlowe (born the same year as Shakespeare) transformed it into the "mighty line" of such plays as *Tamburlaine* (1587) that the power and flexibility of the form made it the baseline of English drama.

Marlowe—who, unlike Shakespeare, had attended college—led the "university wits," a clique of hard-living free thinkers who in between all manner of exploits managed to define a new form of theater. The dates of Shakespeare's arrival in London are unknown—we have no record of him in Stratford after 1585—but by the early 1590s he had already absorbed the essence of Marlowe's invention, and begun producing astonishing innovations of his own.

While the "university wits" had worked with myth and fantasy, however, Shakespeare turned to a grand new theme, English history—penning the three-part saga of *Henry VI* in or around 1590. The trilogy was such a success that Shakespeare became the envy of his circle—one unhappy competitor, Robert Greene, even complained in 1592 of "an upstart crow...beautified with our feathers...[who is] in his own conceit the only Shake-scene in a country."

Such jibes perhaps only confirmed Shakespeare's estimation of himself, for he began to apply his mastery of blank verse in all directions, succeeding at tragedy (*Titus Andronicus*), farce (*The Comedy of Errors*), and romantic comedy (*The Two Gentlemen of Verona*). He drew his plots from everywhere: existing poems, romances, folk tales, even other plays. In fact a number of Shakespeare's dramas (*Hamlet* included) may be revisions of earlier texts owned by his troupe. Since copyright laws did not exist, acting companies usually kept their texts close to their chests, only allowing publication when a play was no longer popular, or, conversely, when a play was *so* popular (as with *Romeo and Juliet*) that unauthorized versions had already been printed.

Demand for new plays and performance venues steadily increased. Soon, new theaters (the Hope and the Swan) joined the Rose in Southwark, followed shortly by the legendary Globe, which opened in 1600. (After some trouble with their lease, Shakespeare's acting troupe, the Lord

pendeſt on to meane a ſtay . Baſe minded men all thꝛee
of you,if by my miſerie you be not warnd:foꝛ vnto none
of you (like mee) ſought thoſe burres to cleaue : thoſe
Puppets (J meane) that ſpake from our mouths, thoſe
Anticks garniſht in our colours. Js it not ſtrange,that
J,to whom they all haue beene beholding: is it not like
that you,to whome they all haue beene beholding, ſhall
(were yee in that caſe as J am now) bee both at once of
them foꝛſaken ': Yes truſt them not : foꝛ there is an vp-
ſtart Crow, beautified with our feathers, that with his
Tygers hart wrapt in a Players hyde, ſuppoſes he is as
well able to bombaſt out a blanke verſe as the beſt of
you : and beeing an abſolute Iohannes fac totum,is in
his owne conceit the onely Shake-ſcene in a countrey.
O that J might intreat your rare wits to be imploied in
moꝛe pꝛofitable courſes : ⁊ let thoſe Apes imitate your
paſt excellence, and neuer moꝛe acquaint them with
your admired inuentions . J knowe the beſt huſband of

Greene's insult, lines 9–14

Chamberlain's Men, had disassembled "The Theatre" and transported its
timbers across the Thames, using them as the structure for the Globe.)
Shakespeare was a shareholder in this new venture, with its motto "All the
world's a stage," and continued to write and perform for it as well. Full-
length plays were now being presented every afternoon but Sunday, and
the public appetite for new material seemed endless.

The only curb on the public's hunger for theater was its fear of the
plague—for popular belief held the disease was easily spread in crowds.
Even worse, the infection was completely beyond the powers of Elizabethan
medicine, which held that health derived from four "humors" or internal
fluids identified as bile, phlegm, blood, and choler. Such articles of faith,
however, were utterly ineffective against a genuine health crisis, and in times
of plague, the authorities' panicked response was to shut down any venue
where large crowds might congregate. The theaters would be closed for
lengthy periods in 1593, 1597, and 1603, during which times Shakespeare

was forced to play at court, tour the provinces, or, as many scholars believe, write what would become his famous cycle of sonnets.

THE NEXT STAGE

Between these catastrophic closings, the theater thrived as the great medium of its day; it functioned as film, television, and radio combined as well as a venue for music and dance (all performances, even tragedies, ended with a dance). Moreover, the theater was the place to see and be seen; for a penny

Famous scale model of the Globe completed by Dr. John Cranford Adams in 1954. Collectively, 25,000 pieces were used in constructing the replica. Dr. Adams used walnut to imitate the timber of the Globe, plaster was placed with a spoon and medicine dropper, and 6,500 tiny "bricks" measured by pencil eraser strips were individually placed on the model.

you could stand through a performance in the yard, a penny more bought you a seat in the galleries, while yet another purchased you a cushion. The wealthy, the poor, the royal, and the common all gathered at the Globe, and Shakespeare designed his plays—with their action, humor, and highly refined poetry—not only to satisfy their divergent tastes but also to respond to their differing points of view. In the crucible of Elizabethan theater, the various classes could briefly see themselves as others saw them, and drama could genuinely show "the age and body of the time his form and pressure," to quote Hamlet himself.

In order to accommodate his expanding art, the simplicity of the Elizabethan stage had developed a startling flexibility. The canopied platform of the Globe had a trap in its floor for sudden disappearances, while an alcove at the rear, between the pillars supporting its roof, allowed for "discoveries" and interior space. Above, a balcony made possible the love scene in *Romeo and Juliet*; while still higher, the thatched roof could double as a tower or rampart. And though the stage was largely free of scenery, the costumes were sumptuous—a theater troupe's clothing was its greatest asset. Patrons were used to real drums banging in battle scenes and real cannons firing overhead (in fact, a misfire would one day set the Globe aflame).

With the death of Elizabeth, and the accession of James I to the throne in 1603, Shakespeare only saw his power and influence grow. James, who considered himself an intellectual and something of a scholar, took over the patronage of the Lord Chamberlain's Men, renaming them the King's Men; the troupe even marched in his celebratory entrance to London. At this pinnacle of both artistic power and prestige, Shakespeare composed *Othello*, *King Lear*, and *Macbeth* in quick succession, and soon the King's Men acquired a new, indoor theater in London, which allowed the integration of more music and spectacle into his work. At this wildly popular venue, Shakespeare developed a new form of drama that scholars have dubbed "the romance," which combined elements of comedy and tragedy in a magnificent vision that would culminate in the playwright's last masterpiece, *The Tempest*. Not long after this final innovation, Shakespeare retired to Stratford a wealthy and prominent gentleman.

Beyond the Elizabethan Universe

This is how Shakespeare fit into his age. But how did he transcend it? The answer lies in the plays themselves. For even as we see in the surface of his drama the belief system of England in the sixteenth century, Shakespeare himself is always questioning his own culture, holding its ideas up to the light and shaking them, sometimes hard. In the case of the Elizabethan faith in astrology, Shakespeare had his villain Edmund sneer, "We make guilty of our disasters the sun, the moon, and stars; as if we were villains on necessity." When pondering the medieval code of chivalry, Falstaff decides, "The better part of valor is discretion." The divine right of kings is questioned in *Richard II*, and the inferior status of women—a belief that survived even the crowning of Elizabeth—appears ridiculous before the brilliant examples of Portia (*The Merchant of Venice*), and Rosalind (*As You Like It*). Perhaps it is through this constant shifting of perspective, this relentless sense of exploration, that the playwright somehow outlived the limits of his own period, and became, in the words of his rival Ben Jonson, "not just for an age, but for all time."

Conclusion of the Sourcebooks Shakespeare
Othello: *Derek Jacobi*

track 47

Acknowledgments

The series editors wish to give heartfelt thanks to the advisory editors on *Othello*, David Bevington, Barbara Gaines, and Peter Holland, whose brilliance, keen judgment, and timely advice were irreplaceable during the process of assembling this book.

We are incredibly grateful to the community of Shakespeare scholars for their generosity in sharing their talents, collections, and even their address books. We would not have been able to together such an august list of contributors without their help. Thank you to Tom Garvey, Doug Lanier, Lois Potter, Janet Suzman, and Andrew Wade for their marvelous essays. Extra appreciation goes to Doug Lanier for all his guidance and the use of his personal Shakespeare collection. Thanks also to the following professors for answering questions and discussing our ideas, no matter how unusual they may have sounded: Michael Best, Regina Buccola, Mark Burnett, Paul Cantor, Michael Cordner, Larry Friedlander, Suzanne Gosset, Katherine Maus, and David Nicol. We want to acknowledge the editors of our future editions who have already contributed much to the series: Terri Bourus, Rob Ormsby, and William Williams. We are especially grateful to William for his astute guidance and hand-holding on all issues textual.

We want to single out Tanya Gough, the proprietor of The Poor Yorick Shakespeare Catalog, for all her efforts on behalf of the series. She was an early supporter, providing encouragement from the very beginning and jumping in with whatever we needed. For her encyclopedic knowledge of Shakespeare on film and audio, for sharing her experience and collaborating on the explanatory notes, for introducing us into her estimable network, and for a myriad of other contributions too numerous to mention, we offer our deepest gratitude.

Our research was aided immensely by the wonderful staff at Shakespeare archives and libraries around the world: Jane Edmonds and Ellen Charendoff from the Stratford Festival Archives; David Way, Richard Fairman, and the Sound Archives group from the British Library; Susan Brock and the staff at The Shakespeare Birthplace Trust; Georgianna Ziegler, Richard Kuhta, Jeremy Erlich, and everyone at the Folger Shakespeare Library; Lynne Farrington from the Annenberg Rare Book & Manuscript Library at the University of Pennsylvania; and Gene Rinkel, Bruce Swann, Nuala Koetter, and Madeline Gibson, from the Rare Books and Special Collections Library at the University of Illinois. These individuals were instrumental in helping us gather audio: Justyn Baker, Janet Benson, Annie Hughes, William Housely, Linn Lancett-Miles, Janet Suzman, and Tamar Thomas. We appreciate all your help.

From the world of drama, the following shared their passion with us and helped us develop the series into a true partnership between between the artistic and academic communities. We are indebted to: Graham Abbey, Kate Buckley, Paul McCleary, Steve Pickering, Joseph Plummer, Bob Scogin, Julia Watson, Scott Wentworth, Marilyn Halperin and the team at Chicago Shakespeare Theater, Beth Emelson from The Folger Theatre, Beth Burns and the team at the Guthrie Theater, Michael Kahn, Catherine Weidner, Lauren Beyea, and the team at The Shakespeare Theatre, Steven Tabakin and The Public Theater, Jeffrey Horowitz from Theater for a New Audience, George Joseph, Cleo Haynes, the 2005 *Othello* cast of Actors From The London Stage, and Lucien Riviere from the RSC. Special thanks go to Nancy Becker of The Shakespeare Society.

With respect to the audio, we extend our heartfelt thanks to our narrating team: our director, John Tydeman, our esteemed narrator, Sir Derek Jacobi, and Daryl Chapman and RNIB Talking Book Studios. John has been a wonderful, generous resource to us and we look forward to future collaborations. We owe a debt of gratitude to Nicolas Soames for introducing us and for being unfailingly helpful.

Our personal thanks for their kindness and unstinting support go to: Charlie Athanas, Ray Bennett, Marie Bennett, Marissa Colgate, Josie Macaisa, Maribeth Macaisa, Sheila Madigan, Mary Ellen Zurko, and our families.

Finally, thanks to everyone at Sourcebooks who contributed their talents in realizing The Sourcebooks Shakespeare–in particular, Samantha Raue, Todd Stocke, Andrea Edl, Dan Williams, and Megan Dempster.

Audio Credits

In all cases, we have attempted to provide archival audio in its original form. While we have tried to achieve the best possible quality on the archival audio, some audio quality is the result of source limitations. Archival audio research by Marie Macaisa. Narration script by Marie Macaisa and Joseph Plummer. Audio editing by Marie Macaisa and RNIB. Narration recording, Audio engineering, and mastering by RNIB Talking Book Studios in London, UK. Recording for "Speaking Shakespeare" by Guthrie Theater.

Photo Credits

About The Contributors

SERIES EDITORS

Marie Macaisa is a lifelong Shakespeare fan who has seen at least one production of each of the plays in the canon. Her first career, lasting twenty years, was in high tech. She has a B.S. in Computer Science from the Massachusetts Institute of Technology and a M.S. in Artificial Intelligence from the University of Pennsylvania. Macaisa contributed the "Cast Speaks" essay for this book. She is currently working on the next books in the series.

Dominique Raccah is the founder, president and publisher of Sourcebooks. Born in Paris, France, she has a bachelor's degree in psychology and a master's in quantitative psychology from the University of Illinois. She also serves as series editor of *Poetry Speaks* and *Poetry Speaks to Children*.

ADVISORY BOARD

David Bevington is the Phyllis Fay Horton Distinguished Service Professor in the Humanities at the University of Chicago. A renowned text scholar, he has edited several Shakespeare editions including the *Bantam Shakespeare* in individual paperback volumes, *The Complete Works of Shakespeare*, (Longman, 2003), and *Troilus and Cressida* (Arden, 1998). He teaches courses in Shakespeare, Renaissance Drama, and Medieval Drama. He also contributed the essay "As Performed" to the Sourcebooks Shakespeare *Othello*.

Barbara Gaines is the founder and Artistic Director of Chicago Shakespeare Theater. She has directed over thirty productions at Chicago Shakespeare, and she serves on the artistic directorate of Shakespeare's Globe Theatre in London as well as on Northwestern University's Board of Trustees.

Peter Holland is the McMeel Family Chair in Shakespeare Studies at the University of Notre Dame. One of the central figures in performance-oriented Shakespeare criticism, he has also edited many Shakespeare plays, including *A Midsummer Night's Dream* for the Oxford Shakespeare series. He is also General Editor of Shakespeare Survey and co-General Editor (with Stanley Wells) of Oxford Shakespeare Topics. Currently he is completing a book about Shakespeare on film and editing *Coriolanus* for the Arden Third series.

Essayists

Thomas Garvey (In the Age of Shakespeare) has been acting, directing, or writing about Shakespeare for over two decades. A graduate of the Massachusetts Institute of Technology, he studied acting and directing with the MIT Shakespeare Ensemble, where he played Hamlet, Jacques, Iago, and other roles, and directed *All's Well That Ends Well* and *Twelfth Night*. He has since directed and designed several other Shakespearean productions, as well as works by Chekhov, Ibsen, Sophocles, Beckett, Moliere, and Shaw. Mr. Garvey currently writes on theatre for the Boston Globe and other publications.

Douglas Lanier (*Othello* and Pop Culture) is an Associate Professor of English at the University of New Hampshire. He has written many essays on Shakespeare in popular culture, including "Shakescorp Noir" in Shakespeare Quarterly and "Shakespeare on the Record" in *The Blackwell Companion to Shakespeare in Performance*. His book, *Shakespeare and Modern Popular Culture*, was published in 2002. He is currently working on a book-length study of cultural stratification in early modern British theater.

Lois Potter (In Production) is Ned B. Allen Professor of English at the University of Delaware. She has also taught in England, France, and Japan, attending and reviewing as many plays as possible. Her publications include the Arden edition of *The Two Noble Kinsmen* and *Othello* for the Manchester University Press's series Shakespeare in Performance.

Janet Suzman (As Performed) has twice won The Evening Standard Best Actress Award, and earned Academy Award and Golden Globe Nominations for *Nicholas and Alexandra*. Suzman's distinguished acting career includes playing many major roles at the RSC and in the West End of London. Other films include *The Draughtsman's Contract*, *The Singing Detective*, *A Dry White Season*, and Fellini's *E La Nave Va, Nuns on the Run*. Her *Hedda Gabler* was chosen as the BBC's 50th Anniversary Play of The Month repeat. In 1987 she directed *Othello* with John Kani in her native South Africa, and filmed it for Channel Four TV. She has written and directed her own response to Chekhov's *Cherry Orchard* set in post-democratic South Africa and renamed *The Free State*. She directed *Hamlet* in South Africa, again working with John Kani, in the summer of 2005.